Fraternity Gang Rape

PEGGY REEVES SANDAY

FRATERNITY GANG RAPE

Sex, Brotherhood, and Privilege on Campus

Second Edition

New York University Press   •   *New York and London*

NEW YORK UNIVERSITY PRESS
New York and London
www.nyupress.org

Library of Congress Cataloging-in-Publication Data
Sanday, Peggy Reeves.
Fraternity gang rape : sex, brotherhood, and privilege on campus / Peggy
Reeves Sanday. — 2nd ed.
p. cm.
Includes bibliographical references and index.
ISBN-13: 978-0-8147-4038-5 (pbk. : alk. paper)
ISBN-10: 0-8147-4038-3 (pbk. : alk. paper)
1. Gang rape—United States—Case studies.   2. Greek letter
societies—United States—Case studies.   3. College students—Sexual
behavior—United States—Case studies.   I. Title.
HV6561.S25 2007
306.77—dc22   2006038925

New York University Press books are printed on acid-free paper,
and their binding materials are chosen for strength and durability.

Manufactured in the United States of America
p 10 9 8 7 6 5 4 3 2 1

To three women who resisted

Carol Tracy

Andrea Ploscowe

Meg Davis

They emancipate women in universities and in law courts, but continue to regard her as an object of enjoyment. Teach her, as she is taught among us, to regard herself as such, and she will always remain an inferior being. (The Kreutzer Sonata, Tolstoy, 1889)

When I'm older and turning grey, I'll only gang bang once a day. (Ditty, American College Fraternity, 1983)

Contents

Introduction to the Second Edition

In the dark cold days of February several weeks into the spring semester, a student of mine at the University of Pennsylvania, whom I'll call Laurel, got high on a combination of LSD and beer before going to a fraternity party on campus in search of a good time. People at the party reported that during the course of the evening her behavior attracted quite a bit of attention as she danced provocatively to the beat of music only she could hear. She seemed disoriented and out of touch with her surroundings, oblivious to the various fraternity brothers who danced with her during the course of the evening. Some of the brothers spun her around until she was so dizzy she couldn't find her way out of the room.

According to various eyewitness and hearsay accounts, after the party was over five or six of the brothers had sex with Laurel. When Anna, who had observed Laurel's behavior at the party, heard the brothers bragging about their sexual escapade the next day, she concluded that Laurel had been raped. According to Anna, Laurel was incapable of consent due to her drunken-drugged condition. At a rally held to protest the event weeks later, after word got out on campus about what had happened, Carol Tracy, then director of Penn's Women's Center, referred to the 1983 legal definition of rape when she said:

> The law is clear—if a woman does not consent and is forced to have sexual intercourse, it is rape; if a woman *cannot* consent, it is rape.

By the year 2000 the Pennsylvania rape statute spelled out the meaning of consent even more clearly than in 1983:

> A person commits a felony of the first degree when he or she engages in sexual intercourse with a complainant:

1   By forcible compulsion.
2   By threat of forcible compulsion that would prevent resistance by a person of reasonable resolution.
3   Who is unconscious or where the person knows that the complainant is unaware that the sexual intercourse is occurring.
4   Where the person has substantially impaired the complainant's power to appraise or control his or her conduct by administering or employing, without the knowledge of the complainant, drugs, intoxicants or other means for the purpose of preventing resistance.
5   Who suffers from a mental disability which renders the complainant incapable of consent.
6   Who is less than 13 years of age.

On many campuses, then and now, sex with a drunken, nearly comatose, or passed-out woman is not defined as rape by the male participants. One cannot understand campus rape without seeing it in the context of the sexual culture that breeds the behavior. Often the male leaders characterize their role as passive despite the fact that they stage scenarios which they call "hitting" or "riffing" on women. The passivity the men attribute to themselves is the prelude for blaming the victim later.

A woman who gets drunk is said to be "asking for it." This is true despite the fact that fraternity brothers admit that the goal of their parties is "to get 'em drunk and go for it" and that they make the women's drinks "really strong to loosen up some of those inhibitions." As a rule, getting women drunk as a prelude to "getting laid" is as far as it goes. However, in some cases the "go for it" attitude spills over into the acquaintance rape of an inebriated party guest who is unable to give informed consent. When a woman is particularly vulnerable, acquaintance rape turns into gang rape as a group of brothers take advantage of a woman who is clearly "out of it."

In the case of Laurel the XYZ (a pseudonym for the fraternity) brothers claimed that she had lured them into a "gang bang" or "train," which they described as an "express." They thought of what had happened as a routine part of their "little sisters program," something to be proud of. Reporting the party activities on a sheet posted on their bulletin board, they described what had happened as interviewing for the little sisters program. They proposed that the name for the program should be "little wenches," and "the XYZ Express."

The XYZ brothers never publicly admitted to wrongdoing. I concluded (as did the local DA) that what had occurred at the XYZ house was rape as the term was legally defined. This conclusion was based on my talks with Laurel and interviews with students who had observed her behavior at the party, as well as other evidence presented in these pages.

My purpose in conducting the research for this book was to understand the shadow sexual culture that ensnared a drunk, vulnerable woman who was out of control. I wanted to bring to the public eye an event that I learned was common on college campuses. My goal was to erase the divide between what is well known to many male college students but hidden from the public sphere of debate and action. In the aftermath of the incident, the brothers' first instinct was to brag about what had happened, thinking it would increase their status on campus. When the fraternity faced a one-year expulsion from campus, the brothers claimed that it was common knowledge that such events took place frequently. Defending their actions in a lawsuit against the university, they testified that excessive drinking occurred not only on weekends but at all times. They also testified that it was *common for multiple consensual sexual intercourse to occur in one evening on the University campus approximately one to two times per month.*

Appalled at the glimpse of university life presented to her, the hearing judge, Lois Forer, asked whether there were rules regarding consumption of alcoholic beverages and having visits by members of the opposite sex at fraternities. She was told in response by the counsel for the plaintiff: "The only thing in the University Code of Conduct says members of the university community shall not act immaturely, whatever that means."

The meaning of "whatever that means" is the subject of this book. After some sixteen years, there is still a need to address this topic. The many cases reported since the book was published confirm the repetition of a common pattern up to the present. In 2003, reporting on the sexual assaults at the Air Force Academy, for example, *USA Today* wrote that it was "hardly alone in having problems with sexual assaults." According to this article,

Harvard University has reported 50 forcible sex offenses on campus over the past three years. The Naval Academy in Annapolis, Md., has had 11 midshipmen accused of indecent assault in the same period.

The U.S. Military Academy in West Point, N.Y., has investigated 15 cases over the same period. (*USA Today,* Kenworthy and O'Driscoll, March 13, 2003)

Recent cases have also been reported at Notre Dame (*USA Today,* May 24, 2002); Brigham Young University (Stephen Hunt, *The Salt Lake Tribune,* Aug. 10, 2005); the University of Colorado, Boulder (NOW, Feb. 19, 2004);[1] Morehead State University (Campus Watch 2002, 2003); and the University of Tennessee, Chattanooga (Bill Poovey, Associated Press, Nov. 8, 2005). Charges of forcible rape brought in March 2006 by an exotic dancer involving three members of Duke University's lacrosse team who were present at a team party attended by more than forty players received nationwide publicity, including front-page attention from the *New York Times* (*New York Times,* Drape and Bernstein, March 29, 2006—"Rape Allegation against Athletes Is Roiling Duke").

These and other incidents in secondary schools and gangs demonstrate that the same underlying behavior occurs across the U.S. social spectrum, not just on college campuses. It is reported in elite and nonelite secondary schools and among street gangs. It is not restricted to whites, blacks, or other ethnic groups. American campus–style gang rapes also occur in other countries; most notable is the high-profile case reported at Waseda University in Tokyo. Between 2001 and 2003 a leader of a university club and other members used strong alcoholic drinks to intoxicate their victims to the point of unconsciousness, whereupon they were raped on various occasions by up to a dozen members of the club. The explanation given was that rape created solidarity among members and those who did not participate in the gang rapes were not members (Yumi Wijers-Hasegawa, *The Japan Times,* Nov. 3, 2004).

In this new Introduction I broaden the explanatory framework for understanding fraternity gang rape by putting the subject in its personal, social, and historical context. In the new Afterword I focus on what has and has not changed at the University of Pennsylvania and on other campuses since I wrote this book. Not wanting to convey the impression that all of Penn's fraternities are rape prone, in the Afterword I include a profile of a rape-free fraternity. This profile was first written by two brothers who approached me in 1995 saying that they were organizing their fraternity according to rape-free values. In 2006 I talked with two current members of this fraternity to determine whether the rape-free values were still in place.

When the book was originally published in 1990, I did not identify the University of Pennsylvania by name despite the fact that the local press had done so at the time of the incident in 1983. After publication, a book review in the *New York Times* divulged the name of the university and the name of the fraternity. I had not identified either because I did not want to put the onus on one campus or one fraternity for fear that both would be thought of as unique. My goal at the time was to draw attention to a sexual culture in which the line between consensual and nonconsensual sex is often blurred. Now that the incidence of acquaintance and gang rape on college campuses has been widely publicized and the identity of many campuses revealed, choosing to identify Penn is not a revelation, nor is the sexual culture described in this book unique to Penn's fraternities.

When Duke University was confronted with allegations of forcible rape brought by one of the African American dancers hired for a party attended by over forty members of the lacrosse team, in a letter addressed to the university community Duke's president, Richard H. Brodhead, instituted a mechanism for examining the campus sexual culture (*New York Times,* April 7, 2006). Although not all of the facts in the Duke case have yet come to light, enough is known of the context surrounding the alleged gang rape to suggest that the activity is similar to what I describe in these pages: male bonding and sexual dominance fueled by pornography, heavy drinking, and dehumanizing references to women as sexual objects. Regardless of the legal outcome of the alleged sexual acts reported in the Duke case, the culture revealed when the charges were made raises serious questions about the continuation of sexism and racism on campus. Most campus administrations know where the problems lie. The question is why no action is taken until charges such as those brought at Duke and those associated with the XYZ Express erupt into the media.

The sexual culture associated with the XYZ Express and the university's response at the time yielded a picture of entrenched sexual inequality on a campus where fraternities had historically occupied a privileged place in campus social life. After prolonged self-examination and pressure from faculty and students, the policies and educational programs initiated some years later made Penn one of the earliest campus leaders in the anti-rape movement. In the Afterword I ask whether and to what extent the sexual culture has changed in response to these efforts. In answering this question I include the results of a student-conducted examination of fraternity sexual culture conducted in the spring of 2005. The evidence suggests a complex mix of continuity and change.

WRITING *FRATERNITY GANG RAPE*

I was an early member of the anti-rape movement that began in the late 1960s and took off with the publication of Susan Brownmiller's landmark book *Against Our Will* (1975). Throughout the 1970s I researched the social context of rape in a cross-cultural sample of ninety-five band and tribal societies in order to question the then prevalent assumption that rape was universal. By demonstrating variation in rape cross-culturally, the findings broke the back of the then prevalent biological argument that all men will rape if given a chance (Sanday 1981).

Rape was rare in 47 percent of the societies studied and common in 18 percent of them. Most interesting about this study was the evidence that the relative frequency of rape was significantly correlated with gender roles and status. In the more rape-free societies there was evidence of male-female integration in the affairs of everyday life, especially in domestic activities. Women had higher status in these societies. In the more rape-prone societies there was greater sexual segregation, male social dominance, interpersonal violence, and the subordination of women (Sanday 1981b, 2003).

Different social factors are also associated with rape-prone as opposed to rape-free fraternity environments. The isolation of fraternities and athletic teams may enhance a sense of privilege and entitlement that spills over into interpersonal violence against outsider males or violence against female party guests that takes the form of sexual abuse. When I heard the story of what happened to Laurel, I was struck by how the sexual activity was not unlike the rapes in rape-prone societies in the band and tribal world in which men use rape to establish social dominance.

Lest it be thought that all fraternities are rape-prone, it is important to note that this is not the case. At the time of the XYZ Express there were fraternities on campus known to treat women with respect. As mentioned, I will have more to say about the rape-free mores in one of the houses described to me in later years in order to demonstrate that sexual segregation is not necessarily a formula for disaster (although this fraternity was and still is leaning toward requesting coed status).

The striking similarity found in incidents of gang rape on many college campuses in the 1980s led to the book's title, *Fraternity Gang Rape*. I did not use the word "fraternity" in the title to refer to fraternities generally as an institution. The phrase "fraternity gang rape" refers to bonding through sex. This does not mean that all fraternities engage in this activity. Nor does it mean that this kind of bonding is found only in fraternities. It is also commonly found in athletic teams and other male-segregated settings. I use the word "fraternity" in its broader sense to mean a group of persons associated *by or as if by* ties of brotherhood, or, any group or class of persons *having common purposes and interests* (Random House Unabridged Dictionary 1999).

The commonality is male bonding in sex acts in which the males involved aid and abet the activity. In party settings, boys examine the girls as they come in the door and play the host by plying them with drinks as they pick partners for dancing. One never knows when or if a date-rape drug is part of the mix. The success of the night, who "scored" and who didn't, is discussed either at the end of the evening or the next day—or is written up. Once a girl has been sexually "snagged" at a party, she is forgotten because the object is always to score with new targets. The more new girls a brother can boast about, the higher his status. There is a thin line separating consensual sexual activity in this scenario from acquaintance rape. The next day the girl herself may not be sure what happened.

If, as sometimes happens, the behavior mushrooms into group sex, there is always the question of whether the girl consented. The boys may not even consider the possibility that she may have been too drunk to consent. They assume that by drinking she signaled her desire for sex. The woman involved is a tool, an object, the centerfold around which boys both test and demonstrate their power and heterosexual desire by performing for one another. They prove their manhood on a wounded girl who is unable to protest. Her body stands in for the object of desire in porno-staged acts of sexual intercourse that boys often watch together. She is the duck or the quail raised and put in place for the hunter. Who she is doesn't matter and she is quickly forgotten after it's all over—sloughed off like a used condom. The event operates to glue the male group as a unified entity; it establishes fraternal bonding and helps boys to make the transition to their vision of a powerful manhood—in unity against women, one against the world. The patriarchal bonding functions a little like bonding in organized-crime circles, generating a sense of family and establishing mutual aid connections that will last a lifetime.

REACTION TO *FRATERNITY GANG RAPE*

With its graphic description of abusive sexual behavior fueled by sexist attitudes, *Fraternity Gang Rape* exploded onto the campus scene and was widely reported upon in the media. I was invited to many campuses to raise student consciousness and to talk to administrators about what could be done by way of prevention. I also appeared on numerous television programs and was interviewed by reporters and radio commentators across the country.

To this day I am called whenever a new incident is reported. Recently a CNN reporter called to ask about the case at the University of Tennessee, Chattanooga, involving six football players who were charged in November 2005 with taking turns raping a drunken student after a party. Vetting me for an appearance on CNN, this reporter asked with a tinge of outrage in her voice, "Why do things like this happen?" I was surprised because I had already given explanations to CNN several times after the book was published. I should not have assumed that what I said over fifteen years ago would be remembered today. The source of the problem is still not common knowledge. After I started to answer her question, I realized that she was only looking for a sound bite: one minute into my answer she got another call and hung up on me.

Around the same time, a local newspaper reporter called about another incident, this time at a Florida university. He asked the same question as the CNN reporter, adding, "Is it the pack mentality?" This phrase always carries with it the assumption that there is something evolutionary in the behavior. I pointed out that whatever might be evolutionary in sexual behavior, among humans it is shaped primarily by group values, sexual mores, and taboos. After all, man is not just an animal, but the premier culture-bearing being. (See Sanday 2003 for a response to the argument that rape is evolutionarily programmed.)

When I was called about the Duke case, the reporter asked me why the athletes involved engaged in such "pathological behavior." I answered that what he was calling pathological was commonplace in the sexual culture of some young males, replete with the joking and bragging that was evident in the email written later by one of the lacrosse team players, along with the dehumanizing, racist language that reportedly occurred during the party. My point was that however pathological the behavior may be, it is necessary to understand its roots before effective change is possible.

We know (or should know) that rape is common in the United States, which is in all likelihood one of the most rape-prone societies in the world. According to the National Violence Against Women Survey (NVAWS), conducted from November 1995 to May 1996 by the National Institute of Justice and the Centers for Disease Control and Prevention, more than 300,000 women and almost 93,000 men are raped annually. Researchers analyzing the survey results found differences in rape prevalence (defined as lifetime experience of rape) relating to age, gender, and race/ethnicity, as well as other factors such as whether victims were first raped as minors. In their report they concluded that "despite widespread public education, rape remains a largely underreported crime; and despite increased levels of research over the past few decades, significant gaps remain in understanding rape victimization" (Tjaden and Thoennes 2000, 2006).

The studies conducted by University of Arizona psychologist Mary Koss and her colleagues in the 1980s provided the first data on rape prevalence among college students (see Koss et al. 1987 and Warshaw 1988.) The data indicated that one of every four women on campus had been subjected to rape or attempted rape. These findings have been replicated in many studies since then. Between 13 percent and 25 percent of the participating females respond affirmatively to questions asking if they had ever been penetrated against their consent by a male who used force, threatened to use force, or took advantage of them when they were incapacitated with alcohol or other drugs (for a summary of these studies see Koss and Cook 1993:110; see also Sanday 1996:193, 251–255).

More recent studies, conducted in the late 1990s, report similar results. A nationally representative survey of 4,838 college students funded by the Centers for Disease Control and Prevention reported that 20 percent of college women, recalling their entire lifetime, said they had been raped (Brenner, McMahon, Warren, and Douglas 1999).[2]

According to a report issued by the National Institute of Justice and the Bureau of Justice Statistics in December 2000 entitled "The Sexual Victimization of College Women,"

> [c]ollege campuses host large concentrations of young women who are at greater risk for rape and other forms of sexual assault than women in the general population or in a comparable age group.

This study was based on a telephone survey of a randomly selected, national sample of 4,446 women attending a two- or four-year college or university during the fall of 1996. The questions were asked between February and May 1997. Responding to a question asking about sexual victimization incidents before 1996, the study found that about

> 1 in 10 college women said they had experienced a rape, while the same proportion stated that they were victims of an attempted rape. Almost the same proportion also had sexual intercourse or contact in which they were subject to threats of nonphysical punishment or promises of reward. Unwanted or uninvited sexual contacts were widespread, with more than one-third of the sample reporting these incidents. (Fisher, Cullen, and Turner 2000:17)

IS RAPE BIOLOGICAL OR CULTURAL?

Anthropologists argue that while the capacity for sexual pleasure may be constitutional, human sexual behavior "is rather a sociological and cultural force than a mere bodily relation of two individuals" (Malinowski 1929: xxiii; see also Sanday 2003). This means that human sexuality sits precariously on the divide between individualized sensations and culturalized meanings, making it both preeminently social as well as physiological. As sexuality straddles two worlds—the biological and the social—the major question forresearch concerns the social purposes served by types of sexual behavior. This question is answered by introducing the concept "sexual culture."

Because human sexual behavior is a sociological and cultural force guided by public sexual cultures—such as reflected in pornography, the media, and religious education—we must begin by examining popular, historically based models for human sexual expression. Understanding how sexual behavior has been conceived at various times in our history uncovers trends that promote female sexual choice in some contexts and deter it in others.

Early Americans had a much different conceptualization of male and female sexuality than we have now. They came to these shores with beliefs characteristic of Western thought before the eighteenth century, reaching as far back as Aristotle and Galen, that men and women were basically alike physiologically speaking. Women had the same genitals as men, with the difference that the male organs were outside and the female organs were inside the body. The word "vagina" only entered the language around 1700. Before that the vagina was imagined as "an interior penis, the labia as foreskin, the uterus as scrotum, and the ovaries as testicles" (Laqueur 1990:4, 159; see also Sanday 1996:67).

Thomas Laqueur calls this the "one-sex model" (ibid.; see also Sanday 1996:67, 297). Although the two sexes might differ in such important characteristics as the amount of vital heat or in their capacity for moral perfection, by this model sex differences were a matter of degree, not of kind. Aristotle and Galen thought of women as colder and weaker than men. Women did not have sufficient heat to transform inner fluids into the more perfect form of semen. In conception women contributed only the material substance and the place of incubation, while men supplied "the form and the efficient cause."

Over the two thousand years that this model ruled Western thought, it entailed certain dangers for those who valued sex differences. Men could turn into women and women into men just by associating with the opposite sex or by emulating the behavior of that sex. A penis could spring out from the girl who was too active. The interior balls of women who meddled too much in men's affairs were thought to have slipped down to her loins. By consorting closely with women, men might lactate or lose their hardness, becoming more effeminate and like a woman (see Laqueur 1990:5–6, 7, 123, 125).

Today, we live in a sexual culture in which some boys are terrified of being viewed as effeminate by other boys who bully them mercilessly. Who wants to be called "nerdy," a "dork," or a "fag" at school? In most adolescent peer groups, a young male is expected to display his "hard-wired" maleness, lest he be thought of, or, perhaps, think of himself as homosexual. This is odd in light of the obvious homoeroticism of fraternity gang rape—unless one understands it as a ritual of "silencing the feminine," by those subscribing to the one-sex model.

According to one-sex thinking, it was routine for both sexes to experience orgasm during conception. The seat of sexual pleasure for women has been located in the clitoris for centuries before Masters and Johnson rediscovered the clitoral orgasm. In the second century A.D., Galen wrote about the "raging desire" and the "great pleasure" that precedes "the exercise of the generative parts." Although people debated which sex enjoyed "the pleasures of Venus more," libido, as we call it today, had no gender then. Aristotle regarded the possibility of women conceiving without pleasure as highly unlikely. Renaldus Columbus, who claimed to have discovered the clitoris in 1559, just a half-century after the discovery of America by the more famous Christopher Columbus, took it upon himself to name the new discovery the "female penis." He referred to the organ as "the seat of woman's delight" and said that when it was touched it became a "little harder," and "oblong to such a degree that it shows itself as a sort of male member." Later, in the seventeenth century, an English midwife likened both the vagina and clitoris to the penis, giving women two penises, so to speak. One was inverted, creating a passage for the male penis, and the other, the clitoris, stood and fell just like the male organ, making women "lustful" as well as giving them "delight in copulation" (see Laqueur 1990:43, 48, 64–65).

Colonial New England appears to have enjoyed a low incidence of rape. A woman's "no" meant something in Puritan New England. Despite the current definition of "puritanism" that emphasizes prudery, it was the only time in our history when males and females as a group were thought to have the same sexual appetite. Sexual desire was conceived of as explosive and in need of a vent for both sexes. It is also true that the laws of the colonies kept passion in check, forbidding "fornication" outside of marriage. Within marriage sexual passion was encouraged. Women married to an impotent husband could sue for divorce on those grounds alone. If a woman was raped, community officials tended to believe her because of the belief that a woman would have no

reason to lie. If she said "no," a man was more likely to desist from making sexual advances (Sanday 1996:66–81).

The birth of the nation saw the flowering of the cult of "true womanhood" and a radical change in the conception of female sexuality.
While the conception of male sexuality remained the same, the conception of female sexuality became dualistic: women were either pure or
promiscuous, and sexuality was either private and marital or public
and prostituted. While males were expected to be as lustful as ever,
proper females bore the burden of giving the new nation a semblance of
respectability. At a time when male licentiousness in the cities was well
known and poor women often turned to prostitution as their only
source of income, chastity became the dominant symbol of a polite, re-
fined America.

True womanhood gave women of means moral superiority, but its
definition robbed them of a sexual appetite. When these women
reached beyond the feminine sphere of the home and entered the arena
of public debate to take up abolition, temperance, social purity, and the
women's rights movement, they wore true womanhood like a chastity
belt to protect themselves from the discourse of public sexuality that demeaned and subordinated all women to the demands of male sexuality
(Sanday 1996:82–99).

In the public domain of nineteenth-century sexual culture, the expansion of the culture of pornography and prostitution deepened belief
in the inherent lustfulness of men and their female companions in the
bawdy houses of the times. Public women served men, while private
women, mothers and wives, nurtured their moral backbone. In the public domain, any woman who disagreed too openly with a man—such as
in rape cases—was automatically subject to the suspicion of having
"asked for it," of being inherently lustful like her sister the prostitute. In
the courtroom, a woman's past was examined for evidence of prior lustful acts on the grounds that, once "fallen," a woman was always ready
for sex. The complainant's credibility might also be impeached by suggesting she was a false accuser, a scorned or vindictive woman. The
tenacity of these suspicions is seen in the legal ruling of the nineteenth
century that complainants had to provide evidence of having resisted to
the utmost (Sanday 1996:100–120).

As the nineteenth-century discourse on women's rights expanded,
a group of women began a campaign of sexual politics. Activist women

(the term "feminist" had not yet been adopted in American sexual discourse) argued for more sexual autonomy and started a sex-rights campaign to reinstall the right to female lust. In true backlash fashion, the science of sexology was born at this time and ushered in another trend in American sexual discourse. The new sexual scientists posited a dualistic model based on man's biologically based aggression and woman's lustful sexual passivity. This was a dualistic sexual model with a difference. While lust was common to both sexes, the sexes split along the active-passive gradient.

Basing his position on Darwinian thought, Havelock Ellis, one of the founders of the American sexology movement, glorified male sexual aggression as a biological, evolutionary necessity. As women rediscovered lust, to ensure female sexual subordination Ellis and later Freud defined the female sex drive as inherently passive and responsive to forceful male seduction—even rape. Freud defined the sex instinct as a basic biological drive, which in its active form was masculine and in its passive form was feminine. Thus, these men returned the sex drive to women with the restriction that the proper female was to be a sexually passive, but now willing, recipient of male passion.

The new version of the true woman still said No when she meant Yes, not because of moral superiority but in obedience to her alleged biological desire to be dominated. Under her demur demeanor, however, Freud assumed the raging fires of desire still lurked in the female breast, giving her an overactive sexual imagination that sometimes led to false accusations of rape. Thus, Freud created a new version of the lustful female false accuser. Whereas in the nineteenth century the woman who cried rape was "fallen," in the early twentieth she was a hysteric.

These ideas influenced rape law through the most important and widely cited legal treatise on rape of the twentieth century penned by the noted jurist John Henry Wigmore. Using Freudian terminology, Wigmore cautioned the legal establishment to beware of the female hysteric and the pathological liar and advised that all rape complainants be examined by a psychiatrist for nefarious complexes of a Freudian nature. Predictably, those few rape cases that were prosecuted often ended in acquittal (Sanday 1996:121–139).

The sexual truisms of the two-sex model outlined above functioned to maintain a community of males in opposition to and superior over females. Although some of the details of the discourse changed during the twentieth century, its ability to maintain male bonding and male dominance was unaffected until feminists began to challenge the underlying gender inequity. The discourse of "No means Yes," which in the third sexual revolution was transformed to "No means No," can be traced back to the nineteenth-century cult of true womanhood and to the Freudian concept of female sexual passivity. At that time, to preserve her reputation and to show that she is not an aggressive hussy, a woman had to say No so that a man could take pride in his seduction and assure himself that she is not "loose." Turning a No into a Yes by getting a girl drunk, slipping her a "date rape pill," or using aggressive seduction was a common practice on college campuses when I wrote *Fraternity Gang Rape*.

SEXUAL REVOLUTIONS OF THE TWENTIETH CENTURY

The sexual ideologies described above were associated with three revolutions for change in the twentieth century. By revolution I refer to a social movement led by high-profile individuals interested in promoting certain gender-based sex rights and privileges. *Fraternity Gang Rape* grew out of the third revolution inspired by late-1960s feminism.

The first sexual revolution began in the late nineteenth century and was waged by a few outspoken women who objected to the restrictions on their sex lives imposed by the social-purity movement earlier in the century. They talked about the "naturalness of female sexual desire" and said that women had the "right" to a "frank enjoyment of the sensuous side of the sex-relation." A group of women living in Greenwich Village in the early decades of the twentieth century were the first to call themselves feminists in reaction to women who were activists for Victorian sexual prudery. Claiming that the sex drive was as important to woman's nature as to man's, the first feminists argued for female "sex rights," sexual freedom for women, and a single standard for both sexes (Sanday 1996:121–139).

Based on the theories of Ellis and Freud, the second revolution promoted unfettered sexual freedom for both sexes, with women expected to be passive but lustful for sex while men were the aggressors. The cultural superstructure for this revolution was laid by the novels of Henry Miller and D. H. Lawrence and by the work of Wilhelm Reich and Alfred Kinsey. Their ideas were based on Freud's theory of the libido and Havelock Ellis's contention that male sexual aggression and female passivity were natural.

A somewhat different theory was expressed in Wilhelm Reich's book *The Sexual Revolution* (1963). First published in German in the 1930s and in English in 1945, Reich argued that venting sexual energy through orgasm made for a better society. According to Reich, sexual energy had to be released in any way possible or society would crumble. He claimed that controlling sexual desire only produced "sex-negative" activities such as warfare, social oppression, and human anxiety, leading to other sex-negative social expressions. Alfred Kinsey's famous studies of male and female sexuality were both based on Reich's theories. Like Reich, Kinsey believed that the more orgasms people had, the better off they would be.

Kinsey was the first of America's great sexual entrepreneurs. Unlike the others who came after him, such as Hugh Hefner and Larry Flynn, Kinsey did not build a money-making sex industry. He only laid its scientific and moral foundation by suggesting that multiple orgasms was a good thing and that human sexual behavior was no different from animal sexual behavior. Kinsey writes with approval about a man he interviewed who reported having thirty orgasms a week for thirty years. Kinsey's only allusion to sexual abuse was to write disdainfully of an incident in which an old man was put in jail because he sought release with little girls. According to Kinsey, people should have shown more sympathy for this man's natural need.

The sexual entrepreneurs changed the American sexual culture in dramatic ways, promoting pornography as big business and leading to a tremendous increase in reported rape rates. Between 1935 and 1956, the time when Reich and Kinsey were the most popular, arrest rates for rape nearly doubled, as did the rates for other sexual offenses, while those for prostitution fell by two-thirds. *Playboy* got its start in the 1950s with Hugh Hefner declaring his undying gratitude to Reich and Kinsey. Together Reich, Kinsey, Miller, Lawrence, and eventually writer Norman Mailer reaffirmed the Social Darwinist notion that male sexual aggression was natural, that "boys will be boys," a mantra that acts as a defense for gang rape in middle-class environments.

The basic message of the 1950s and 1960s from literature, science, and popular culture was that masculinity should be defined primarily in aggressive and sexual terms. Once denied a readership in the United

States because of obscenity laws banning the publication of their books, Henry Miller and D. H. Lawrence were widely read during the 1950s. In their novels the hero is the potent, virile male, who, like an animal, takes his woman without asking. The male is presented as all potency—the active agent in sex—while the woman is presented as the passive receptor whose sexual desire is sparked by the male's overpowering manhood (Sanday 1996:140–160).

MY EXPERIENCE WITH THE MORES OF THE
SECOND SEXUAL REVOLUTION

Since sexual revolutions tend to come in reaction to what has gone before, it is helpful to summarize my experience of the second revolution which led me to join with others in seeking sexual equity through the third sexual revolution. In the sexual culture of my teenage years—true to the two-sex active-passive model—a woman was thought to communicate her sexual desire wordlessly by the way she looked at a man or by the way she dressed. I had my first lesson in the requirement that woman waits and man proposes when I was thirteen. I was in the eighth grade and invited a fellow student (in the ninth grade) to a square dance in the park. We had a nice time and went out a few more times. Nothing much happened on these dates. Looking back on it, I realize that the boy I idolized was simply unable to relate to me as a human being as opposed to a sex object. I projected onto him my hopes for companionship not realizing that he was tied up in knots by his sense of masculine vulnerability.

One day when he saw me at our church gym, this boy invited me to play basketball with him and his friends. During this activity, which seemed to me innocent, his friends got me into a corner. The leader in the group, who was the oldest and biggest, the one the other boys looked up to, took the ball and approached me menacingly, as if I was the basket. Terrified by the looks on the faces of the boys and the stillness in the room, I ducked under their outstretched arms and ran, without looking back, all the way home. Later I learned that the boy whom I idolized as my first date told his buddies I was "hot" for him because it was I, not he, who asked for the first date. In terms of the boy sexual culture I encountered in the gym that day, my interest in him was defined as "she wants it." Because of my girlish (or he would have said not-so-girlish) aggression in asking him out, I was fodder for the boys' sexual talk.

Within the context of this sexual culture, the male projects his own sexual tension on to the female, fetishizing her desire as being reducible to "wanting it." I first heard the phrase "she wants it" at this time. For a long time I was perplexed about what the "it" I supposedly wanted was. Later, I learned that the *it* was the male member. Much later, after I had read the French theorist Jacques Lacan, I understood that the *it* in question was the signifier of the *lack* that all women are supposed to feel because they do not have a penis. In *Fraternity Gang Rape* I suggested that the presumption of the *lack* (or penis envy, as Freud called it) has nothing to do with psychosexual development but a great deal to do with socialization for male dominance and power in patriarchal societies. What Freud and Lacan described as a hardwired psychological problem experienced by all women was in reality a cultural doctrine that functioned to give men a stage on which to socialize one another for power. The *it* embodied (stood for) the male power which women were denied solely because they were female. Boys who buy the idea that only power counts in the adult male game are much more likely to think in terms of "she wants it," because they know how much they themselves will be defined by power. These boys also assume that the closest most women will ever get to power is through sex, because it is mainly through sex that women have power over men. Thus, when anyone says "she wants it" they are talking more about a male-defined power game than about female desire.

For women of the late 1960s the sexual freedom of the second sexual revolution meant many things. An increasing number of young women liberated themselves from the idea that they had to save themselves for their husbands. They also began to think more in terms of give and take in sexual relationships. This was the period when women reclaimed their right to sexual pleasure. Women consulted one another and books about how to have an orgasm. Their male partners, on the other hand, were mostly concerned with "getting laid," a euphemism for release of sexual tension. Both sexes were concerned with the mechanics of sex. With one difference. Women tended to look for sexual release in the security of a relationship, while men tended to look for sex wherever they could get it. Men used the new sexual freedom as a ploy to get women in bed. Women who didn't rush into a man's bedroom at the first request were labeled frigid or lesbian. If she didn't want it, it was allowable to coerce and cajole her either by verbal pressure, alcohol, or physical force.

Rather than leading to greater sexual freedom and peaceful relations as Reich had theorized, this kind of thinking was associated with an increase in the incidence of acquaintance rape. Beginning in the 1970s, scientifically designed surveys replicated the same statistic: one in four women on college campuses reported that they had experienced unwanted sex by the age of twenty-one (see summary of studies in Sanday 1996:184–207). During the 1960s women found that their private experience of sexual abuse stood in sharp contrast to the civil rights rhetoric of the time. Talking to one another about their sexual experiences in consciousness-raising groups gave women the power and strength to start a separate women's movement. This movement, of which I was a part, was the ground in which the third sexual revolution took root.

THE THIRD SEXUAL REVOLUTION

Today, few people realize that the feminism of the 1960s got its impetus mainly from women's shared experience of sexual abuse. There is nothing like the experience of threatened or actual sexual abuse to impress the social meaning of male dominance permanently on the brain. When I saw the faces of those boys in the gym illuminated by the setting sun as they turned menacingly toward me, reaching out, pinning me against the wall wanting to have their way, the American dream of equality and freedom was smashed in my psyche. In a few seconds I went from human being to object—the deer they had lined up in their sights, the centerfold they were about to share, the glue that would bring them together in shared abuse. In that one split second the phrase *liberty, equality, and fraternity for all* took on an entirely different, male-defined meaning. Being made the object of shared male lust in such a grossly unequal situation, I lost all sense of myself as subject.

The sexual freedom encouraged by the work of Reich, Kinsey, Hefner, and Mailer et al. meant that although the women of the sixties were having sex in greater numbers, they were not seen as equal sexual partners with the enforceable right to say No. While the so-called sexual revolution together with easy access to birth control might have freed women to have sex, it was on male, not female, terms. Getting together in consciousness-raising sessions, women began to discover the degree to which sexual expression for them was marked by either "giving in" or being forced. Few of them could say that they were in egalitarian sexual relationships characterized by mutual consent.

The discovery of the ubiquity of acquaintance rape led to a significant lobbying effort in the early to mid-seventies that resulted in rape-law reform in most of the states. "Earnest," "sufficient," or "utmost" resistance was abolished as being necessary to indicate nonconsent in most states. The legal reform was an attempt to equalize rape trials so that fear of false accusers and examining a woman's reputation no longer played decisive roles.

The reform changed outmoded laws and practices that had remained on the books since the seventeenth and eighteenth centuries. For example, in many states the death penalty for rape persisted up to the 1960s, making convictions highly unlikely. Another holdover from the seventeenth century was the practice of reading to the jury the pro-defense cautions of the seventeenth-century English judge Sir Matthew Hale. Defining rape as the "carnal knowledge of any woman above the age of ten years against her will, and of a woman-child under the age of ten with or against her will," Hale warned juries that

> rape is a most detestable crime, and therefore ought severely and impartially to be punished with death; but it must be remembered that it is an accusation easy to be made, hard to be proved, but harder to be defended by the party accused, though innocent.

By giving semilegal status to the fear of the false accuser, Hale's warning was read verbatim to jurors in many states until the 1970s, being removed, for example, from the California code of criminal procedure only in 1975 (Sanday 1996:58).

The innovation introduced by feminism to the American sexual culture was female sexual choice and affirmative consent. Women sought to return a passion to women that was on a par with men. The role of the clitoris was rediscovered and women rejected Ellis's and Freud's belief that female passion needed to be passive to spark the fire of male lust. The basic proposition was that "No means No" and that sexual consent was to be established through discourse. Although articulated in the 1970s, these ideas only began to reach the American public in the 1990s. Today, the anti-rape movement on many college campuses teaches men and women the necessity of *affirmative verbal consent*. The latter development is the most significant change in American sexual discourse of the past three centuries. It brings us back to the one-sex model with a difference: the equivalence of sexual appetite it assumes for both sexes is now joined with a corresponding call for female sexual choice and sexual equality in all aspects of social life. In the Afterword, I call this the new sexual revolution.

NOTES

1. http://www.now.org/lists/now-action-list/msg00138.html.

2. See "Interview with Mary P. Koss." http://vip.msu.edu/theCAT/ CAT_Author/MPK/interview.html. "Acquaintance Rape: A Critical Update on Recent Findings with Application to Advocacy." http://vip.msu.edu/theCAT/ CAT_Author/MPK/colorado.html.

Foreword

In this book, Professor Sanday explains the societal background that permits and, indeed, encourages male violence against women. All too often gang rape is perceived as a phenomenon of the underclass—the poor, deprived, and minorities. Sociologists, jurists, and political pundits look for the causes in poverty, racism, illiteracy, and the anomie of the young in the adult world. I, too, accepted these facile explanations in the many cases of gang rape over which I presided as a trial judge.

My initial acquaintance with fraternity gang rape also occurred in the court room. In this case no one had been arrested. The victim, instead of going to the police, had made a complaint to the university. This case is discussed extensively by Professor Sanday. I was amazed to learn that the attitudes, language, behavior, and literacy levels of these fraternity members are identical to those of young, underprivileged criminals. Both groups frequently engage in sexual behavior that others call gang rape. Both call it "playing train" or "pulling train" (one man follows after another). Both groups consider it a form of male bonding for which the female is merely an available instrument. Both may prepare themselves for this test of manhood by ingesting quantities of alcohol and fortifying themselves with drugs. Both consider this acceptable, indeed normal, conduct. Both are amazed to learn that such actions could be crimes. These fraternity brothers, like slum hoodlums, are often semiliterate and unable to present coherent and intelligible statements in their own defense even though they are high school graduates and students in good academic standing at elite universities. The difference between the two groups is that fraternity brothers are rarely, if ever, prosecuted for their conduct whereas slum youths are prosecuted, convicted, and imprisoned.

There is a similarity of pattern in these incidents. The men are on their own "turf," whether it be a part of a park, a shack, or a fraternity house. The identity of the woman is irrelevant. Anyone who happens to be at or near the premises will suffice. All the men drink a great deal of liquor. Then, in the presence of the entire group, each has sex in turn with the female.

The participants are always part of a male gang. While individually they probably would not engage in such brutal and degrading conduct, when reinforced by their companions they exhibit no sense of what most men and women consider decency or compassion.

In one case tried before me, the girl was fourteen years old and lived in a public housing project. She was on her first date. He was a neighborhood boy, her classmate in junior high school. She thought they were going to a party. I learned in the course of the trial that each member of the gang was obligated in turn to provide a girl for the benefit of all the gang. The boys had a clubhouse, an old shed bizarrely furnished, which was regularly used for group sex.

In another case, the rapists were unemployed youths in their late teens or early twenties. They had taken over an abandoned house as their headquarters. On the afternoon of the gang rape tried before me, one of the group was chosen to go to the blood bank, sell his blood, and with the proceeds buy liquor for all. Another was designated to obtain a female, also to be shared by all. The woman in this case was a married, thirty-year-old nurse. She was lured to the apartment by a man she knew on the pretext that he would sell her a TV set cheap. She was held captive for three days and repeatedly raped. When all the men were extremely drunk, she managed to make her escape.

In yet another case the young men were all married buddies who had a weekly night out. It was their practice to go to the park. One of them would pick up a young girl and ask her to go with him for something to eat or to the movies. Instead, he would take her to a secluded area where his pals would be waiting and each would have sex with her in turn.

Another gang rape occurred in the back room of a supermarket. A store guard caught a young woman shoplifting and ordered her to follow him. She did so and discovered that instead of being charged with petty larceny, she was gang raped by the guard and his pals. After a few hours she was released. She promptly went to the police, who accompanied her to the supermarket and arrested her assailants.

In all these cases, as soon as the female victim was able to make her escape, she reported the incident to the police. After some persistence on the part of the victim, the police did investigate and make arrests. The accused men were brought to trial, convicted, and sentenced to prison. In every instance the victim knew at least one of the rapists by name or nickname, and she knew where the crime had taken place. The men certainly should have known that they would be identified and apprehended. At trial, all the defendants admitted what they had done but insisted that they had not committed any crime. To them it was a customary form of amusement for normal males, which is how they saw themselves. And, of course, they blamed the victim. She "asked for it"; she should not have been where she was; she should not have complained; she wasn't harmed.

The average men and women who sat on the juries in these cases had an entirely different perspective. They brought in guilty verdicts. And when the victim sued the rapists in civil court, as did the woman who was raped in the supermarket, that jury awarded her very substantial damages.

As a judge who has presided over the trials of many gang rapists, my perspective is focused on legal principles, remedies, and procedures. My knowledge is more limited than that of Professor Sanday. It is derived wholly from the evidence produced in court. She has had the benefit of conversations with some of the male participants in these incidents, the female victims, and other men and women on college campuses. There are some differences between college gang rapes and street gang rapes, particularly in the behavior of the victims. But the similarities are more striking.

Before I was assigned the case of the alleged gang rape described by Professor Sanday and began reading the literature, I did not realize that such behavior is a pervasive phenomenon in American society. Professor Sanday, with the skills and insights of an anthropologist, illuminates and explains the underlying social attitudes that give rise to and condone such acts. She suggests far-reaching, long-term solutions as well as short-term programs to prevent such conduct. I suggest immediate changes in legal procedures on campus. The conduct of the university in the case tried before me is a paradigm of what college administrators should not do.

In that case the fraternity was in court suing the university, which had suspended it. No action had been taken against the individuals involved. Following an outcry by campus coeds after the alleged rape was reported, the university made an inquiry and issued the suspension order. I used the word *alleged* because there was never a prosecution, and so the fact of the gang rape was never legally proved.

I was, under the law, obliged to set aside the order of suspension because the hearing held by the university was conducted without a semblance of due process: hearsay, rumor, and conjecture were admitted in evidence; even though there were dozens of eye witnesses, none was called to testify; and members of the university investigating staff sat on the hearing body. This most irregular procedure was followed even though counsel for the university had been consulted during the investigation and was present during the hearing.

At the hearing, counsel for the accused fraternity was not permitted to cross-examine any of the witnesses or to present oral testimony. I remanded the matter to the university to hold a proper hearing, make findings of fact, and enter an appropriate order.

The principal evidence on behalf of the fraternity consisted of a written statement that the members had prepared and offered into evidence. Not only was it ungrammatical and replete with misspellings but it was also garbled and incomprehensible. Two excerpts from the introduction read as follows:

> Although there has [sic] been serious public allegations made against our fraternity we feel that they are gross exaggerations, maliscous [sic] fabrications, and unsubstantiated judgements.

> To try to judge such serious allegations and such subtle questions of consent and collective responsibility without a complete report, [sic] would be grossly unjust. Although the University's investigation is willing to make conclusions about such subtle questions, this is not a significant statement about what occured [sic], but rather a reflection on the process which the University and its investigators are willing to make such subtle judgments.

Following my Order, another hearing was held but no testimonial evidence was taken with respect to the charge of rape. Accordingly, the hearing officer, a law professor, found that the charge that the female victim was unable to consent to the multiple acts of intercourse was not proved. The fraternity was ordered suspended for six months. No action was taken against any of the individuals involved.

The president of the university issued a public statement in which he declared, inter alia, "Our deep concern for the woman involved in this matter remains as does our undertaking to help her." She was, it is reported, paid a substantial sum of money by the university. Whether buying off a victim who might have brought a civil suit against the university is a proper use of tax-exempt institutional funds was never publicly discussed. The university was satisfied with this resolution because the adverse publicity ceased. The alumni who are substantial contributors were mollified. The fraternity brothers were relieved that they would not be tried or punished. The women's groups were outraged but impotent. And so the matter was closed.

An experienced judge does not expect perfect justice in the courtroom. Vindication of rights often becomes secondary to pragmatic considerations. Although I could appreciate the reasons for terminating the litigation, this case troubled me for many reasons.

The glimpse of university life disclosed was appalling. At first I assumed that the behavior of these fraternity brothers was anomalous. In every large institution, no matter how careful the selection process, there will be mistakes. Miscreants have found their way into the highest levels of government, the clergy, industry, and the arts, and therefore it is likely that academe will also have its share of wrongdoers. However, both the evidence in the case itself and reports from other campuses indicate that this kind of conduct, moral myopia, absence of rules, and low level of literacy is not uncommon.

During the hearing the fraternity brothers plaintively asked what rules of university conduct they had violated. I asked a number of questions about this matter. The transcript reads in part:

> Is there any standard about consumption of alcoholic beverages? Are there any rules or regulations about having visits by members of the opposite sex? Are there any rules or regulations about anything like that? (snicker from the audience)
>
> *Counsel for the plaintiff:* He says no, Your Honor. The only thing in the University Code of Conduct says members of the University community shall not act immaturely, whatever that means. Counsel for the University assents to these answers.

Further evidence in the case disclosed that excessive drinking on campus occurred not only on weekends but at all times. Female students regularly slept in fraternity houses. There was no privacy when sexual intercourse took place. According to the fraternity members, gang sex is a common practice on campus. Their proposed finding of

Fact No. 66, submitted to the hearing officer, reads as follows: "It is common for multiple consensual sexual intercourse to occur in one evening on the University campus approximately one to two times per month." Of course, this may be treated as a self-serving statement by the fraternity members who defended themselves by saying, in effect, "We only did what everyone else was doing." The fraternity's definition of consensual sexual intercourse differs widely from the legal definition of consent, since the former takes no account of the circumstances in which the incident occurred.

Under the law, valid consent to an act, a contract, or a statement cannot be obtained if the party is coerced. Coercion need not be by physical force or threat of force or violence. The court looks at all of the circumstances surrounding the transaction to determine whether the party acted volitionally. When a legally arrested crime suspect is in the custody of the police, courts have held that the situation is inherently coercive and that statements given by the prisoner under such circumstances may not be received into evidence unless the individual has been told that he has a right to a lawyer and a right to remain silent, and that anything he says can and will be used against him. How much more coercive is the situation of a single female in the company of a half-dozen drunken males on their premises who demand that she engage in sex with all of them? There is no one to whom she can turn for protection. The circumstances are inherently coercive. But this issue was not addressed by the university hearing officer who dismissed the charge of gang rape.

A cursory review of the daily press and the literature dealing with higher education discloses some shocking facts. Professor Sanday cites the statistics on the percentage of college women who state that they have been raped. In *Coping with Crime on Campus*, Michael Clay Smith (1988) lists dozens of cases in which students and their parents have sued universities for crimes committed against them on campus. These cases are only the proverbial tip of the iceberg. Most criminal acts by students are not reported to the police. They are quietly papered over within the college or university.

Many universities shrug off responsibility on the ground that fraternities and clubs are private organizations over which they have no control. They do, of course, have control over the students who could be expelled or suspended. In most cases, however, unless the offending students are criminally prosecuted, they are shielded from the consequences of their misconduct. Even when death occurs, many institutions attempt to protect the miscreant students. In some communities the local police do not come onto the campus except at the invitation of the university.

In one case tried before me a university student was charged with burglary and theft. He admitted that he had broken into his girlfriend's dormitory room and stolen her computer and her color TV. She was the last in a series of coeds whose expensive possessions he had stolen and fenced. These items included skis, watches, jewelry, typewriters, radios, and television sets. All the victims had complained to the university authorities. But nothing was recovered and no disciplinary action was taken against the thieving student.

He was a National Merit Scholarship winner who was on a full four-year scholarship and also received a stipend from the university. I convicted him and as a condition of probation ordered him to leave the university, get a job, repay the victims of his crimes, and also pay a stiff fine. The university protested that he was a promising student and should not be forced to give up his scholarship and a bright academic future. I replied that this young man was a criminal and that the university by its actions was condoning his crimes. There was no meeting of the minds. Under my sentence this young man cannot return to college until he pays these penalties in full. If at the termination of probation the university chooses to reward him with more scholarships, that is beyond my jurisdiction.

Similar extraordinarily tender concern is shown by many colleges and universities to their students who commit serious and inexcusable crimes. For example, fourteen Rutgers students who were charged in the drinking death of a fraternity pledge were permitted to plead guilty and accept a counseling program in lieu of any other penalty. Those who successfully complete the six-month program will have the charges removed from their record.

At Harvard, a resident in one of the teaching hospitals sexually assaulted several patients. Derek Bok, president of Harvard, writes, "Rather than discipline the culprit or insist upon appropriate psychiatric treatment, those in charge arranged for him to leave quietly and then sent letters of recommendation to other hospitals without mentioning the circumstances of his departure." Bok recognized that this was wrong, but he ignored the right course of action: criminal prosecution. A criminal record might prevent the man from ever practicing medicine, but why should a university protect one of its members from the legal consequences of criminal behavior and the penalties to which other less favored persons who commit crimes are exposed?

Willard Gaylin, in his book *The Killing of Bonnie Garland*, notes the concern for the criminal shown by the university. Bonnie Garland, an exemplary Yale student, was brutally murdered in her parents' home by another Yale student. He was academically unsuccessful. Apparently he was her boyfriend and she had sought to terminate the relationship. Instead of recoiling in horror from such a crime, the university community—administration and faculty—as well as an order of Catholic priests gave aid and comfort and housing to the murderer. The victim's father, himself a Yale alumnus, was understandably outraged.

Other parents of female students who have been crime victims have reacted by suing the colleges and universities. Some parents of students and prospective students have demanded information, hitherto concealed, with respect to campus crimes. For example, Pennsylvania has enacted a law requiring that such information be made available to students, prospective students, and their parents.

I do not believe that draconian prison sentences or the death penalty fulfill the aims of the proponents of such sentences. Few prisoners are reformed by their experiences in prison. Most street criminals get a graduate course in crime while in prison; many are raped by other inmates and abused by prison guards; few receive education or counseling. Impetuous young people who commit crimes in moments of rage or fear are seldom deterred by the thought that if they are caught the penalty will be severe. Even white collar criminals are not deterred from their carefully plotted crimes by the sentences imposed on others. Nonetheless, the credibility of the law and the concept of equal justice require that regardless of wealth and privilege, wrongdoers should be tried and convicted and some meaningful punishment should be imposed.

But even those most familiar with campus crime continue to view it as an in-house problem that can be solved within the college community. A naively benign solution, frequently expressed, proposes building community among students and encouraging them to report incidents of violence and rape. Such steps are necessary, but all too often universities do little, if anything, to discipline the offending students, and hardly ever are criminal offenses handed over to the police for criminal prosecution.

The exceptional position of members of the college community and their immunity from legal process has a long history dating to the establishment of universities in Europe in the twelfth century when the academic community consisted of a homogenous group of privileged males. This tradition was replicated in the United States and continued relatively unchanged for many years. The campus scene changed dramatically with the GI Bill of Rights and with the influx of women into universities that had been elite male institutions. Academic achievement and college board scores became more important in the admission process than old money and family connections. The turmoil of the 1960s, affirmative action, and student control of the curriculum accelerated the process of change. In the 1960s fraternities were viewed with suspicion, if not scorn.

In the 1980s, Reaganomics and the push for money and power have taken priority over the goals of public service, equality of opportunity, and intellectual inquiry. Fraternities have had a resurgence of popularity. They are probably the last bastion of male exclusivity and privilege on the campus. Fraternity life is again characterized by excessive drinking, idleness, and sexual liberties. But the females with whom these fraternity brothers indulge themselves are no longer exclusively "townies," they are also classmates.

These young women and their parents do not view such incidents with benign indulgence or subscribe to the view that "boys will be boys" whose careers should not be blighted because of sexual misconduct. They see this solicitude for male student malefactors as blatant evidence of sexism.

Although 53% of students at American universities and colleges are females, only 10% of the presidents of these institutions are females. Apparently old-boy feelings of solidarity by college administrators operate to protect male students from the consequence of their misconduct at the expense of their female victims.

Derek Bok, writing in the May—June 1988 issue of *Harvard Magazine*, discusses the problems of ethics and the university. He recommends a "comprehensive program of moral education" on campuses consisting of these elements: courses in "applied ethics," discussing and administering rules of student conduct, programs of community service, striving for high ethical standards in dealing with moral issues, and sending signals to the students that the university will support basic ethical norms. These proposals, although probably good in themselves, will not suffice to meet the problem. *Applied ethics* is a vague and novel term. As Bok himself recognizes, didactic courses in ethics have not been effective in the past, nor have strict codes of student conduct. I have little confidence that new nomenclature and the addition of supplemental discussions and explanations will make courses and codes of conduct more effective in the future unless enforced by severe sanctions. Mere discussion of the impropriety of gang rape is unlikely to be persuasive. Community service has little to do with the problem of ethics and crime on campus.

The strongest signal a university can send to its students that unethical and illegal conduct will not be tolerated is to take two simple measures: file criminal complaints and suspend or expel all members of the college community who violate the law or basic norms of decent behavior. This applies to groups such as fraternities as well as to individual students.

At present, American colleges and universities are failing to meet their obligations to the students and their parents. They do not provide a safe, secure environment. Professor Sanday shows with a wealth of horrifying detail the indecent acts of male bonding, the dehumanizing of young men, and the disregard of women as human beings that occur in an environment in which these men consider themselves beyond the strictures of law. And she shows that these are not innate biological traits of violence but learned social patterns that can be changed. Academe is entrusted with educating the brightest and best of the next generation not only for positions of leadership in science, the humanities, arts, society, and government, but also to be decent, law-abiding citizens of a democracy. So long as any university tolerates crime, vicious behavior, and dubious ethical standards, it betrays the students and the entire nation.

Lois G. Forer

Introduction to the First Edition

This book presents an anthropological case study and analysis of certain group rituals of male bonding on a college campus. In particular, this study is focused on a phenomenon called "pulling train." According to a report issued by the Association of American Colleges in 1985, "pulling train," or "gang banging" as it is also called, refers to a group of men lining up like train cars to take turns having sex with the same woman (Ehrhart and Sandler 1985, 2). This report labels "pulling train" as gang rape. Bernice Sandler, one of its authors, recently reported that she had found more than seventy-five documented cases of gang rape on college campuses in recent years (*Atlanta Constitution*, 7 June 1988). Sandler labeled these incidents gang rape because of the coercive nature of the sexual behavior. The incidents she and Julie K. Ehrhart described in their 1985 report display a common pattern. A vulnerable young woman, one who is seeking acceptance or who is high on drugs or alcohol, is taken to a room. She may or may not agree to have sex with one man. She then passes out, or is too weak or scared to protest, and a train of men have sex with her. Sometimes the young woman's drinks are spiked without her knowledge, and when she is approached by several men in a locked room, she reacts with confusion and panic. Whether too weak to protest, frightened, or unconscious, as has been the case in quite a number of instances, anywhere from two to eleven or more men have sex with her. In some party invitations the possibility of such an occurrence is mentioned with playful allusions to "gang bang" or "pulling train" (Ehrhart and Sandler 1985, 1–2).

The reported incidents occurred at all kinds of institutions: "public, private, religiously affiliated, Ivy League, large and small" (ibid.). Most of the incidents occurred at fraternity parties, but some occurred in residence halls or in connection with college athletics. Incidents have also been reported in high schools. For example, in the spring of 1989 news reports described an incident involving the cocaptains of an elite suburban high school football team, who with three schoolmates were charged with sexually assaulting a teenage "mentally handicapped" girl while at least eight other boys watched (*Record* (Hackensack, N.J.), 23 May 1989).

Just a few examples taken from the Ehrhart and Sandler report (1985, 1–2) are sufficient to demonstrate the coercive nature of the sexual behavior.

- The 17-year-old freshman woman went to the fraternity "little sister" rush party with two of her roommates. The roommates left early without her. She was trying to get a ride home when a fraternity brother told her he would take her home after the party ended. While she waited, two other fraternity members took her into a bedroom to "discuss little sister matters." The door was closed and one of the brothers stood blocking the exit. They told her that in order to become a little sister (honorary member) she would have to have sex with a fraternity member. She was frightened, fearing they would physically harm her if she refused. She could see no escape. Each of the brothers had sex with her, as did a third who had been hiding in the room. During the next two hours a succession of men went into the room. There were never less than three men with her, sometimes more. After they let her go, a fraternity brother drove her home. He told her not to feel bad about the incident because another woman had also been "upstairs" earlier that night. (Large southern university)
- It was her first fraternity party. The beer flowed freely and she had much more to drink than she had planned. It was hot and crowded and the party spread out all over the house, so that when three men asked her to go upstairs, she went with them. They took her into a bedroom, locked the door and began to undress her. Groggy with alcohol, her feeble protests were ignored as the three men raped her. When they finished, they put her in the hallway, naked, locking her clothes in the bedroom. (Small eastern liberal arts college)
- A 19-year-old woman student was out on a date with her boyfriend and another couple. They were all drinking beer and after going back to the boyfriend's dorm room, they smoked two marijuana cigarettes. The other couple left and the woman and her boyfriend had sex. The woman fell asleep and the next thing

she knew she awoke with a man she didn't know on top of her trying to force her into having sex. A witness said the man was in the hall with two other men when the woman's boyfriend came out of his room and invited them to have sex with his unconscious girlfriend. (Small midwestern college)

Although Ehrhart and Sandler boldly labeled the incidents they described as rape, few of the perpetrators were prosecuted. Generally speaking, the male participants are prosecuted and the victim is blamed for having placed herself in a compromising social situation where male adolescent hormones are known, as the saying goes, "to get out of hand." For a number of reasons, people say, "She asked for it." As the above examples from the Ehrhart and Sandler report suggest, the victim may be a vulnerable young woman who is seeking acceptance or who is weakened by the ingestion of drugs or alcohol. She may or may not agree to having sex with one man. If she has agreed to some sexual activity, the men assume that she has agreed to all sexual activity regardless of whether she is conscious or not. In the minds of the boys involved the sexual behavior is not rape. On many campuses this opinion is shared by a significant portion of the campus community.

In this book I apply the anthropological method to an investigation of the values, social expectations, and institutional practice encouraging "pulling train" on a college campus. Since the value of the anthropological method lies in its focus on particular actions rather than on large-sample surveys, I begin by reporting an incident that occurred in one setting—a college fraternity. However, information from other campuses where "trains" have been reported is also included to indicate that the sexual behavior I describe is widespread.

Professional ethics demands that anthropologists do not reveal the identity or location of the people they study. Therefore, none of the students mentioned in this study are referred to by his or her real names. Unfortunately, it is more difficult to conceal the identity of the location of the study because the case on which I focus was widely reported in the press. Thus, I wish to emphasize at the outset that the specific location is not relevant to the subject of this book. The kind of behavior this case illustrates appears to be widespread not only among fraternities but in many other exclusively male contexts at colleges and universities in the United States, such as organized sports. It or its equivalent is also found outside universities where men band together in clubs, work groups, athletic teams, military units, and business conventions—in all the settings we associate with the term "stag party." To help focus the reader's attention on the issues, therefore, I shall refer to the university simply as U. and to the fraternity as XYZ.

I also wish to stress at the outset that the sexual discourse and practices I describe are associated with a small, although highly visible, subculture of male students. The reader should not assume that all college males or all fraternity brothers act in the manner described below. The tragedy of "pulling train" and other forms of sexual harassment on college campuses is that although a minority of men on campus may be involved in promoting or participating in the acts of sexual aggression, a large number of women are affected. Although few female students are gang raped, an alarming number of them (as many as 92 percent at one campus) report that they had "experienced at least one form of unwanted sexual attention and had reacted negatively to it" (Hughes and Sandler 1989). Additionally, news of just one incident of group sexual aggression against a lone college woman that goes unpunished and is accepted as standard practice can have an intimidating affect on large numbers of women students, making them feel insecure and unsafe in the college environment.

THE XYZ EXPRESS

I first learned about "pulling train" in 1983 from a student who was then enrolled in one of my classes. Laurel had been out of class for about two weeks. I noticed her absence and worried that she was getting behind on her work. When she came back to class she told me that she had been raped by five or six male students at a fraternity house after one of the fraternity's weekly Thursday night parties. Later, I learned from others that Laurel was drunk on beer and had taken four hits of LSD before going to the party. According to the story Laurel told to a campus administrator, after the party she fell asleep in a first-floor room and when she awoke was undressed. One of the brothers dressed her and carried her upstairs, where she was raped by "guys" she did not know but said she could identify if photographs were available. She asked a few times for the men to get off her, but to no avail. According to her account, she was barely conscious and lacked the strength to push them off her.

There is no dispute that Laurel had a serious drinking and drug problem at the time of the party. People at the party told me that during the course of the evening she acted like someone who was "high," and her behavior attracted quite a bit of attention. They described her as dancing provocatively to the beat of music only she could hear. She appeared disoriented and out of touch with what was happening. Various fraternity brothers occasionally danced with her, but she seemed oblivious to the person she was dancing with. Some of the brothers teased her by spinning her around in a room until she was so dizzy she couldn't find her way out. At one point during the evening she fell down a flight of stairs. Later she was pulled by the brothers out of a circle dance, a customary fraternity ritual in which only brothers usually took part.

After the other partyers had gone home, the accounts of what happened next vary according to who tells the story. The differences of opinion do not betray a Rashomon effect as much as they reflect different definitions of a common sexual event. No one disputes that Laurel had sex with at least five or six male students, maybe more. When Anna, a friend of the XYZ brothers, saw Laurel the next day and heard the story from the brothers, her immediate conclusion was that they had raped Laurel. Anna based her conclusion on seeing Laurel's behavior at the party and observing her the following day. It seemed to Anna that Laurel was incapable of consenting to sex, which is key for determining a charge of rape. Anna's opinion was later confirmed by the Assistant District Attorney for Sex Crimes, who investigated but did not prosecute the case for reasons to be discussed later (see chapter 3).

The brothers claimed that Laurel had lured them into a "gang bang" or "train," which they preferred to call an "express." Their statements and actions during the days after the event seemed to indicate that they considered the event a routine part of their "little sisters program," something to be proud of. Reporting the party activities on a sheet posted on their bulletin board in the spot where the house minutes are usually posted, Anna found the following statement, which she later showed me:

> Things are looking up for the [XYZ] sisters program. A prospective leader for the group spent some time interviewing several [brothers] this past thursday and friday. Possible names for the little sisters include [XYZ] "little wenches" and "The [XYZ] express."

The XYZ brothers never publicly admitted to wrongdoing. Although there was no criminal prosecution and conviction in this case, I concluded that what had occurred at the XYZ house was, in fact, rape, as the term is legally defined. This conclusion was based on my talk with Laurel and interviews with other students who had observed her behavior at the party, as well as other evidence presented in this book. Like Anna, I believe that Laurel was unable to give consent. Therefore, I will refer to the incident as "rape" instead of "alleged rape."

PURPOSE AND GENERAL APPROACH

After Laurel reported the incident to me and other feminists on campus, a rally, sponsored by five campus women's organizations, was held to protest violence against women. At that rally a number of us spoke about the kind of environment that encourages a climate of sexual exploitation. Carol Smith-Rosenberg, a feminist historian, challenged her colleagues to bring the issue of sexism into "the classroom for discussion within the frame of a liberal arts education and a community of scholars." Carol Tracy, Director of the Women's Center at the time, reminded us of the role campuses can play in social change. This book responds to these concerns and to the many others arising from the growing knowledge about the prevalence of coercive sexual behavior on college campuses. My purpose is to explore and analyze the sexual subculture that encourages and supports "pulling train."

As an anthropologist I have studied the cross-cultural incidence of rape in tribal societies (see Sanday 1981a and 1981b) and have conducted intensive fieldwork in one society (located in Southeast Asia; see Sanday 1986, 1988, 1990a). This research falls within a long-standing theoretical tradition in anthropology that emphasizes the cultural construction of norms for sexual behavior. As Malinowski noted long ago, although the capacity for sexual pleasure may be constitutional, human sexual behavior "is rather a sociological and cultural force than a mere bodily relation of two individuals" (Malinowski 1929, xxiii. For more recent discussions by anthropologists of the cultural construction of sexual behavior see Vance 1984 and Caplan 1987).

Occurring frequently in some societies and rarely in others, rape in tribal societies is demonstrably part of a cultural configuration that includes interpersonal violence, male dominance, and sexual separation.

In these societies, as the Murphys (1974, 197) say of the Mundurucu, "Men . . . use the penis to dominate their women." Such a configuration evolves in societies faced with depleting food resources, migration, or other factors contributing to a pervasive sense that the natural environment is out of control and that human beings are dependent on male efforts to control and harness destructive natural forces. It is significant that in societies where nature is held sacred, and the mother-child bond is respected as the primary and enduring social relationship, male sexual aggression is rare. On the basis of these and other differences between rape-prone and rape-free societies, I suggest that rape is not an integral part of male nature, but the means by which men programmed for violence and control use sexual aggression to display masculinity and to induct younger man into masculine roles (1981b).

SEX AND POWER ON CAMPUS

In this book I turn away from the societies I have studied in the past to investigate the values, social expectations, and institutional practices encouraging male sexual aggression in the environment in which I work: the university setting. In this setting, as in the others I have investigated, my research demonstrates that sexual aggression is the means by which some men display masculinity and induct younger men into masculine power roles. It will be useful for me to summarize the theoretical framework I have developed for understanding the meaning of "pulling train" before presenting this research.

Echoing the early conclusions of writers like Malinowski, many contemporary writers (see Weeks 1985 for examples) conceive of sexual behavior not as a "stubborn drive" but rather as "an especially dense transfer point for relations of power" (Foucault 1980, 103). Many feminist writers have commented on the relationship between sexual aggression and male dominance. This is a central theme in Susan Brownmiller's treatment of rape (1975) and Andrea Dworkin's (1987) discussion of intercourse. In one of the most extended theoretical and historical analyses of the relationship between sex and power, Michel Foucault argues that sexual expression is channeled by strategies of knowledge and power used for defining the nature of desire so as to deploy male and female bodies in certain ways. Foucault's analysis is particularly relevant because he illustrates the degree to which sexual expression, although motivated by considerations of power, is communicated and learned through discourse.

For purposes of analysis it is useful to distinguish between sexual expression and sexuality. Sexual expression deploys polymorphous sexual desire in a given social relationship; the desire is channeled by strategies of knowledge and power. Sexuality, on the other hand, considered without regard to the social relationship in which it is expressed, can be defined as polymorphous desire, involving conscious and unconscious fantasies and eliciting "a range of excitations and activities that produce pleasure beyond the satisfaction of any basic physiological need" (Mitchell 1982, 2). Sexuality is polymorphous because "it arises from various sources, seeks satisfaction in many different ways and makes use of many diverse objects for its aim of achieving pleasure" (ibid.). Only with difficulty does polymorphous sexuality move from being a drive with many component parts "to being what is normally understood as sexuality, something which *appears* to be a unified instinct in which genitality predominates" (ibid.).

I suggest that "pulling train" is a form of sexual expression that is defined as normal and natural (hence normative) by some men and women. In the act of "pulling train" polymorphous sexuality is focused primarily on the penis and, hence, is phallocentric. The sexual act is not concerned with sexual gratification but with the deployment of the penis as a concrete symbol of masculine social power and dominance. The male sexual bonding evident in "pulling train" is a sexual expression and display of the power of the brotherhood to control and dominate women. The discourse associated with acts of "pulling train" defines this form of control and domination as part of normal male sexual expression. Thus, this discourse operates as a strategy of knowledge that sanctions the deployment of male power in acts of sexual aggression.

Discourse is "a domain of language-use, a particular way of talking (and writing and thinking)" (Belsey 1980, 5). We can speak of a phallocentric discourse, which like all discourse involves certain shared assumptions, in this case concerning the nature of male sexual needs. Related to the phallocentric discourse is an ideology or a set of assumptions about the way things naturally are, in this case the way things are and should be sexually. A phallocentric ideology cannot be separated from phallocentric discourse and practice because the ideology is inscribed and represented in discourse and practice.

The ideology that promotes "pulling train" is seen in the discourse and practices associated with some parties on campus. Party invitations expressing this ideology depict a woman lying on a pool table, or in some other position suggestive of sexual submission. The hosts of the party promote behavior aimed at seduction. *Seduction* means plying women with alcohol or giving them drugs in order to "break down resistance." A drunken woman is not defined as being in need of protection and help, but as "asking for it." If the situation escalates into sexual activity, the brothers watch each other perform sexual acts and then brag about "getting laid." The event is referred to as "drunken stupidity, women chasing, and all around silliness." The drama enacted parodies the image of the gentleman. Its male participants brag about their masculinity and its female participants are degraded to the status of what the boys call "red meat" or "fish." The whole scenario joins men in a no-holds-barred orgy of togetherness. The woman whose body facilitates all of this is sloughed off at the end like a used condom. She may be called a "nympho" or the men may believe that they seduced her—a practice known as "working a yes out"—through promises of becoming a little sister, by getting her drunk, by promising her love, or by some other means. Those men who object to this kind of behavior run the risk of being labeled "wimps" or, even worse in their eyes, "gays" or "faggots."

The rationalization for this behavior illustrates a broader social ideology of male dominance. Both the brothers and many members of the broader community excuse the behavior by saying that "boys will be boys" and that if a woman gets into trouble it is because "she asked for it," "she wanted it," or "she deserved it." The ideology inscribed in this discourse represents male sexuality as more natural and more explosive than female sexuality. This active, "naturally" explosive nature of male sexuality is expected to find an outlet either in the company of male friends or in the arms of prostitutes. In these contexts men are supposed to use women to satisfy explosive urges. The women who satisfy these urges are included as passive actors in the enactment of a sexual discourse where the male, but not the female, sexual instinct is characterized as an insatiable biological instinct and psychological need.

Men entice one another into the act of "pulling train" by implying that those who do not participate are unmanly or homosexual. This behavior is full of contradictions because the homoeroticism of "pulling train" seems obvious. A group of men watch each other having sex with a woman who may be unconscious. One might well ask why the woman is even necessary for the sexual acts these men stage for one another. As fraternity practices described in this book suggest, the answer seems to lie in homophobia. One can suggest that in the act of "pulling train" the polymorphous sexuality of homophobic men is given a strictly heterosexual form.

Polymorphous sexuality, a term used by Freud to refer to diffuse sexual interests with multiple objects, means that men will experience desire for one another. However, homophobia creates a tension between polymorphous sexual desire and compulsory heterosexuality. This tension is resolved by "pulling train": the brothers vent their interest in one another through the body of a woman. In the sociodrama that is enacted, the idea that heterosexual males are superior to women and to homosexuals is publicly expressed and probably subjectively absorbed. Thus, both homophobia and compulsory heterosexuality can be understood as strategies of knowledge and power centering on sex that support the social stratification of men according to sexual preference.

In group sex, homoerotic desire is simultaneously indulged, degraded, and extruded from the group. The fact that the woman involved is often unconscious highlights her status as a surrogate victim in a drama where the main agents are males interacting with one another. The victim embodies the sexual urges of the brothers; she is defined as "wanting it"—even though she may be unconscious during the event—so that the men can satisfy their urges for one another at her expense. By defining the victim as "wanting it," the men convince themselves of their heterosexual prowess and delude themselves as to the real object of their lust. If they were to admit to the real object, they would give up their position in the male status hierarchy as superior, heterosexual males. The expulsion and degradation of the victim both brings a momentary end to urges that would divide the men and presents a social statement of phallic heterosexual dominance.

By blaming the victim for provoking their own sexual aggression, men control and define acceptable and unacceptable female sexual behavior through the agency of fear. The fear is that a woman who does not guard her behavior runs the risk of becoming the target of uncontrollable male sexual aggression. Thus, although women are ostensibly the controlling agent, it is fear of the imagined explosive nature of male sexuality that ultimately reigns for both sexes. This fear instills in some men and women consciousness of their sexual and social identities.

In sum, the phenomenon of "pulling train" has many meanings. In addition to those meanings that have been mentioned, it is a bonding device that can permanently change a young man's understanding of masculinity. The bonding is accomplished by virtue of coparticipation in a "forbidden" act. As Ward Goodenough (1963) points out, sharing in the forbidden as part of initiation to a group is a powerful bonding device. For example, criminal gangs may require the initiate to perform a criminal act in order to be accepted as a member, an act that once performed is irrevocable. Participation in a "train" performs the same function of bonding the individual to the group and changing his subjectivity. Such bridge-burning acts of one kind or another are standard parts of ritualized identity-change procedures.

THE CONDITIONS PROMOTING "PULLING TRAIN"

We cannot assume that all entering college students have well-established sexual and social identities or ethical positions regarding sexual harassment and abuse. Recent research by psychologists on human subjectivity argues that subjectivity is dynamic and changes as individuals move through the life cycle (see chapter 8). The evidence presented here suggests that the masculine subjectivity of insecure males may be shaped, or at least reinforced, by experiences associated with male bonding at college.

For example, three fraternity initiation rituals are described in chapters 6 and 7 in which young men who admit to feelings of low self-esteem upon entering the college setting are forced to cleanse and purify themselves of the despised and dirty feminine, "nerdy," "faggot" self bonded to their mothers. The ritual process in these cases humiliates the pledges in order to break social and psychological bonds to parental authority and to establish new bonds to the brotherhood. The traumatic means employed to achieve these goals induces a state of consciousness that makes abuse of women a means to renew fraternal bonds and assert power as a brotherhood.

One of the most important social conditions promoting the act of "pulling train" has to do with the university's response when particular incidents are reported. There is a widespread tendency on the part of college administrators to ignore or cover up reports of specific incidents. In protecting the male students involved, the school also protects its image. Such a response only encourages a repetition of rape-prone party activities. The absence of a strong set of sanctions against abusive party sex on many campuses not only encourages incidents of gang rape but also helps explain the high incidence of sexual harassment and date rape at colleges, such as reported by Mary Koss and her colleagues (1987). Much of the material presented in this book helps to explain the mentality that makes sexual harassment and date rape so much a part of the college dating culture.

THE DEFINITION OF RAPE

A number of readers of drafts of this book have raised questions about the women I describe who agree to some sexual activity and then pass out while a group of brothers continue to have sex with them. These readers believe that there is complicity on the part of women who submit to the sexual demands of a few or who dress and act provocatively. It is important to stress here that in the state where the XYZ incident occurred, the law implies that regardless of a woman's past sexual history or provocative behavior, when she says no and asks a man or men to stop, they are legally bound to stop all sexual activity. Additionally, the law states that *if a woman is incapable of consent, any sexual activity with her is legally classified as rape.*

Currently there seems to be widespread ignorance about the legal definition of rape. Many people believe that rape is sexual intercourse accomplished either by direct force or a threat of force. They do not understand that in most states rape applies also to sexual intercourse where the victim, by reason of unconsciousness, mental derangement or deficiency, retardation, or intoxication, is incapable of consent. To this we can add the points raised by Judge Forer in the Foreword. Legal consent to an act, a contract, or a statement cannot be obtained if the party is coerced. Coercion need not be accomplished by physical force or threat of force but may be inherent in the circumstances surrounding the transaction. The circumstances in which a single female is in the company of a half-dozen drunken males on their premises who demand that she engage in sex with them are inherently coercive. University administrators who permit the contexts in which these circumstances occur or who do not investigate charges stemming from the behavior that takes place in these settings contribute to a rape-prone environment on college campuses.

SPECIFIC APPROACH AND METHOD

In keeping with my emphasis on ideology, discourse, and practice, as noted above, in the first part of this book I present the context—the ideology, discourse, and institutional setting—in which a specific incident of "pulling train" was defined as "no problem" by the men involved and lightly punished by the institution. The first section of the book is devoted to a description and analysis of what happened to Laurel and how the university administration responded. In addition to my conversations with university administrators about the incident, my understanding of the incident is based on my conversations with students who were at the party and with the assistant district attorney who investigated the case. I also talked extensively with journalist Mark Bowden, whose account of the incident appeared in the *Philadelphia Inquirer Magazine* (see Bowden 1983).

In order to achieve an understanding of the broader social context making "pulling train" an expectable part of sexual behavior for certain groups of men on campus, I trained students to interview men and women at parties and in fraternity houses. The interviewing took place during the course of two years. In all cases, with the agreement of the persons interviewed, conversations were tape recorded and the interviews transcribed. Additionally, several students wrote about their own experiences in fraternities, including the fraternity in which the incident occurred. The data I present are culled from these sources. The result is a unique documentation by students of a sexual subculture on a college campus. The social prevalence of the ideas and values reported by these students and reflected in their conversations is suggested by the fact that these same values and attitudes are repeated in the information derived from other campuses.

Another part of the book describes incidents that occurred on other campuses. I interviewed the victim of a gang rape that occurred on another campus and searched for reports of events in newspapers and magazines. I also gained access to the police report of a gang rape on still another campus. Additionally, I cite the nationwide study of sexual experiences of college students conducted by Koss and her colleagues (see Koss et al. 1987). From this material, together with information I include on fraternity initiation rituals, one can conclude that the attitudes and behavior connected with "pulling train" are part of a nationwide sexual subculture.

This book is organized into two sections. In the first, I devote chapter 1 to describing the institutional contexts and the discourse that made the "XYZ Express" natural, seemingly expected, and fun to the perpetrators. In chapter 2 the story of the XYZ Express is told from the point of view of two female students who were very familiar with life at the XYZ house. These stories help us to understand the motivation of young women who get involved in fraternity party life. In chapter 3 I give an account of the aftermath of the XYZ incident, describing the reaction of the brothers, the legal implications of the incident, and the university administration's reaction. In order to demonstrate that the XYZ Express is a national and not a local phenomenon, this section ends with a chapter describing cases on other, geographically distinct campuses. These cases demonstrate how some young women are unknowingly caught in the fraternity party net while pledging a sorority or because they have put their trust in female roommates or in fraternity brothers at a party. The complicity of other, usually more experienced, women in some incidents of gang rape indicates that the phenomenon is not necessarily restricted to men alone. Thus, it is misleading to assume that men are necessarily the only aggressors in these cases. Women who aid men in their search for victims are as responsible as the men who participate in the sexual behavior.

The next section of the book begins with a chapter examining the processes by which the discourse and practices of phallocentrism are communicated among male students: chapter 5 focuses on the sexual discourse of fraternity brothers in several houses. In their late night talk among themselves these brothers demean women as sex objects as they promote brotherly feeling among themselves. As they talk among themselves about a variety of topics—pornography, homosexuality, the XYZ incident—the brothers display an unwitting sense of their dominance over the women they invite to their parties and their right to exploit these women sexually. These points are illustrated by transcripts of conversations between fraternity brothers talking about "working a yes out" and "getting laid." In their talk as well as at their parties these brothers use women and sex to rehearse the dominance and control expected of successful American men. It is interesting to note that in the discussions reported here none of the brothers resist the dominant discourse. The unstated goal is agreement and fraternal unity. Talking about sex and "working a yes out" unites men who might otherwise experience intense rivalry as they prepare themselves to enter the competitive marketplace.

A sexist consciousness is stamped on the bodies and psyches of pledges during some initiation rituals. Chapters 6 and 7 describe three rituals drawn from several universities that illustrate the "truth games" brothers may play to mold a new generation of pledges into a masculine, brotherly image. One of the truth games is subjugation of the self to the bonds of brotherhood in order to become a "brother" and thereby a "man." This game is played out in the abusive behavior of the ritual that includes "killing the woman" and cleansing "the fag" in the pledges. The humiliation, pain, and sheer physicality of these acts can be interpreted as a radical resocialization, a physical brainwashing that alters consciousness. The pledge who survives and accepts the abuse earns the right to be a "true brother," a true man, and to dominate the next generation of pledges. We can speculate that, as is true of the sexual abuse of children in the family, the physical abuse of pledges may have lasting effects. At the least we must recognize that the abuse of pledges in some fraternities on college campuses is a training ground for an abusive and sexist subjectivity. This recognition is the subject of chapter 8. A society that confuses masculinity with abuse can expect its adult male members to act accordingly.

CONCLUSION

The material presented in this book is derived from interviews and observations in a few of the many fraternities at U. and on several other campuses. The sexual aggression evident in these particular cases does not mean that sexual aggression is restricted to fraternities or that all fraternities indulge in sexual aggression. Sexist attitudes and the phallocentric mentality associated with "pulling train" have a long history in Western society. For example, venting homoerotic desire in the gang rape of women who are treated as male property is the subject of several biblical stories. Susan Brownmiller describes instances of gang rape by men in war and in street gangs. Male bonding that rejects women and commodifies sex is evident in many other social contexts outside of universities. Thus, it would be wrong to place the blame solely on fraternities. However, it is a fact also that most of the reported incidents of "pulling train" on campus have been associated with fraternities.

Cross-cultural research demonstrates that whenever men build and give allegiance to a mystical, enduring, all-male social group, the disparagement of women is, invariably, an important ingredient of the mystical bond, and sexual aggression the means by which the bond is renewed (Sanday 1981b, 1986). As long as exclusive male clubs exist in a society that privileges men as a social category, we must recognize that collective sexual aggression provides a ready stage on which some men represent their social privilege and introduce adolescent boys to their future place in the status hierarchy.

Why has the sexual abuse of women and the humiliation of generations of pledges been tolerated for so long? The answer lies in a historical tendency to privilege male college students by failing to hold them accountable. Administrators protect young men by dissociating asocial behavior from the perpetrator and attributing it to something else. For example, one hears adult officials complaining about violence committed by fraternity brothers at the same time they condone the violence by saying that "things got out of hand" because of alcohol, adolescence, or some other version of "boys will be boys." Refusing to take serious action against young offenders promotes the male privilege that led to the behavior in the first place. At some level, perhaps, administrators believe that by taking effective action to end all forms of abuse they deny young men a forum for training for masculinity. Where this is the case women students cannot possibly experience the same social opportunities or sense of belonging at college as their male peers, even though they spend the same amount of money for the privilege of attending. As colleges and universities face an increasing number of legal suits deriving from rape, murder, and the other forms of abuse reported in fraternities, athletic settings, and dorms, change is clearly imminent. This book is dedicated to the proposition that the direction of change must be based on an understanding of the multifaceted nature of the problem.

Acknowledgments

This book could not have been written without the cooperation of Judge Lois Forer, who gave me access to all of the documents pertinent to the case argued before her by counsels for the university and the fraternity. Equally crucial to the success of this book has been the cooperation and hard work of a number of courageous students who worked on this project and hoped that I would publish the results. Most of these students cannot be named, but they know who they are. I particularly want to thank Laurel, Anna, Amy, Laura, Alice, Sean, Bob, and Rick, whose lives were in one way or another significantly affected by the incidents described in this book and who worked with me as co-investigators by supplying the details of their own experiences. Additionally, many other students worked as interviewers on campus.

Carol Tracy, who as Director of the Women's Center worked for many years to combat sexism and violence against women on campus, was a constant source of inspiration. I dedicate this book to her and to Andrea Ploscowe and Meg Davis, students who showed uncommon courage in resisting the sexual exploitation of women on their respective campuses.

I also want to thank William Heiman, Mark Bowden, and Peter Canellos for the interest they took in this work and for their own courage in speaking out against the behavior I describe. These men have taught me that feminism is a way of thinking and not a matter of gender.

I received support during this project from the university's administration, particularly the Office of Computing Facilities and the Office of the Vice Provost for University Life. I am also very grateful to the president of the university, who from the beginning of the project supported its intention.

This has not been an easy book to write. A number of individuals played a significant role in the editing process. Kathleen Barry, Linda Brodkey, Michelle Fine, and Lucienne Frappier-Mazur read some of the many drafts of the manuscript and provided thoughtful comments as well as encouraging support. Ward and Ruth Goodenough, anthropological colleagues, and Kitty Moore, Senior Editor at New York University Press, worked very hard helping me to shape the final draft. To these individuals I am extremely grateful for their time, effort, and encouragement.

PART I

THE XYZ EXPRESS

One

Campus Party Culture

For entering students college represents a break from the restrictions of high school and family life. College life provides not only the means to prepare for a profession and develop intellectual skills but also the opportunity for developing independence and forging a self. Among the social traditions of interest to entering students is the sexual culture and the opportunities this culture offers for sexual expression. On many campuses the sexual culture includes the notion that sexual exploitation is part of normal male sexual expression.

In recent years we have learned a great deal about the prevalence of acquaintance rape on college campuses (see Warshaw 1988 for a summary of numerous studies). The most comprehensive study was conducted by Mary Koss and her colleagues in the mid-eighties. This national study of 6,159 students enrolled in thirty-two institutions of higher education in the United States reported that nearly half of the over three thousand women students surveyed had experienced some form of sexual coercion since the age of fourteen (see Koss et al. 1987). These women respondents reported several different types of sexually coercive behaviors. For example,

- 44 percent of them reported that they had "given in to sex play (fondling, kissing, or petting, but not intercourse) when [they] didn't want to because [they] were overwhelmed by a man's continual arguments and pressures";
- 15 percent said they had experienced attempted intercourse by threat of force;
- 12 percent said they had experienced attempted intercourse by the use of alcohol or drugs;
- 25 percent said they had sexual intercourse because they "were overwhelmed by a man's continual arguments and pressure";
- 9 percent said they had experienced sexual intercourse because of the threatened or actual use of physical force;

- 6 percent said they had experienced anal or oral intercourse or penetration by objects other than the penis because of the threatened or actual use of physical force.

The problem of date rape and gang rape is not restricted to the college setting. A long-term study of female teen victims of rape found that 97 percent knew their attackers (Ageton 1983). Many teenagers believe that sex means "guys pounce on you, you struggle, then forget the whole thing" (quoted in Warshaw 1988, 119). According to a recent study of adolescents, aged fourteen to eighteen, "more than half the boys and nearly half the girls thought that it was okay for a male to force (that is, rape) a female if he was sexually aroused by her" (Warshaw ibid., 120, referring to study by Goodchilds et al. 1988). Additionally, high school social life, like that in college, is often centered on alcohol or drugs, which further exacerbates a rape-prone environment.

Contrary to high school, the college environment is usually a total world of living and learning. This means that colleges have more control over individual behavior than do high schools. Colleges also have the opportunity to educate students and the right to punish students who engage in rape-prone behavior. Unfortunately, few colleges choose to exercise either the opportunity to educate or the right to punish. In this vacuum we find that self-governing all-male fraternities can control much of the party life on some campuses. Sometimes at these parties a sexual discourse is transmitted and a sexual culture promulgated that makes sexual exploitation a condition of manhood.

At U., as at many other campuses, fraternities are the primary focus of party life because fraternities are more numerous than sororities and there are usually no other places on campus to party. Fraternities enjoy their superior status as places to party and use this fact as an incentive to incoming freshmen to become members. Because of their privileged social position, the sexual ethos publicly displayed during some fraternity parties may play an important role in shaping the sexual expectations of many young men whether or not they join fraternities. This ethos includes denial of any responsibility for sexual abuse that might take place at parties or in the dorms and projection of fault onto the women who come to the parties or participate in dorm activities looking for a good time.

It is important to understand that the privileged position enjoyed by fraternities is in part a legacy of history at U. For many years of U.'s history women were not admitted. Today the conspicuous location of fraternities along the spine of the campus, called the Walk, gives an unbalanced sense of the current representation of women in the student body, which equals that of men. However, equality ends with the numerical composition of the student body. The exclusion of women is evident in the predominantly male composition of the faculty and administration. At the time of the XYZ Express, there were twenty-five residential fraternities and four sororities at U. None of the sororities are located on the Walk. Their absence furthers the impression of U. as a predominantly male campus. Additionally, the prominence of fraternities along the Walk grants the fraternity subculture more visibility than any other subculture of students on campus, with the exception of the student-run newspaper.

The Walk is one of the first landmarks a new student encounters when first visiting or arriving at U. Winding past old, ivy-covered stone halls, the Walk is the main route through campus, connecting the dorms at the edge of campus with classroom and administrative buildings, the main library, the campus bookstore, and fraternities at the center of campus. In order to attend classes or almost any other function, most students make the trek down the Walk daily.

At first sight students are impressed by the contrast between the old, ivy-covered stone halls and the strikingly modern figure of the School of Business, the Center for Performing Arts, and the modern sculptures that dot the few grassy areas surrounding the Walk. Yet more impressive is the sheer amount of space taken up along the sides of the Walk by the various fraternities. Many of these houses resemble beautiful private homes rather than college living quarters; only the glaring Greek letters above the door and the banner painted with a skull and crossbones and the announcement "Party Tonight—10 P.M.!" reveal that these are fraternities. One massive stone house is built to look like a castle, complete with turrets and flying flags. Other houses boast ivy-covered stone walls, stained glass windows, and towers and columns, which stand in marked contrast to the industrial-like appearance of the twenty-five-floor high-rise dorms where most students live on the campus periphery.

When they first get to U., women students have various reactions to the conspicuous location of the fraternities. Some don't notice it, or if they do, they accept it as part of college. Others complain bitterly, saying it is unfair that only males get to live so close to campus in such nice houses. Some women students avoid what they call the "gawk walk," saying that they don't want to experience the "degrading sensation of being gawked at by frat brothers sitting on their front wall or checking out the scene from their rooftop balconies."

Fraternity brothers respond to complaints regarding their privileged residential status by pointing out that the houses are supported by many rich alumni who donate money to the university and who wield considerable political influence. The buildings are held by long-term leases, which would be difficult to break. According to one brother, the tradition of all-male fraternities on the Walk would be "more difficult to abolish than slavery."

Another brother admitted that fraternities discriminate against women, saying, "It's an irrefutable fact, and I agree with anyone who has levied this charge against fraternities." However, he felt that it was wrong to admit women into membership. In his opinion, any man who says women should be admitted "either knows nothing about fraternities, or has missed one of the best times of a boy's life, or both." This brother likened being in a fraternity to being eleven years old again. He felt that the movie *Stand By Me*, about four eleven-year-old boys, was the best movie of the year, "as close to perfect as any movie can be." He liked the movie so much because it reminded him of his fraternity life.

Not all fraternity brothers are comfortable about the advantages they have. One house on the Walk is coed. Another house declared that they wanted to go coed, but their national chapter wouldn't let them. A brother at this house explained that if they went coed, the national chapter would "yank our charter and we'd be dog meat." At present these are exceptions. Most brothers defend their status as exclusive all-male organizations with the advantages of beautiful houses on the Walk by saying such things as, "We were there first," "Women have sororities if they want to join a house, so why should we let them into our fraternities?" Whether or not fraternity brothers recognize their advantages over their female counterparts, the fact remains that students walking along the Walk cannot help noticing that in five short blocks there are nine fraternities lining the Walk, with several more standing on side streets within a few hundred feet.

It is not only the actual physical existence of the houses that affects life at U., but, more importantly, the atmosphere they exude. On a warm day one is accosted by the sight of fraternity brothers on the steps and lawns of their houses and by the sounds of men talking loudly, often shouting out commentary at the passersby and blasting loud music through their windows. Whether women see the loud row of fraternities as places for great parties, or, as many do, a gauntlet of prying eyes that they must walk through, all students will sooner or later be affected by an atmosphere that ostensibly displays white, male, middle-class privilege. Women students frequently complain about the situation. On her first visit to campus, one woman's impressions of the fraternities were very negative:

> I first came to [U.] during the spring of my senior year in high school. I came with a friend who was also checking out prospective schools. As we walked down the Walk we passed a frat house where ten or so guys were hanging out front drinking and being loud. They leered at me and my friend as we walked by, and shouted out numbers, rating us and the other women who were passing by. They were being really gross with their comments. It made me think twice about coming to [U.].

Offensive remarks from fraternity brothers can do more than antagonize women students. Sometimes they are frightening. It is common for first-year students to go to fraternity parties because these are the most widely advertised and accessible places to socialize for those who are unfamiliar with the social environment. Freshmen women, ignorant about the fraternity culture, may enter some houses naively, expecting help and goodwill. Instead, they may be assaulted with stares and thumbs-up or thumbs-down gestures, indicating their sexual suitability. One student reported that when she went to a house looking for help with her homework from a fellow classmate, she was greeted by a nearly stampeding group of pledges and brothers, yelling, "Girl in the house! What the fuck!"

Many first year women express ambivalence about fraternities. They are happy to have been accepted at U. and are glad finally to be walking down the Walk as a student. They notice the fraternities and feel suspicious but are torn because they want to have a good time. They express curiosity about what goes on behind the imposing facades. They are particularly curious about the parties. Often they are warned not to go to a brother's room and not to accept a drink from a stranger because it may be drugged.

Admission to the parties is usually a dollar or two for men, nothing for women. The posters advertising parties announce this with loud lettering, saying "Women Free." The implication on many posters is that women pay for their booze with sex. On one poster a woman is depicted scantily clad with the frat dog tugging at the bottom of her bikini. Another, particularly offensive poster showed a woman's pair of legs portrayed as a bowling lane with a frat brother depicted as the ball ready to roll down the lane. When feminists on campus objected to such posters, a rule was established requiring fraternities to get approval for party posters. This rule was later revoked in response to the objection that it infringed on the rights of fraternities to free speech.

Most fraternities have a large living room, which serves as a dance floor when all the furniture is removed. During a party the lights are usually turned out. It is difficult to recognize even close friends. The music is overwhelmingly loud making conversation virtually impossible. In one house the party centers around a "black bag," a room in which the lights remain off and couples enter to fool around, miming orgiastic sex. Although nobody may actually use the "bag" for sex, its presence and the joking it invites establishes a sexually charged party mood. At another house, the centerpiece for one party was a model of a bride clothed in white and stretched out on the pool table with head back and legs open. The theme for the evening at this party was advertised as "Loss of Innocence."

A centerpiece of every party is the bar. Before 1988, when a new alcohol policy was introduced by the administration, beer was readily available along with grain-alcohol punch. Everyone was served. It is known that to avoid causing sickness the best ratio for mixing grain alcohol punch is twenty-three to one. Most of the fraternities, however, mix their punch in a ratio between three and seven to one. Heavy drinking and getting drunk are the norm. Drinking serves as a social aid. It helps men to find a willing sexual partner. Many men say that they look for drunken women and encourage women at the parties to drink.

Most women who go to fraternity parties are not seeking sex. They want to "have fun," see people, and "just hang out." Many men, however, are looking for sex, and some men claim they join fraternities for the sex and the parties. It is unclear how much sex actually occurs during or after parties; there appears to be much more talking and bragging than actual sexual activity. As testimony to their major goal in giving a party, some fraternities advertise the occasion on other campuses where the women have the reputation of enjoying "one-night stands" with fraternity brothers at U.

During the party the guys "scope" for likely prospects. Blonde, buxom women heavily made up and wearing tight clothes are likely targets. A senior said, "I want a girl who looks friendly and who will come over and talk to me. I like a girl who wears clothes that reveal some of her body, so I can, I don't know, so I can see what she looks like."

A senior said, "I look for a girl who is having a good time and who looks at me in a certain way. If I'm just looking to pick someone up, she doesn't have to be beautiful. I just have to like the way she looks and she has to be open to being picked up. She's sending off signals that she wants me."

Neither of these men is interested in establishing a relationship. "The whole idea is that they come cheap," one of them said. "I don't ever need to see them again unless I want to."

Women at nearby colleges have the reputation of being "sleazy" and looking for sex. *Sleazy* means displaying a suggestive sexual attitude and looking "kind of low class." A sleazy woman is scantily dressed, wears lots of make-up, and looks like she is "ready for action." Men label a woman who fits this description "slut," "cheap," "hot," and "fair game." She appears sexually receptive and hence "wants it," "is asking for it," "is setting herself up," "is looking to get fucked," and/or "is sending off signals." About one local college, a favorite expression heard at many fraternities is "Harkem, Parkem, Farkem in the Darkem."

The procedure for picking up is as follows. A man sees a woman who is described as "fair game." He determines this by "scoping," which means "giving her the eye," "choosing," or "going on the prowl."

"I roam around the room sort of looking at the girls who are there," Mike said. "If I see one I like, I'll stop and give her the eye and see how she responds. If she smiles or something, I go over and talk to her."

He then approaches her and has some preliminary contact, which includes talking, dancing, and drinking. The men hope to "score" with her. Other terms for having sex are "having a fling," "having a one-night stand," "getting an easy lay," "getting it," "fooling around," "screwing around," and "getting action."

"Part of it is just the thrill of getting an easy lay," Mike said. "A lot of my friends do it just for fun."

"It's just screwing around," another brother said. "The idea is that after you're out of college, you don't have much of a chance to do things like this. You know, just hang out in your house and get action on a weekend."

If a brother "scores," he goes upstairs to fool around or "get it." Women students report that in at least two fraternities the brothers leave their blinds open so that others in the house can watch. Sometimes the door to the room is purposely left unlocked so that anyone can walk in. Women in the know at U. say that they would never go upstairs with a brother in these fraternities because they are afraid that others will walk in on them.

At one fraternity house, located on the Walk, the brothers use the terrace that runs around the second-floor of the house for a practice called "beaching." From the beach, formed by the roof of the larger first story of the house, it is possible to see into the rooms on the second floor. "Beaching a girl" means watching a brother or a male guest have sex from this vantage point. The view into the windows is very clear, but it is not so easy to see the people on the beach. Thus, the girls involved do not know they are being watched. Usually, the male knows that he is being watched; indeed, he may communicate his intention to the brothers and leave the light on to make it easier for brothers to watch from the beach.

In most instances of casual party sex, the girl is expected to leave as quickly as possible. One young woman who was the object of "beaching"—a fact she discovered only when the phone rang and hands reached in from outside of the window to answer it—reported that the man involved never spoke to her again, not even to say hello. Joking about party sex in general, one brother said, "The definition of eternity is the time between the boy coming and the girl leaving." About "one-nighters," another brother said, "I don't want to know them, really. I mean, I'll exchange a few words with them, laugh a little, but it's all flirting and just joking around. If I want conversation I talk to the girls from [U.]."

Another brother explained that these sexual partners from another college are very willing. "They come to our parties because they want to fool around with frat men, and we're glad to oblige." The next day the brothers brag to one another, saying, for example, "She couldn't talk because she had her mouth full." In their conversation the brothers degrade both the woman they have slept with and the sex act by using such terms as "gashes," "hosebags," "heifers," "scum," "scum bags," "queens," "swanks," "scum buckets," "scum doggies," "wench," "life-support systems," "beasts," "bitches," "swatches," and "cracks." This kind of conversation and the fact that the girls are out of sight on another campus serves the brothers' need to "get it" without intimacy and to use the event to bond among themselves. It also means that there are no witnesses to the validity of their claims.

Campus women students do not respect the women who come to parties from other colleges. Their impression of these women is similar to that voiced by the brothers. Karen, a sophomore, said that these women show their availability through clothing, intentionally or unintentionally. "Guys respond to how a girl looks and acts, and clothing is a big part of that," she said. "A girl knows when she gets dressed that other people are going to see her, especially if she's going to a fraternity party."

This woman and others do not feel at risk walking into a fraternity party because they are convinced that frat brothers are looking elsewhere for sex. Echoing the prejudice voiced by the brothers, Karen said, "The girls who the guys pick up for sex are usually slutty. They are there just for sex, and the frat guys don't want anything else from them except a cheap fling."

Not all fraternity parties are hunting grounds for female prey. Brothers in some houses feel disgusted and embarrassed by what they see as the offensive behavior of other fraternities toward women. One woman who lived in a fraternity off the Walk for two summers commented on her experience at the house:

> I have never seen any of the rude, sexist behavior that I know occurs at some other frats here. Even though there is as much drinking and partying here as anywhere else, I have never known the brothers to treat women who come to the house as prospective conquests rather than prospective friends.

Another group of brothers claimed that they could never take advantage of a drunken woman who appeared to want sex. Indeed, brothers in this fraternity expressed disgust at the idea of engaging in group sex with a semiconscious or unconscious woman.

At U. there are several contexts outside of frat parties where men express their dominance and sex is treated as a commodity. On many college campuses pornographic movies are shown in response to student demand, which nets a profit for the student organization responsible for arranging campus entertainment. In one year at U. (1984) the student organization showed two pornographic movies and made a profit of $3,000, more than twice the revenue of other films. The student members of the sponsoring group claimed that money was not the issue but that screening pornography "accurately reflects the interests on the campus" because pornography gives students a chance to learn about sex. Arguing against showing the films, feminists on campus claimed that pornography represents abusive sex not only as entertaining but also as depicting what sex is really like to students who have never seen representations of explicit sex. There may be truth to this claim, given the comment made by one of the XYZ brothers that the XYZ Express didn't seem odd to him because of the stories he had heard about gang bangs in other houses and because of the movies he watched on TV. According to this brother,

> We have this Select TV in the house, and there's soft porn on every midnight. All the guys watch it and talk about it and stuff, and [the XYZ Express] didn't seem that odd because it's something that you see and hear about all the time. I've heard stories from other fraternities about group sex and trains and stuff like that. It was just like, you know, so this is what I've heard about, this is what it's like, what I've heard about. (quoted in Bowden 1983)

Some male students strongly objected to feminist protests against showing pornography on campus. To display their objection these men mimicked feminists' concern about violence against women in the movie *Deep Throat* by shouting sadistic remarks during the showing of the film. The male members of the audience outnumbered female members by about five to one. Some of them shouted "Fuck her," "Hurt her," "Rip her," as if to encourage the male actors in the movie to act violently. Toward the females on the screen they screamed comments such as "Ugly bitch," and "Whore." They also exhibited a strange fascination for Linda Lovelace's bruises, shouting out "Bruises! Bruises! Bruises!" continually during the film. These comments were made in response to a rally held a few days previously in which Linda Lovelace described her 21/2-year-long virtual imprisonment by the producer of the film, her husband at the time, who beat her constantly. In this reaction phallic dominance was being asserted in response to the women outside the theater protesting the sexual degradation and rape of Linda Lovelace in the movie.

The public expression of phallocentrism is also found in graffiti at U. The average male graffiti writer in men's bathrooms takes the action of the penis in either homosexual or heterosexual intercourse as his subject. Size of the penis is an obsession and schematic drawings of a penis appear not only in bathrooms but also in stairwells and hallways in various campus buildings. Typically these drawings are large, some more than three feet high—standing as a kind of monolith to male sexual power. Words like "cock," "bone," "prick," and "rod" portray the penis as an instrument of power and are employed in a context connoting male sexual aggression and female passivity. The female body is degraded with comments focusing on genitals and odor. The degradation of women as a prerequisite for masculinity is reflected in one particularly revealing exchange. On a bathroom wall where graffiti writers pen their response to someone else's remarks, one man wrote, "Sexism oppresses everyone (but women get the brunt of it)." Underneath this remark another man responded, "Who cares, you prickless bastard." Thus, a man who rejects sexism for himself and expresses compassion for women is verbally castrated and demeaned. In the eyes of the second man, compassion for women implies castration.

CONCLUSION

Every society reproduces its culture—its expected social and sexual identities, its attitudes, behaviors, and meanings—in the individual in the form of subjective dispositions. These dispositions are affected by the individual's access to the structure of opportunity, experience with social privilege, and internalization of sexual expectations. Psychologists argue that subjectivity—the sense of self as male or female, or as a living, acting human being—is an ongoing process constructed from experience (Hollway 1984). Subjectivity is formed by the experience of interaction with the external world. Subjectivity is thus produced by one's personal engagement in the practices, discourses, and institutions that lend significance to one's daily life.

If subjectivity is constructed from experience, we must ask, what does it mean for female students' sense of their autonomy and power if they are constantly confronted by males whose social power receives institutional support and whose sexual aggression at parties appears to be sanctioned? What does it also mean when these men live in residences, unavailable to women and located at the center of campus, where phallocentric parties are staged, sometimes with the explicit intention of getting sex from the women who attend? Women students sense that the phallocentrism they encounter at parties is geared toward constructing a masculine subjectivity. They are affected by this behavior because of the implicit assumption that their own admission to the heterosexual social order is based on their accepting, or at least tolerating, a passive role in the phallocentric social order. By accepting this role they become second-class citizens in the college social order.

When young men go to college they know that entering a fraternity positions them in a privileged social hierarchy, one that can, in some instances, control a significant portion of campus social life. In the houses that line the typical fraternity rows that are found on many campuses and in the parties that fuel campus social life, young men experience what it is like to dominate and control. At these parties, the brothers control the lights, the music, the alcohol, and their inner feelings. In these settings they avoid commitment and feeling for their sexual partners by choosing "sleazy women" from other schools, whom they need not face on campus the next day. They dominate these women by denigrating them for being willing to have sex. The women are described as inferior—"low-class," "cheap," or "slutty"—or they are dehumanized with animalistic terms. By belittling their sexual partners the brothers achieve more than a sense of social and sexual dominance. They also degrade the dependency sexual desire arouses in them. As they dominate and control the women who satisfy their sexual desire, the brothers separate sexual feelings from emotions of love and compassion. Such emotions are reserved for brothers. Party sex is the glue that binds the brothers to the fraternity body. The fraternal bond helps to transform infantile feelings of dependency on women by transferring these feelings to men.

In party sexual activities that are demeaning to their sexual partners, fraternity brothers learn to split lust from love. Such a split is necessary for homophobic men living in groups structured by ties demanding mutual loyalty. These men must be careful not to act out sexual feelings for a loved brother lest it compromises their status as privileged, heterosexual males, nor can they show loyalty or love for a party woman lest this weaken the fraternal bond. While love for a woman might dilute the strength of their bonding, lust enables the brothers to solidify the "mystical bonds" that unite them by sharing or discussing a party woman. Party women who believe that their sexual activities are all in good fun do not, perhaps, realize the extent to which they play an important role in the formation and celebration of ties of brotherhood.

Two

The XYZ Express

The XYZ Express occurred in February 1983 after one of the fraternity's weekly parties. Parties at XYZ were similar to those at some other fraternities. A very strong grain punch was served, made with the flavor of Kool-Aid. One student reported that she had seen brothers "do coke" before or during XYZ parties. According to her, drinking and dancing took place on the first floor, and taking drugs was relegated to the second floor. Occasionally there were threats of fights when people from other frats tried to crash a party.

Alice and Anna, women students at U., describe the sexual culture that made the XYZ Express a logical part of party activities. The stories they tell are important because they are told from the point of view of young women who were attracted to life at the house. Their stories illuminate not only the sexual culture of the house but also the motivation of women who participate in this culture.

I begin with Alice's story. Alice lived at the XYZ house one summer. She describes the importance of drinking and "hitting on" women to the brothers' lifestyle. She introduces the concept of "riffing," the practice of getting sex from a woman in exchange for a good time and alcohol. She also describes the ritual of the "circle dance," a ritual that illustrates the emphasis on male bonding in the life of the house. Alice is sympathetic to the brothers, many of whom were her friends, and yet she realizes that the sexual mores at the house could easily lead to gang rape.

ALICE'S STORY

Alice lived at the XYZ house during one summer. Finding a job at home that summer didn't interest her, even though she didn't have a job at school. She was very low on money, and the cheapest place to live on campus during the summer was in a fraternity house. She looked at a

66

room in the XYZ house even though she knew that the brothers were "the people who hung out on the benches in front of their house drinking beer and screaming obscene things at passersby." Her sense of adventure got the better of her, and she took a room for the summer.

Alice became part of the XYZ drinking lifestyle, which gained her acceptance into the group. From the beginning she drew clear-cut boundaries in order to communicate how she expected to be treated by the brothers. She claimed her own bathroom and rejected a sexual move made on her by a male party guest by kicking him down the stairs. With this action she felt like "one of the guys" rather than a woman the brothers could "riff" on. Another female boarder that summer, Susan, became a prime target for sexual attention because of her flirtatious and, as Alice describes it, "cute" behavior. In the eyes of the brothers, by acting "cute" Susan seemed to be "asking for it." As we shall see, however, neither woman was fully accepted: while Susan was treated as an object, Alice was treated as a pet.

Soon after moving in, Alice went to the shore with the brothers for a graduation party, where she "sat around and drank like a fish from the well-stocked bar." She felt that she ought not get too drunk so that she could protect herself if one of the guys started paying a little too much attention to her. Everything worked out fine. She was given her own room to sleep in, and she locked the door.

Over the summer, Alice's drinking increased, and she noticed that by drinking every day for most of the day she avoided serious hangovers. It is not clear whether she was attracted to the house because the climate enabled a drinking habit or whether her drinking was an attempt to maintain comradery with the brothers. Although she felt equal to the brothers by drinking as much as they did, she felt that she had to guard herself against unwanted advances. At an all-night picnic she felt that she could not "comfortably sack out" because of what might happen if she lost control. Although she liked the brothers, she expresses the feeling that she could never trust them. Alice notes that Susan was less guarded and slept with one of the brothers, named Ed. By becoming one of Ed's girls, Susan lowered her status because of Ed's already considerable reputation for "riffing" or "hitting" on women. From Susan's experience, Alice recognized that she could never be "one of the guys" because as a woman she would always be a potential sex object.

Alice describes life at the XYZ house during that summer. The brothers marked time in relation to their favorite TV show. Their heroes were taken from TV, and house legends were built around brothers who defied the campus norm of the hard-working, successful student from an upper-middle-class family. Brothers classified as "five-year-men" were considered heroes, as were members of the "no-A club." This inversion of the normative demonstrates the brothers' sense of privileged freedom. The brothers lived by the rules of their frat-house collective, not by the rules of the broader campus society.

Drinking and sex played prominent roles in house activities. As in other fraternities on campus, the XYZ brothers looked for party girls from local colleges. Alice describes an event with one of these girls that she now believes probably ended in a gang rape. At the time she thought of it as a "gang bang." The event began when a girl from another college began flirting with some of the XYZ brothers at a local hangout. She sat on one brother's lap and agreed to join the brothers in a party back at the house. The invitation to party included Alice, but when the group arrived back at the house Alice went to her room and passed out to the tune of a Doors album and a fair amount of noise coming from downstairs. After hearing about the incident with Laurel, which happened much later, Alice reflected on what probably happened that night after she fell asleep.

> The Doors were a kind of musical mascot at the house. I think that the music is used in the initiation ceremony in some way. But that's just an educated guess. I do know that "LA Woman" is the song to which brothers do the circle dance. The circle dance is called for without fail at every party I have been at. Usually it is later at night as it requires some floor space. The song comes on and the brothers start yelling "Ho! Ho! Ho!" All the brothers link arms and join in a circle. Then the whole circle moves around so fast that the shortest members are lifted off the ground. The "Ho!"s continue until the circle loses control and the entire group piles on top of each other, squashing the smallest members. The whole thing is scary to watch. It looks almost manic and unconscious of the individual—a single personality made up of a couple of dozen of people. I have no idea what the dance means or why it is done. I could hypothesize that "LA Woman" and "Ho" were words for whore and the group was jumping on an imaginary woman. This is an interpretation I have arrived at since the rape case. The only other thing that the circle dance ever brought to mind was that for a bunch

of guys who were always so full of nasty, ugly, homophobic remarks, they seemed to enjoy jumping around on top of each other very much.

When I got up the next morning the girl from the lap was sitting on the stairs crying. She said she was locked in. Occasionally someone would lock the front door from the inside, which was stupid since only one or two sets of keys were to be found. I asked her if she was okay. She said that her head hurt and asked if I had been at the party too. She said she didn't remember seeing me there. I said no and told her that I lived here. She just stared at me and I showed her how to climb out the back door. It occurred to me then that I had missed something and I immediately felt like I was glad to have missed whatever it was. Ignorance was fine with me. It wasn't any of my business what other women chose to do or not do. Later that night I asked the guys if they had a good time after I went to bed. All I got were snickers. One of the brothers laughed and said that the girl was a great bimbo. I was very suspicious.

Although she suspected a gang rape, Alice preferred to remain ignorant. Like many women seeking acceptance in the fraternity culture, she needed to mask from consciousness the reality of her own and others' inferior positions vis-à-vis the brothers.

At the end of the summer Alice moved back into the high-rise dormitory. She missed her new friends and frequently returned to the house to party. Early in the school year she got involved with Cliff and her status in the house then became that of "wench." She assumed that she and Cliff would be mentioned in the minutes of the house meetings, as usually happened when someone slept with a brother. After Cliff left the house she was classified as a "regular." Regulars were women who attended every party but were not girlfriends of any of the brothers. In addition to "wenches," "regulars," and "bimbos," there was a strong inner circle of women who were girlfriends of the brothers. The girlfriends came to the parties to make sure their boyfriends didn't take up with any of the other women at the party. The girlfriends didn't like the regulars and made ugly remarks about their virtue. This would seem to be fairly normal jealous behavior if it weren't for the fact that many of the girlfriends had once been regulars themselves. The various types of women never bonded with one another, as their primary interest was in the brothers, which is the way the brothers seemed to want it to be.

Alice was at the house the night the brothers raped Laurel. According to Alice, Laurel was one of the regulars who came to the house. Alice had also seen Laurel at various bars around campus. Alice describes what she remembers about Laurel.

Laurel was one of the regulars or at least she came around on a fairly frequent basis. She did a lot of drugs and was rumored to be pretty loose. I didn't know her better than to say "Hi," which she always did. She was friendly but never seemed able to remember my name. I also ran into her several times at a local bar. One night she was so fucked up she ran her hands up and down the backs of most of the men at the bar. This bar had a half-student half-neighborhood clientele and was pretty rough. One of the guys at our table was an engineer, a bouncer, and a boyfriend of a good friend of mine. When Laurel got around to talking to Bill, she was nearly incoherent. When she wrapped her body around him, he picked her up and carried her out like a "sack of potatoes." He wanted to get her out before anything happened. When he came back he said she had passed out before they got home and he had to pound on the door and do a lot of explaining to her roommate. The roommate was probably scared of Bill, who is well over six feet tall and black.

Bill said Laurel was always hanging around bars fucked up out of her mind and she always found someone who didn't mind being picked up. He said that everyone knew about Laurel. I guess it didn't occur to anyone that she might have real psychiatric problems. It didn't cross my mind either.

I had another view of Laurel at the next XYZ party. I remember asking someone there if she was always like that. (She was dancing like someone possessed.) They laughed and said "Yeah." I arrived at the party around midnight. Maybe a little after. I said hello to several of the brothers and went to get a glass of punch. It was not as crowded as it sometimes was, but there were still close to fifty people milling around. The music was as loud as usual and more people were arriving. I stopped to talk to Pete, who was well on his way to being very drunk. He is one of those people whose ears and face get red when they drink. He was saying the usual "How are you" and I talked with him briefly. Tom asked me to dance at some point after I had been there for a while. We danced to two songs and then went back to the room with the punch. While we were dancing we both saw Laurel dancing in the middle of the dance floor by herself and not to the music that was being played. I made some comment and Tom said something to the effect that she was really out of it tonight. I stayed at the party for an hour longer. I drank some more and every time I walked to the dance area Laurel was still dancing. Occasionally she danced with some of the guys for a song or two. I don't remember seeing her talk, but I wasn't paying a whole lot of attention. When I left she had been dancing with Sam for some time. It must have been around three when I left. I stumbled to the high-rise, turned on my TV, and fell asleep to the music issuing from the XYZ house not more than fifty yards away from my window.

The next thing I knew there were headlines everywhere about a gang rape at XYZ. My first thought was that it was ridiculous. I was there and didn't see a thing. A lot of people said to me things like, "Look what your nice friends did." My female friends had never understood why I spent any time with the XYZ brothers. I went over to the house, but no one would talk. Someone said something to the effect that I had better not start. I assumed that every female they knew was irate and giving them all kinds of shit. They were just hostile and I didn't stay.

I got the story from Zeke. He said that the brothers had really fucked up. He had been working at the time and had come home after the whole thing was over. He told me who had been involved and I was shocked. The most polite and the nicest of the whole XYZ crew seemed to be in on it. I had to wonder if Laurel had agreed to the whole thing. They were all probably drunk beyond their limit. I didn't know whether the guys were capable of such a thing. Zeke pointed out that *capable* meant some sort of premeditation and he assured me that there certainly was none. In his words a lot of people who had passed the point of being able to control their actions made simultaneous errors in judgment. In retrospect I think this is the correct assessment. But when I remember the importance the guys attach to "riffing," I realize that they were always "hitting" on girls and maybe the thing with Laurel was just another way of "hitting."

In her description of Laurel, Alice raises several key issues concerning collective responsibility. First, it is evident that Laurel had a serious drug and alcohol problem. The night Alice saw her at a local bar, Laurel was drunk and actively seductive. One male's response to this behavior was to take her home before anything could happen. Another male response is seen at the XYZ party. During the evening it was clear to everyone that Laurel was "really out of it." Alice's description of Laurel's behavior confirms this impression. However, when Alice heard who was involved in the incident—the "most polite and the nicest of the whole XYZ crew"—she wondered if Laurel had agreed to the whole thing despite the general observation that Laurel was in a semiconscious state. Zeke's point that there was no premeditation because everyone was drunk beyond his limit raises the question of why collective responsibility was not extended to Laurel earlier in the evening. Why didn't one or more of the brothers in the house get Laurel home before things got out of hand, as Bill had done? Alice's account of the XYZ ethos suggests that there was no one there to take her home because "hitting or riffing on women" was a more relevant script for these men than demonstrating compassion and responsibility for a woman unable to care for herself.

According to Alice, "riffing" means getting sex from a woman through talking, dancing, or drinking. Brothers who were expert riffers gained status in the house. The brothers were always telling riffing stories, which were uproariously funny to them. These stories always contained slapstick humor with a good deal of sadism mixed in. It was as if the men gained power and position in the group at the expense of the women they slept with.

In general, "riffing" means talking your way into a situation. Some brothers were better riffers than others. There is skill involved in being good at riffing, because it involves persuading someone to do something. There are many kinds of riffs. There is the "nice guy" riff, which means offering to walk a woman home when it is late at night. By being well mannered and almost chivalrous the "nice guy" riffer hopes to induce the woman to invite him in. There is no good reason to believe that because a woman agrees to be walked home she also wants to invite the man inside for something more. However, the brothers saw this as a legitimate form of riffing.

Alice does not remember hearing the brothers ever refer to consciously getting a woman drunk in order to "take advantage of her." Perhaps this explains the meaning of the phrase "she asked for it": if a woman gets drunk it is considered perfectly acceptable to riff on her, the idea being that she got drunk not because the brothers plied her with alcohol or mixed large amounts of grain alcohol in the punch but because she accepted drinks from the brothers. Alice believes that the brothers didn't have to make women drunk because the men and women at the parties were there to get drunk voluntarily. No one seemed to be there for any reason except getting drunk, dancing, and riffing, or getting picked up, depending on who you were. Alice admits that she went to the parties to get drunk.

The parties she describes always had loud dance music. It was part of some riffing techniques to ask women to dance. This is not to imply that all brothers danced in order to riff on a woman, but many of them did. The longer a woman danced with someone, the more open to the riff she became. Dancing for a long time with one brother meant a woman was interested in him. If the woman continued talking to the brother after the dancing, this meant that she might agree to go upstairs.

According to Alice, the XYZ brothers know that eventually most girls will give in because most girls are looking for someone to tell them nice things about themselves. Alice believes that a woman will eventually give in once she has put herself into a certain situation and that by putting herself there she is essentially "asking for it." Alice knows that she has put herself into situations where, due to her own passivity or because she simply doesn't care, she has no reason to say no. She does not see herself as being victimized because she is under the impression that she has given consent. She suspects that maybe Laurel consented because she didn't care enough to protect herself. She can't give a name to either her experience or Laurel's, but initially she did not think of it as rape. In the aftermath of the incident she knows that others called Laurel's experience a rape, but this naming doesn't really fit her understanding of what happened, especially since she believes that she herself was never forcibly victimized.

Alice compares the behavior of the XYZ brothers to that of weekend alcoholics who work hard all week long and drink from Friday evening after work until Sunday afternoon. She feels that the question of alcoholism may be relevant and speculates that "some of us were probably alcoholics." Later she came to realize that she had a problem with alcohol because she could never have just one drink; rather, she drank until she got drunk. Eventually, she stopped drinking altogether. She concluded that what happened to Laurel was caused by too much drinking and by the importance the brothers attached to riffing.

What happened that night happened in a context defined by getting something from a woman and getting drunk. From the brothers' point of view I guess you could say that women come to the parties to get something—a boyfriend, a drink or drugs, or just a good time.

The brothers were good to me the summer I lived at the house and yet I guess I knew all along that they were capable of gang rape. As a woman I want to feel that they are a savage bunch of criminals or at least despicable human beings, but they were my buddies. They drank too much and tried to riff on a lot of women. But, at any party the trying and talking were infinitely more numerous than the actual successful riff. There were a few brothers who had a better riffing technique than the others because it always seemed like it was the same two or three who actually got laid on the evening of any particular party. The rest just tried, got turned down, talked about it, and took shit from the rest for failing.

The brothers weren't angels, but the whole summer I lived there they never mistreated me and in fact got me out of more than one potentially ugly situation. They actually protected me if someone tried to hit on me at a party and I looked unhappy. After the incident it was hard to justify being friends with a group that was capable of an attack against a woman. At the same time it was hard to accept that an attack had occurred by people whom I thought were basically nice. Anyway, I stopped going to the house. I don't know why I stopped going. I suppose I was just one more person who abandoned them when they got in trouble. I know they felt this way because whenever I would run into one of them he would give me this impression. I haven't seen most of them since it happened a couple years ago. I ran into one of them on the street recently. We never even hinted at anything beyond what a great summer it had been at the house. Both of us wanted it that way.

ANNA'S STORY

At the time of the XYZ incident Anna had been a house regular for several years. Anna begins her story by describing her relationship with Ed, the brother whose "riffing" on women Alice had noted. Anna's relationship with Ed caused her a lot of pain because she never knew where she stood with him. He was always running after other girls and she felt that he paraded their sexual relationship in front of the other men. It was clear to Anna that his primary loyalty was to the fraternity and his primary bond of affection was to the brothers.

Ed hardly ever took Anna out or came over to her apartment. They always saw each other at the house. It seemed that the only time Anna saw him alone was in bed. Sometimes he would try to make out with her when his roommate was in the room and once he hinted that they have sex as a threesome. There were other innuendos about group sex. This usually happened when Anna was being treated like one of the brothers—as if it were as natural to have sex with her in a group as it was for the brothers to get naked in a circle dance.

Anna's attraction to the power of the collective fraternal body is vividly illustrated in a story she tells about the circle dance.

> One night a couple years before the XYZ incident I got extremely trashed at one of the weekly parties, so much so that I lost an hour. I cannot remember what the hell I did. I do remember that I got heaped in a circle dance. It was amazing. There I was engulfed beneath this mountain of male humanity, and not one body violated mine. They were extra careful to leave a healthy and safe bubble of space about me as they piled on top of each other above me. It was a total acceptance initiation ritual executed with an exceptional degree of consideration. We really spoke each other's language. I felt as if I were being exposed to and being welcomed into a totally new culture. I was wearing a leotard and tights—excellent exercise outfit for the occasion. After the circle dance it was very late and everybody went to sleep.

Anna was very proud of the fact that the brothers treated her as a female version of one of them. Once, on her way back from drinking with the brothers at a local bar, Jack said to her in front of everybody. "You know, Anna, I like your breasts." Anna answered, "Yeah, I like them too. They've given me a lot of pleasure." Reflecting on this exchange later, Anna realized how much she wanted to be treated as an equal.

> Here was I, a woman, but a friend, partying like I was one of the guys. For me, this meant that I had to play by their rules, which in this instance meant that I would have to put up with the abuse and ride with the punches, delivering some of my own as we went along. For the guys this meant that I was not entitled to preferential or deferential treatment because I was a woman. If I was to be included in the

house revelry, I was not to be permitted to cramp anyone's style. Usually this worked pretty well.

In reconsidering my response to Jack, I imagine myself as a man in the locker room comparing my penis with those of the rest of the guys. One guy says, "Hey, Andre, you've got a big dick!" I respond, "Yeah, I like it. It gives me a lot of pleasure. I like fuckin' the broads with my big dick."

In other words, sexuality between the two conversants is not the issue. In real life my relationship with Jack was purely platonic, and I wanted it to stay that way. I adopted a male-identified attitude in order to show that I had no remorse, shame, or hypocritical modesty about my sexuality. At the same time I was also claiming possession of my sexuality. "You can like my breasts/dick all you want, but they're/it's not for you."

Anna exhibits "male-identified" attitudes in several respects. She refuses to be passive in her relationship to the brothers. As Alice used drinking to establish a relationship of comradery, Anna used sex. As with Alice, the brothers protected Anna. Whenever beer wars broke out in the house and everyone got doused, she was always threatened with a drenching. The brothers included her in the spirit of their horseplay, but they protected her from their superior strength. She was, to a certain extent, one of them. She believes that this is the reason why Ed would try to make out with her sometimes while his roommate was in the room. About this, Anna says

> We were so familiar with one another that they and I were confused about my sex-role identification [by which she probably means gender identity]. Having sex with me in front of others was probably a little like getting naked in a circle dance.

This confusion was particularly evident one night when Anna and Ed got very drunk at a local bar. Before leaving, as Anna learned later, one of the brothers at the bar, Sam, took Ed aside and told him to "buttfuck" her. Looking back on the incident, Anna describes what happened later that evening.

> Later, Ed did just that and I was horrified. He did it without lubrication and without warning. I shrieked out in pain and made him stop.

He passed out and then vomited all over himself. I cleaned him up and as I was doing so a whole group of guys, led by Sam, charged through the door. I ordered everyone to get the fuck out and fell asleep.

It never crossed my mind until after the incident with Laurel that these people who were charging through the door were doing so with the knowledge of the distinct possibility that they might have caught us in the middle of something. I can only guess at what they were planning when they charged through the door. Considering Sam's earlier suggestion that Ed "buttfuck" me, I shudder in disgust when I imagine what kind of scene they were expecting to encounter.

When he woke up the next day, Ed was peevish but proud of having vomited all over the place. He went charging through the house waking up everyone. He kept telling everyone about vomiting. All of the brothers seemed proud of having vomited. When he woke up Jack, Jack said to Ed, "Hey, bro! You blew some chunks, eh?"

Ed smiled and they both laughed. When we went into Joe's room, Ed's little brother, we could smell the vomit. Joe woke up smiling and said to Ed, "I threw up, man."

Ed smiled and chanted, "I did too. All right!"

We went down to the basement and woke up Bob. He had fallen asleep in his clothes without taking off his boots. Ed exclaimed, "Bob, man, you look like you butt-fucked a big fat pig!"

I hadn't mentioned the buttfucking episode to Ed yet and I wondered why he said that. Later, when I told him, he asked if I had enjoyed it and I bitched that it hurt like hell and that I hated it. Ed said that he wouldn't have done anything if he hadn't been so drunk. We broke up not long after.

This episode and others made Anna very aware of the importance of male bonding in the XYZ sexual culture. She never saw Ed outside of the fraternity house. In their relationship it seemed as if she was being used as a pawn in a sexual game Ed played with the brothers. Anna put up with this game because she wanted to be accepted as "one of the guys." The importance of being accepted is illustrated by her sense of exhilaration when she was drawn into the collective energy of the group via the circle dance. Like Alice, Anna needed acceptance, a need that deluded her into thinking that because the brothers included her in such activities as the circle dance, she was accepted. However, as she describes her acceptance in the circle dance, she was treated like an outsider, one who must be protected. Like Alice, Anna was a house pet.

Anna is aware that she had adopted a male-identified attitude when she equated the size of her breasts to the size of a penis. She feels that her attitude caused the brothers to treat her like one of them, and yet she points out that they protected her and that she was a sex object for many of them. The "buttfucking" episode illustrates the tension between homosexual acting out and heterosexual intercourse. If she was "one of the guys," as she says, then why was her boyfriend instructed by another brother to "buttfuck" her? In this scene it appears that Anna had become a sexual scapegoat. The conspiracy between Ed and his brothers in this act is clear. One wonders, with Anna, what the brothers expected when they all piled into the room later that same night. What would have happened had Anna been unconscious or unable to vigorously eject the intruders from the room?

The circle dance, as Alice and Anna describe it, gives rein to a different kind of excess, one in which the brothers are literally physically merged as a group. According to Anna, the circle dance is a special XYZ ritual reserved for celebrations. It usually takes place near the end of a party, late in the night, when everyone is sufficiently drunk and loosened up. Usually, only brothers take part in the circle dance, as it is a fraternity bonding ritual. As Anna describes it:

> The brothers assemble together in a circle. The song, "Suffragette City," by David Bowie, is played, and the brothers begin to run around in a circle. Several times in the course of the song a few brothers will break from the circle and move to the inside where they mime various sexual and/or lewd acts. Homosexual intercourse is old standard. The group in the circle moves around faster and faster, getting more and more rough, until the song peaks with everyone shouting, "Awwww WHAM BAM! THANK YOU, MA'AM!!!" Then, as the song nears its end, all the brothers pile on top of one another in an explosive heap. An important feature of this ritual is that it is performed before an audience. It is a kind of demonstration of brotherly solidarity. Another feature is the no-holds-barred, completely uninhibited nature of the ritual in which total loss of control is celebrated. It is characteristically rough, and anybody who attempts to interfere or to join in does so at his or her own risk.

Once, Anna witnessed a circle dance during which some of the male guests got naked, either taking off their clothes or just pulling down their pants. The party had gotten way out of bounds. Anna was already familiar with this particular practice because of stories she had heard about an alumnus brother who would get naked at the end of particularly successful parties and try to freak the remaining women out. Anna describes her reaction:

> I laughed along and was not particularly surprised. I was not at all shocked or threatened because no one made any attempt to touch or intimidate me. I was quite drunk at the time and used to the late night atmosphere of anything goes. Looking back I really don't know how much my sense of security was a false one, or if I would have felt in any danger if I hadn't been so drunk. I suspect that my identity as Ed's girlfriend/property afforded me some immunity from violation.

Anna also describes a ritual similar to the circle dance called "the heap." The heap works as a kind of collective sanction within the group. Whenever someone breaches a house rule or does something silly or embarrassing to the group, that person is heaped. Someone in the group shouts, "Heap!" and everyone follows by piling on top of the offending person, forming a mound or heap of bodies. After the first call of "Heap!" everyone involved echoes the call until everyone completes the heap, and then it calms down as the brothers begin to fall off the heap. The brothers usually help each other get up during this detumescent period, lastly helping up the person on the bottom.

Heaps vary in severity. After a particularly brutal heap, Anna asked Ed if he wasn't afraid that someone would get hurt. He explained that it looks a lot worse than it really is. The men in the heap are careful not to throw down all their weight. Those on the top of the heap may only lean over the top, exerting hardly any weight downward. After Ed's explanation Anna began to watch for this whenever there was a heap, and most of her observations bore Ed's assertions out. She saw some brothers on top almost immediately begin to pull upwards from the body beneath them, or brothers on the bottom part of the heap would push upwards as soon as the heap was completed. In the milder heaps the men on the bottom push upwards while the men on the top withhold most of their weight. This is what happened when Anna was included in the circle dance, which always ends with a heap.

There are some heaps that are as bad as they look. Anna saw brothers dive onto the top of the heap in order to make it collapse downward. She remembers in particular a heap in which Charlie dove onto the heap, fell off, and then jumped back up in a sitting-up position, deliberately trying to force his weight onto the men beneath him. The brothers laughed, acknowledging Charlie's choice to make this heap particularly harsh.

According to Anna, the heap is one of the ways in which the brothers permit themselves physical contact with one another without compromising their "heterosexist male identity." She interprets the circle dance as a fraternity bonding ritual in which loss of control is celebrated. The ritual of the heap parallels group sex. Ritual scapegoating occurs in both cases. In the case of the heap, one brother bears the brunt of group blaming while in the case of a gang rape one woman bears the brunt of group sexual aggression. In both cases, in the eyes of the brothers, the victim "asked for it." A misdeed provokes "the heap," and the sanction is meted out through a collective physical process, not by virtue of a judicially derived solution. As Anna perceptively notes about the heap, the supposed misdeed provides the brothers with an excuse for indulging in physical contact with one another without compromising their heterosexual identity. Anna uses the term "heterosexist" perhaps because she understands that the brothers' practice of affirming their heterosexual identity by taking women as sexual objects while rejecting women as equals gives their house activities a marked misogynist quality.

CONCLUSION

At the XYZ house, sex is treated as a commodity that is acquired by the brothers from women who are looking for acceptance, who want to be "one of the guys," or who are looking for a good time. The more a brother can deal in this commodity the higher his personal credit in the house.

"Hitting on women" means getting sex from a woman through talking, dancing, or drinking. The XYZ brothers think that the women who come to their house are there to have a good time and to look for someone to tell them nice things about themselves. Alice believes that by entering the situation and staying in it, women are agreeing to an unspoken sexual contract. This is what "asking for it" means: consent is given by the very act of coming to the party and getting drunk. Hence, Alice doesn't perceive herself or other women as victims.

If this is the case, then why is "riffing" necessary? Riffing is necessary because it is the means by which the brothers score points in the house status game. The game that Alice and other women end up playing is not the game they contract for—getting drunk and having a good time. These young women are victimized because they are pawns in a status game played by the brothers. Although Alice knew that her private affair with a brother might well become a subject for gossip during the house meeting and recorded in the minutes, she and others like her do not know how the brothers use this kind of information to bond among themselves and to elevate one another to the status of successful "riffer." Regardless of what they might agree to, women end up as losers in the game the brothers play among themselves.

Anna was also the subject of gossip among the brothers. However, Anna turned the lesson she learned about sexual dominance back on the brothers when she accused them of having raped Laurel (see next chapter). By these actions Anna demonstrated that she refused to play the role of passive sex object or victim. Her time in the house was a time for learning how to assert herself vis-à-vis the brothers, just as they assert themselves vis-à-vis women. This training explains why Anna was able to stand up to the brothers after they raped Laurel and hold them responsible. In a sense Anna's stay in the house was a form of assertiveness training.

In the case of Laurel, she became a victim of her own vulnerability and the prevailing ethic of "hitting on" women. As we shall see in the next chapter, Laurel was victimized in what some called the house minutes. In these "minutes," or "Highlights" as they were entitled, sex with Laurel is referred to in terms of interviewing for the little sisters' program. Terms like "corpse riff" and "unconscious riff" that appear in the "Highlights" suggest the possibility that riffing on Laurel was accomplished not by talking but by taking advantage of Laurel's drunkenness. No doubt, in the eyes of the brothers, Laurel was "asking for" the collective sexuality she received. The problem with this interpretation is that although the script that dupes women into sex and then uses the event for other purposes is well known to the brothers, it is not understood by the women involved. No woman ever consents to what she ends up receiving in these cases. In Laurel's case there is the additional fact of her drunkenness. If the brothers admit that they were beyond "premeditation" because they were drunk, then Laurel was beyond the premeditation necessary for consent.

Alice and Anna understand the brothers because they themselves had a strong need to identify with the privilege, power, and freedom the XYZ lifestyle emulates. However, reflecting on the meaning of the XYZ Express, they finally realize their subordinate status in the house hierarchy. Additionally, both women recognize the pathology associated with house activities. Alice understands that she and some of the brothers had become alcoholics, and Anna recognizes that her view of her own sexuality was modeled on the brothers' phallocentrism.

With their dawning insight into themselves, both women also comprehend the role of the circle dance in the collective house ritual and its relationship to group sex. As Alice says, the circle dance "is unconscious of the individual, a single personality made up of a couple of dozen people." She believes the movements mime a "gang bang," and Anna is aware of its homosexual allusions. Both women note the contradiction between the homophobia frequently voiced by the brothers and the homoeroticism enacted in the circle dance.

From the anthropologist's point of view, the juxtaposition of homoerotic behavior and homophobic and sexist attitudes illuminates the logic of XYZ group sex. A woman is caught for a moment in the net of collective male sexual aggression and then she is sloughed off. The woman plays the role of ritual scapegoat who receives the brunt of collective male sexual aggression that would otherwise turn a group of privileged heterosexual males into despised homosexuals. By degrading and extruding the woman who has been the ostensible object of their mutual sex act, the men degrade and extrude forbidden sexual feelings from the group. The overwhelming conclusion is that the XYZ brothers could not take Laurel home before things got out of hand because they were compelled by their house traditions and group sexual dynamics to sacrifice Laurel to fraternal bonding. The emotional hold that male bonding has over these brothers probably meant that the issue of collective responsibility, to which all fraternities at U. must subscribe as a condition of their existence, was never considered.

Three

Rape or "She Asked for It"?

Laurel did not report the incident until five days after the party, when she contacted an administrator and said that on the previous Thursday she had been raped by five or six, maybe more, male students at the XYZ house. She said she had waited five days to report what happened because she did not realize its impact. Her delay and the fact that she had gone back to the fraternity the next day to look for her prescription sunglasses, lost the night before, was construed by many on campus to mean that she did not perceive herself as having been wronged.

The five-day hiatus between the incident and its reporting illustrates the confusion many women feel about the meaning of sexual situations in which they are overwhelmed by one or more men. In most cases the woman involved blames herself either because she got drunk or because she stayed too late at the party, or for some other reason. The men involved seem to feel no such confusion. They brag about the act among their male friends and revel in a sense of enhanced masculinity that comes from a feeling of sexual power and dominance over women.

Given the institutional support for male privilege at U. and the history of sexual abuse at fraternity parties, it is surprising that Laurel resisted the brothers' definition of what happened and reported the incident. From the beginning, when news of the XYZ incident first filtered out, there was vigorous debate over the definition of what had happened. The debate reveals the conflicting sexual discourses that exist on a major college campus. One discourse reinforced the power of male bonding in fraternities by promoting a belief in the explosive, biological nature of male sexual expression—the "boys will be boys" rationalization—and the need for an outlet for this explosive sexuality. According to this discourse, male sexual behavior is not socially constructed but is based purely on hormones that erupt uncontrollably into the realm of culture.

Another discourse, articulated by the university administration, referred to building a responsible community where "dehumanizing incidents are least likely to occur" and to establishing "better procedures to handle such serious situations if they do occur."[1] Because it waits for reports of specific dehumanizing incidents instead of confronting directly the campus contexts that encourage these incidents, the administration only addresses the symptom, not the problem.

Another discourse is the feminist discourse, which in this case included strong female and male voices who spoke out against violence against women on campus and against the institutional practices promoting sexual aggression. In the immediate aftermath of the XYZ incident, feminists tried to protect Laurel by discouraging any news of the incident being reported in the campus newspaper. As it happened, news of the incident reached the campus newspaper, which took a strong editorial stand against the brothers and the fraternity. Because of the publicity generated by the daily accounts appearing in the campus newspaper, the Women's Center and other campus feminist organizations sponsored a rally to protest violence against women. At this rally some six hundred students, faculty, and staff—a high proportion of them men, including some fraternity brothers—heard nine speakers. The Director of the Women's Center clarified for the audience the legal definition of rape. As Anna's remarks in this chapter testify, many college students do not understand that the legal definition of rape is based primarily on the issue of consent. In her speech the director underscored the importance of consent. She said, "The law is clear—if a woman does not consent and is forced to have sexual intercourse, it is rape; if a woman *cannot* consent, it is rape." Reading from the Section 31.21 of the state's Criminal Law and Procedure, she cited the legal definition of rape:

> A person commits a felony of the 1st degree when he engages in sexual intercourse with another person not his spouse
> 1. by forcible compulsion
> 2. by threat of forcible compulsion that would prevent resistance by a person of reasonable resolution
> 3. who is unconscious
> 4. who is so mentally deranged or deficient that such person is incapable of consent.

From the beginning, when word first leaked out about the incident, feminists named the incident rape, a judgment with which the local District Attorney of the Sex Crimes Unit, William Heiman, later concurred. Naming the incident rape was threatening at several levels. First, there was the legal level; if the incident was rape the brothers could be prosecuted. Second, if the incident was rape the university administration would have to take a strong stand against the fraternity. Finally, calling the incident rape meant an effective end to "trains" at fraternity parties. For all these reasons the outcome of the debate had serious political consequences for male privilege on campus. As we shall see, in the end male privilege won. The fraternity was only lightly punished. The offending brothers were required to take a reading course to increase their understanding of feminist issues and to participate in community service. The fraternity house itself was closed for one semester.

The debate began when Anna saw Laurel the day after the XYZ party at the fraternity house. Anna describes Laurel's condition:

> Her face looked red and bloated. She seemed strung out, a little disoriented, and very drained. I noticed that her knuckles were raw. Laurel told me that she had taken four hits of LSD, and she rolled up her sleeve and showed me this huge swollen thumbprint welt on the inside of her upper arm. It looked like someone had grabbed her. She told me that she had bruises all over her body and said, "My whole body is sore."

Anna's description of Laurel's condition is corroborated by the remarks of Laurel's roommate, who commented on Laurel's appearance after the party:

> Laurel looked horrible. Her face was really bloated, really *really* bloated, like after having cried hours and hours when your tear ducts have been operating for so long and all the fluids are in your face and the blood rushing around and everything looks all mottled and terrible. (quoted by Bowden 1983, 21)

When Laurel met Anna at the house the next day, she complained to Anna that she had been locked in a room during the party and that several men (she didn't say how many) pushed and spun her around. She said they wouldn't let her out. When she asked to be let out of the room, they directed her into the bathroom, adjoining the bedroom. She said she screamed and then they let her out. Laurel also complained that someone had stolen her prescription sunglasses. She was very upset about this because they were expensive and she couldn't see well without them.

Several brothers came into the room while Anna and Laurel were talking and one noticed that she had a red triangle on the back of her hand drawn by a magic marker. Laurel explained that she liked triangles, and that she filled it in every day. Anna asked her if she wasn't afraid of getting blood poisoning. She chuckled and said no. She explained that one day she covered her hand with magic marker ink, and that later she got feverish and had chills. She joked about this, saying that she didn't care.

Noticing that Laurel had a pink triangle button on her patchy jeans, Anna asked if she was a lesbian. To this one of the brothers replied, "If she is, she must be bisexual." Another brother walked into the room as Laurel was about to leave. After she left, Anna reported the following conversation that took place among the brothers.

One asked, "What was she doing here?"

Another answered, "I don't know. That woman is fucked up."

Another said, "She got boned last night."

Another added, "Many times."

Anna wanted to know what had happened. John and Joe explained how it happened. Joe said that he had been in the bathroom and that Laurel was lying down on the couch in their room. Chet was passed out drunk in the arm chair. Joe said that when he came out, Laurel was sitting in Chet's lap "sucking face," but Chet was still asleep. Joe said that when he tried to pull Laurel off Chet, she threw her arms around him and started to kiss him. Then they started to have sex on the floor, but Pete and some other guys walked in on them. They stopped having sex and Laurel offered to go somewhere with all the guys and have sex with everyone. John said they all went downstairs into the basement, where they took turns having sex with Laurel on one of the convertible beds.

After hearing this story from the brothers, Anna's response was to ask, "Who did it with her?" When one of the brothers asked her why she wanted to know, Anna said,

> For my own information, I'd just like to know who the potential rapists in this house are. I saw her the night before, and she looked like she was in pretty bad shape. She was not capable of giving legal consent because she was mentally incapacitated.

The brothers defended themselves, saying that it happened much later in the night, long after Anna had left, and that at that time Laurel had been fine. Several of the brothers felt that Laurel had started it all. According to their version Laurel offered to go downstairs with everyone and was saying, "Fuck me! Fuck me!"

"She wanted it," the brothers claimed.

They asked Anna, "So, what did you expect us to do?"

As Anna spoke with the guys about the incident, she began to get a clear idea of their definition of rape. Their conception of rape, she concluded, "is simple, stereotypical, and patriarchal." They believe rape involves forcing a woman to have sexual intercourse against her will. According to their story, Laurel was not raped because no one forced her. The brothers believe that when a man initiates sexual activity with a woman her state of mind is irrelevant. It does not matter if she is drunk or high on drugs. If she does not resist sexual advances, her lack of resistance is interpreted as willing acquiescence. Drunk or straight, the woman is responsible for what happens. She could be unconscious and still be responsible because she has not said no and because no force was applied. The brothers do not consider the possibility that their numbers may constitute force. Furthermore, they regard consenting to some sexual activity a license to indulge in anything. For them, it is perfectly legitimate for a man to have sex (if he can) when he is drunk or high. Under the influence, a man is not responsible for his sexual activity.

In response to Anna's reservations about their taking advantage of Laurel's state, the brothers said, "We were drunk. What did you expect us to do, carry her home?"

THE BROTHERS' POINT OF VIEW

There were two stages in the brothers' point of view as to what happened on the night of the XYZ Express. The first stage came in the immediate aftermath, the week following the incident, before word got around on campus and people started labeling the incident rape. During this period the brothers bragged about the event and many claimed that they had participated. During this period, a "humorous sheet" was pinned on their bulletin board, where the minutes of their weekly meeting are usually posted. Because Anna knew that the XYZ meeting minutes are notorious for recording all the names of the girls the brothers slept with during the week, she looked for the minutes of the first house meeting after the incident with Laurel. In the spot where the minutes are usually posted, Anna found a sheet entitled "Highlights" pinned to the house bulletin board. The sheet was about the incident with Laurel and also mentioned a party at one of the nearby colleges where the brothers had interacted with black women. More than any other commentary, the remarks on this sheet portray the sexism and racism at the XYZ house. Although the brothers claimed later that this sheet was not a record of their minutes for the week, that it was just a joke, its contents are revealing of the house sexual discourse.

> Things are looking up for the [name of fraternity] sisters program. A prospective leader for the group spent some time interviewing several [brothers] this past thursday and friday. Possible names for the little sisters include [name of fraternity] "little wenches" and "The [name of fraternity] express."
>
> [Matt], always the good catholic started lent on the right foot making sure he had fish on Friday.
>
> And our leader says that if we're going to make a mess, especially in his room, that we should be white about it and clean up after ourselves.
>
> Various [brothers] applied several new riffing techniques, including: unconscious riff, good samaritan riff, "let's make a deal" riff, corpse riff, polite riff, Negress riff, & Black-hole riff.

Anna's analysis of the remarks on this sheet help us to understand the point of view expressed. In Anna's opinion these remarks implicate the brothers in a rape. The reference to Laurel as "prospective leader" of the fraternity's little sisters' program and to the gang rape as an "interview" alludes to the fact that some fraternities require women whom they admit as "little sisters" to have sex with the brothers. This particular fraternity did not have such a program at the time of the incident. The brothers told Anna that they would never have a little sisters' program because they could never respect anyone who wanted to be a little sister and a woman who was a little sister could expect a lot of abuse.

The use of the word "express" is, undoubtedly, derived from the more common word "train" for "gang bang." The word "express" used in this context does not convey the passive attitude the brothers claim they took with respect to Laurel, since the word suggests rapidity, force, and nonstop action on the part of the men. It appears that the brothers were the active agents, not Laurel.

The fact that the brothers were active, not passive, is also suggested by the references to riffing on the Highlights sheet. Alice had defined "riffing" as "hitting on women" and getting sex from women at parties. Anna believes that *riffing* means "getting something off a person for completely selfish purposes, for total personal gain." In Anna's opinion "good samaritan riff" meant offering Laurel a place to sleep upstairs after the gang bang had started downstairs. "Unconscious riff" and "corpse riff" can be understood by examining the meaning of "Negress riff" and "Black-hole riff." The latter terms refer to Black women the brothers met over the weekend after the XYZ incident at a party at another school. The terms "Negress" and "Black-hole" obviously refer to women, which suggests that "unconscious" and "corpse" are terms that also refer to a woman. Used in conjunction with the term "riff" it is not far-fetched to conclude that "unconscious riff" and "corpse riff" refer to getting sex from a comatose woman, which supports Laurel's contention that during the incident she was drifting in and out of consciousness. The brothers' racist remarks parallel their sexist behavior. Both bespeak dominance and subjugation through the use of the penis.

At the same time that the Highlights sheet was posted, a letter was posted from the Executive Vice-President of the Interfraternity Council requesting nominations and recommendations for the annual awarding of a prize to the fraternity house "which has made an outstanding contribution to the University community." The following criteria were listed for granting the award: 1. leadership and service; 2. scholarship; 3. active participation in Greek-sponsored events; 4. alumni relations; 5. chapter management.

Next to "leadership and service," one of the brothers had penciled in, "We serviced Laurel."

About a week after Laurel reported the incident, the university brought charges against the brothers involved, through the university's judicial system. When they got this news the brothers asked to speak to the president, whom they referred to as "the Prez." According to the brothers, the president told them that they didn't have to see the judicial inquiry officer who brought the charges and that they could go straight to the vice-president. According to Anna, the brothers seemed really pleased about their meeting with the president.

Going straight to the president of the university suggests that the brothers felt that theirs was a privileged position and that they did not need to go through the usual judicial channels. However, as time progressed the brothers began to feel that the university was out to get them. They didn't understand why Laurel would want to get them in trouble. They stuck to their belief that they had done nothing wrong. Laurel had invited them and they were too drunk to act like saints or to be able to care for Laurel. The brothers were shocked by Anna's assessment that what had happened with Laurel was rape. After the initial period of bragging, they began to realize that Anna's opinion was shared by many on campus, and they stopped boasting. Those who bragged that they had participated but who in fact were not even in the house at the time or were sleeping, now owned up to the truth about their lack of participation. However, the brothers did not change their opinion that nothing wrong had transpired that night. They continued to adopt the position that it was all in good fun, that Laurel had seduced them, and that everyone was too drunk to know better.

Several months after the XYZ incident, in fall 1983, some of the brothers told their story to Mark Bowden, a newspaper reporter. According to Bowden (1983), when interviewed together the brothers gave similar stories. Each one went upstairs alone and entered the room, where Laurel made "advances." They either had sex or they didn't. One brother had sex for the first time that night, and another brother was unable to get an erection, which embarrassed him. When the brothers were interviewed separately, the details of the stories conflicted. Some said they were alone in the room, while others said they were present for the very encounters allegedly conducted in private. Despite the inconsistencies, Bowden concluded that for most of the time more than one of the men was present.

Most of the brothers described Laurel's behavior as "strange," but they said that they thought she was sober, alert, and willing. Describing his reaction one brother said he felt "a kind of excitement going on . . . a different mood," a mood that was "crazy."

> It wasn't normal. It wasn't blatant, though. It was weird. I knew what was going on without ever being told. I think everyone knew. I was kind of in a spell. But what I have to stress here is that it never, in any way, resembled the way in which you have some guy having sex with this girl, coming off and saying, "Ok, you're next." (Bowden 1983, 21)

The brother who had sex for the first time thought that the event was normal because of the pornography he had seen at the fraternity house and because of the stories he had heard at other fraternities about group sex and "trains."

The brother who was unable to get an erection felt "really weird and bothered" because he had not been able to have sex. This was the first time he had had to face impotence and he felt "terribly embarrassed about that." Even when Bowden interviewed him, months after the event, this brother was still troubled about his inability to perform that night. The pressure to perform was felt by others. However, Bowden concluded that male bonding was the most important aspect of all. According to Bowden, the brothers' response to Laurel seemed "foreordained," as if

> they were acting out some brute ritual they can neither understand nor explain. It had something to do with belonging to the fraternity and, deeper than that, with *what "fraternity" meant,* what it meant to belong. Feminist writers argue that implicit in any exclusive organization of men, especially in a society dominated by men, is an assumption of sexual supremacy—an assumption that armies, clubs and fraternities have been acting out in gang bangs for centuries. (Bowden 1983, 21)

Bowden concluded that Laurel was

> a troubled young woman [who] came to the party tripping on acid. She got even higher drinking. Despite the brothers' later accounts, it must have been evident to everyone who saw her that she was not acting in a normal, sober way. There are two things to do with a person in this state: One can either help her or take advantage of her. (ibid.)

Later, after Bowden's story was published, I interviewed two of the brothers who had been implicated in the incident. Both agreed to talk with me, but only one had much to say. Tom and I met twice. The first time we talked alone and the second time in the presence of a student interviewer working with me on this study. Tall, handsome, and broad-shouldered, Tom fit the image of the powerful, desirable frat brother. Throughout the interview he acted as if he had all the answers. His dislike for what I was doing and his sense of superiority to people like me were expressed throughout both interviews. The second interview began just as Mark Bowden was leaving my office after a luncheon meeting with me. Tom's attitude toward Mark was not at all friendly and he took the opportunity to lecture Mark on moral philosophy and journalistic ethics. Despite these barriers to communication, Tom felt inspired to give his own analytic version of the incident in order, I suspected, to compete with what he probably thought would be my prejudiced, softheaded version. Despite his negative attitude, Tom displayed considerable insight in discussing the incident.

Throughout both interviews Tom remained adamant that what had happened could not be described as a rape. He claimed that the incident was motivated by Laurel's "sexual identity problems." He explained that it was Anna, not Laurel, who defined the incident as rape. Nothing wrong happened, he said, because the sexual activity was not against her will—nothing wrong, he added, "at least in the strong legal sense of being wrong."

> Whatever sex she did have, I have no reason to believe was not consenting. She seemed amazingly eager, unrestricted in her sexual desire. It is not often that a woman will come to a fraternity to have sex with someone she doesn't know. What she did was unusual. It was related to her sexual identity problems.

Tom explained that sexual identity problems in both men and women lead them to casual sex. Tom compared Laurel to a friend of his, a male, who was sexually confused in the ninth grade. Tom showed compassion for this friend and explained that often guys doubt themselves and for the first few years of their active sexuality "engage in promiscuous sex to establish their sexuality." This kind of sexual activity, he said, is less well thought out and, hence, not under conscious control. People like this "just allow themselves to be seduced" in order to establish their sexuality. As further evidence of this theory Tom explained that Anna had a series of boyfriends who were brothers because she, too, had sexual identity problems.

Tom went on to point out that male social dominance and sexual identity are frequently based on sexual performance. Casual sex, he said, is the way guys both have fun and experience ego gratification. Casual sex is necessary "because guys don't have a strong enough understanding of their sexuality." The male ego is built on sexual conquests because through sex men gain respect from other men. Because social and sexual affirmation comes through sex, there is a lot of peer pressure to be sexually successful.

Tom admitted that rape "was not festive." When I asked him about Laurel's bruises, he came very close to admitting that a rape had occurred. He pointed out that Laurel had taken a lot of acid and was dancing wildly, perhaps damaging her body without knowing what she was doing to herself. This comment makes it clear that he thought something was wrong with Laurel that night. He added that sex always involves some degree of force and this plus the acid might explain the bruises. He did not elaborate on these surprising admissions and did not want to recognize the contradiction between these points and his certainty that Laurel had willingly engaged in sex.

According to Tom, subconsciously women are mad that they are subordinate in sex and are the objects of force. Sex, he continued, is a way for men to dominate women. A gang bang is an assertion of dominance because the woman is objectified and dominated socially in a gang bang. Historically women are more subject to sexual oppression and this is why psychologically it is more important for women to have a commitment in sexual activity. Tom concluded that the incident demonstrated male dominance only in the lesser sense that the next day the guys bragged about what had happened, not in the sense that the incident was a rape. He added that the guy who wrote the Highlights was bragging also—"story telling, not telling the truth." When I confronted another generation of XYZ brothers with the Highlights sheet years later, they repeated this assessment, saying that the Highlights was "just a joke."

Tom's analysis is an intriguing mix of insight and denial in an effort to protect the brotherhood. Tom came very close to concluding that the brothers had sexual identity problems and that the incident with Laurel was a way of resolving these problems. His conceptualization of male sexuality as naturally involving force suggests that the brothers may have used force with Laurel and that this was to be expected. As an individual Tom displayed considerable intelligence and compassion for his male friends and brothers. As a member of the brotherhood, however, he displayed an undifferentiated moral mentality, splitting good and evil and projecting evil onto Laurel while retaining good to characterize his fraternity. Not once did he display empathy for Laurel. In my discussion with a group of XYZ brothers some years later they, too, defended the fraternity and showed absolutely no concern for the victim. Both this group of brothers and Tom seemed incapable of feeling anything for anyone outside of their organization.

THE LEGAL CASE

Tom's comments illustrate a sexual discourse that rationalizes male sexual aggression against women by defining it as a necessary, indeed natural, ingredient of male sexual expression and heterosexual masculine identity. This discourse is widely held and was reflected in the numerous comments after the incident to the effect that Laurel "asked for it" and "boys will be boys." Tom's comments and subsequent events indicate how this discourse protects privileged young men and punishes the victim by blaming her for instigating the sexual activity.

The public nature of the sexual discourse that blames the victim is evident in the difficulty that arises in prosecuting cases of gang rape on college campuses. Legally, the procedure for prosecution is relatively straightforward. According to Judge Lois Forer, who has tried many rape cases (see Foreword), the issue of consent is central to a charge of rape. A person can be determined incapable of consent by reasons of unconsciousness, mental derangement or deficiency, retardation, or intoxication. In an interview Judge Forer said,

> If [the victim] looked perfectly normal and sounded perfectly normal and didn't appear to be drunk or high and said to a boy, "Come on, let's have sex"—well, that isn't a crime. The university had to prove, first, that there was multiple sex, and second, that the girl was incapable of consenting and that the boys who engaged in this activity with her *knew* or *should have known* that she couldn't consent [emphasis mine].

When I described Laurel's behavior at the party as it had been described many times to me and to student interviewers, Judge Forer said,

> All of these things would have been evidence from which a finder of fact could have concluded that she was incapable of giving consent and that her sex partners knew or should have known that she was incapable of giving consent.

When I asked her to explain the meaning of the phrase "should have known," she answered,

> They should have known from her behavior. They wouldn't have to see her take the drugs or drink. All you would need to know is to look at this person, observe her behavior, and say, "She can't give consent." If it is established that she was drunk or high on drugs then that would be rape because she wasn't capable of giving consent. It would be rape just the same as if she were tied down. It's like—supposing a patient is in a hospital and you have to have a consent before the doctors can operate on you. Now, if the person is raving and out of her mind she can't give valid consent and then you have to go and get consent from somebody who is in a position to give it.

In an interview with the Assistant District Attorney for Sex Crimes at the time of the XYZ Express, William Heiman mentioned similar points regarding the definition of rape. However, in this case he concluded that a conviction would have been unlikely. He pointed out that a charge of rape has to be proved beyond a reasonable doubt. A good character witness can lead to a reasonable doubt. If the brothers had a good reputation, that would be grounds to acquit because of reasonable doubt. The case was also tough because of the problem of proof. If Laurel consented to sex with anybody during the course of the evening, there is always room for reasonable doubt as to whether she consented to all sexual activity, making it virtually impossible to convict in the case of party gang rapes.

From his own investigation of Laurel's state during the party, he concluded that "there was no evidence that she was lucid" and able to give consent. Eyewitnesses who had no reason to lie reported that Laurel "was highly intoxicated and out of it . . . just about passed out." Five years later, in a public seminar dealing with the topic of violence on campus, he referred to the XYZ incident, saying, "The guys were guilty as sin." Despite the evidence and his certainty as to the guilt of the brothers, he felt there was little chance a jury would have convicted them.

> How are you going to convince a judge or a jury that she said yes to two guys and no to the next four after the judge and jury's heard about all the beer she drank, the grass she smoked, the pills she

popped, the tabs she snorted, or whatever? After a person has had all of this, their inhibitions lessen. Maybe their sexual drive increases. I don't know. But it makes her more prone to consensual activities with somebody because they're a little bit goosy-goosy kind of thing. You keep ingesting and you keep drinking. Finally you're like a piece of stone, and you don't know where you are, and you're probably unconscious or in a zombie state. In that regard you would get involved in the incapability of consent. But, as a practical problem, you have to look at the chances you're going to convince a judge or jury that she could say yes to two and no to four, as opposed to yes to six. There's always a difference between what is a matter of law and coming up with the evidence to convince a jury beyond a reasonable doubt.

THE UNIVERSITY'S CASE

An investigation of the XYZ incident conducted by the university administration established that on the night in question at least six brothers had "seriatim sexual intercourse with a single female." Testimony during the investigation also established that the sexual behavior was known to be taking place by others present in the house. In their defense the brothers claimed that "trains" were not uncommon on campus. As the brothers said, "It is common for multiple consensual sexual intercourse to occur in one evening on the university campus approximately one to two times per month."

The university, of course, does not have to prove that a rape occurred, only that some specifically defined rule was violated. A university can decide, as U. did, that ganging up sexually on a woman, regardless of her state, is behavior that will not be tolerated. The line between consent and rape need not be specified for the university to take vigorous action. In fact, a university can say that a fraternity that creates an environment that fosters ambiguity about determining whether a rape has occurred can be expelled.

After Laurel went to the administration and charged that she had been raped, the university took action against the brothers first and against the fraternity second. In these proceedings the focus was on "whether the house members conducted themselves in a mature and responsible manner, with due respect for the rights of all persons." The case against the individual brothers was processed through the University Student Judicial System and resulted in negotiated settlements without a hearing. The settlements required that the specific terms, including sanctions, be kept secret.

The secrecy angered the faculty, and a special committee was appointed by the Faculty Senate to investigate the administrative procedures that were followed.

In its investigation this committee learned that the sanctions were very mild and included reading and writing assignments, discussions, and community service. This type of punishment was supposed "to make the respondents understand why their actions were wrong and to foster their development as mature and responsible adults." The committee felt that the brothers deserved "serious and public punishment" of the sort that would, give an "unequivocal signal" that similar behavior "is not to be tolerated on this campus."

The committee also felt that the administration's treatment of Laurel was unacceptable. At no point during the entire period did the president contact Laurel or her family. Additionally, because of the confidentiality of the settlement agreements, Laurel was never informed as to the nature of the sanctions. The committee noted that Laurel was "deeply distressed by the outcome of the judicial process and that there was an immediate adverse effect on her emotional well-being." There were other instances where Laurel was shown "scant respect." According to the committee "the complainant [Laurel] was not accorded the dignity and compassion she deserved and the financial assistance she required." The committee recommended that the university consider its financial responsibility to Laurel and offered four guidelines for the future.

> First, the investigation of the incident should be complete and accurate. Second, there should be a hearing before a tribunal capable of rendering a decision fair to all parties concerned. Third, the resolution of the incident should transmit a clear message as to what conduct is and is not acceptable on this campus. Fourth, the entire process should show great sensitivity to the stake that the complainant has in the outcome.

The case against the fraternity was heard by the University's Fraternity/Sorority Advisory Board. The charge was that the fraternity "violated the Recognition Policy." Recognition of fraternities and sororities at U. is based on an agreement of self-governance in which certain expectations are set for the conduct of fraternities within the university community. According to the Acting Vice Provost for University Life at the time,

> The Recognition and Self-Governance policy makes clear that it is the responsibility of each fraternity to govern the behavior of its members and that such control is exercised through the fraternity leadership. When the leadership has not exercised that control, then self-governance has not worked.

The recognition status of the fraternity was the subject of formal review in light of Laurel's charges. A report summarizing the events of the party was prepared by the university's Judicial Inquiry Officer and the Office of Fraternity and Sorority Affairs. This report concluded that on the night of the party "there was unrestrained drinking of beer and grain alcohol [and] a group of fraternity members had sex with a young woman who was incapable of controlling her own actions." The authors of this report concluded that

> members of the fraternity, during and following the night of Thursday, 17th February 1983, tolerated conduct by members that seriously violated the rights of an individual who was a guest of the fraternity, and treated that conduct lightly until a complaint was filed. They have demonstrated a fundamental lack of understanding of the values that hold together this community and that protect the basic rights of individuals. Because of the incident, which was led by house officers, and the failure by the members to treat it seriously, we believe [name of fraternity] failed in its responsibilities to the community and has jeopardized its recognition status.

This report was reviewed at a meeting of the Fraternity/Sorority Advisory Board convened to determine possible action against the fraternity. The Fraternity/Sorority Advisory Board consists of university alumni, faculty, and student representatives and is considered a significant part of the governance of fraternities. Before its meeting the fraternity was given a copy of the report and the opportunity to defend itself against the charges. In response they prepared a statement giving their own version of what had happened. In their report, filled with misspellings, they claimed that they had done no wrong, and they described the charges against them as "gross exaggerations, maliscous [sic] fabrications, and unsubstantiated judgements." After hearing the fraternity's case and other evidence, the board recommended that the chapter be suspended immediately and remain suspended until 31 January 1984.

After considering all reports, including the report presented by the fraternity and the recommendation of the Fraternity/Sorority Advisory Board, the Acting Vice Provost for University Life imposed stronger sanctions. His final decision on the case stated that

- Effective immediately, the University's recognition of [XYZ] is withdrawn.
- The National [XYZ] Fraternity may submit a detailed plan for reconstitution of the chapter and for provisional recognition for the University to review. However, no active chapter of [XYZ] will be permitted to exist on this campus earlier than September, 1984.
- No present member (or pledge) of [XYZ] will be permitted to participate in any recolonized chapter in the future.

In reaching this decision the Acting Vice Provost stated that he was satisfied that the fraternity "had full opportunity to be heard." His decision was based on what he understood to be the context of the incident, which for him was significant. He characterized this context as one "in which excessive drinking and hazardous social activities, [were] tolerated by the Fraternity" and which "created an atmosphere in which concern for the respect and dignity of others, which we have the right to expect from members of this community, disappeared."

The Acting Vice Provost's decision was published on 25 March 1983, just five weeks after the incident. The fraternity responded by bringing suit in the local courts to restrain the university from enforcing the withdrawal of recognition. This suit began a complex legal process that was not resolved until 7 February 1984.

The basis for the fraternity's suit against the university was that they were denied a fair hearing. Judge Lois Forer of the Court of Common Pleas agreed with this charge. In her final opinion she cited the minimal procedural standards to be followed in a university disciplinary hearing:

a) Furnish the student or student organization specific notice of charges. . . .

b) Provide an impartial hearing tribunal and final arbiter. . . .

c) Afford an opportunity for the accused to present relevant documentary and testimonial evidence on its behalf. . . .

d) Be permitted presence of counsel at the hearing. . . .

e) Disclose all evidence against the accused. . . .

f) Supply an accurate transcript of the hearing. . . .

g) The tribunal or hearing officer must make findings of fact. . . .

Referring to the hearing conducted by the Fraternity/Sorority Affairs Board, Judge Forer concluded, "With the exception of the presence of counsel at the hearing, none of these requirements was met at the hearing conducted on March 23, 1983."

Judge Forer ruled that the case be sent back to U. for another hearing "before an impartial tribunal or hearing officer," who could be designated by the university. She outlined the procedures to be followed in this hearing so as to protect the accused's right to due process. In a Memorandum of Understanding agreed upon by Judge Forer and counsels for the fraternity and the university, guidelines for the hearing were listed. A professor of the law school would be the hearing examiner. It was suggested that the victim "will probably be unavailable to testify at the hearing." Consequently, counsel for the fraternity urged that testimony with respect to the victim "is hearsay and inadmissible." The Court ruled that while persons to whom the complainant made her complaints could testify, their testimony regarding the charge of rape would be considered "hearsay and not admissible for the truth of the substance of the complaint but may be material and relevant as to the circumstances surrounding the making of the complaint." It was also agreed that the issue to be examined was not to be "limited to the behavior of people who allegedly engaged in sexual activities but also includes the behavior of people who were aware of sexual incidents occurring openly and under improper circumstances and who stood by and did nothing." Finally, and most importantly as it turned out, it was agreed that even if the victim was "competent and willing and a series of actions took place within the knowledge of a large group of people, such conduct, if the hearing officer finds that it occurred and that under the circumstances it was inappropriate, may constitute a violation of the Code of Conduct."

Subsequently, the parties agreed that "the decision of the hearing examiner and the sanctions recommended by him, if any, be binding without further review within the University or in court."

The decision and opinion of the hearing examiner were published in February 1984. In a section entitled "Major Findings" the hearing examiner addressed two issues. The first concerned "the charge of rape," the second concerned "other sexual offenses." Regarding the charge of rape, the examiner listed all the reasons why the task of proving rape "was a formidable one." The victim did not appear at the hearings, as predicted. Additionally, it was necessary to maintain the confidentiality of the brothers charged, as had been agreed to in the Memorandum of Understanding as well as ensured by the settlements with the individual brothers in the course of disciplinary proceedings against them. Finally, the examiner noted that, with one "notable exception," the fraternity did not provide evidence with respect to the sexual activity that did take place in order to protect itself because the statute of limitations for rape was five years. The examiner pointed out that this concern "was neither frivolous nor unreasonable" and should not be taken as proof of rape, because "even a formal invocation of the privilege of self-incrimination at a trial will not support the inference of guilt."

With these constraints on his investigation, the examiner found that "forcible rape has not been proved," and "moreover, the credible evidence disproves any such charge." With respect to the charge that the complainant "was either so drunk, or so drugged, as to be incapable of consent," the examiner found "that the charge has not been proved." To this he added,

> It should be made clear, however, that this is not a finding that the charge has been disproved. Careful consideration has been given to the credibility of the eye witnesses, to bias or lack of bias on the part of each, to the precise condition of the Complainant that would have to be found, and to the specific details of the testimony produced.

The examiner's decision effectively exonerates the brothers, despite the fact that the victim did not testify and much of the evidence regarding her condition was ruled inadmissible. Given these limitations, the degree to which the examiner's decision favors the brothers is surprising. He finds, for example, that the "charge that the Complaint [sic] was either so drunk, or so drugged, as to be incapable of consent" was not proved. He also refused to find that "people [presumably Laurel] who slipped or tripped on the steps did so because they were drunk or drugged." Rather, he accepts the fraternity's explanation that the steps were slippery because "the beer slops about and makes the steps wet." He also pointed out that it was not necessary "to determine whether one of the brothers, passed out on a chair, . . . was tired or inebriated." Having refused to find that a rape had occurred or that anyone was drunk (despite the beer slopping on the steps and a brother "passed out on a chair"), it seems logical that the examiner would conclude by exonerating the brothers and the fraternity. Instead, he condemns the "environment," calling it "a ready host of ambiguity" and says that the obligations imposed upon the fraternity and its leadership are "intended to be conducive to a very different type of environment." It would be wrong, he concludes, to clear the fraternity of the charges

> because of the inherent, perhaps unavoidable ambiguity and then to condone conditions which are conducive to creating that very ambiguity. The University owes more to its undergraduate community.

Regarding the second major finding, concerning "other sexual offenses," the examiner stated:

> The evidence is clear and convincing that there was on the night of February 17–18, 1983, seriatim sexual intercourse with a single female by . . . brothers at the [XYZ] house. It is not important to fix a precise number of brothers engaged in that conduct, but it appears there may have been six. Moreover, the circumstances described by the evidence were such as to negate the possibility that this conduct, commonly referred to as a "train," in each instance was private and unknown to all others in the house. The circumstances present a classic case for collective responsibility.

The examiner referred to a witness presented by the fraternity who said that he had personally witnessed a "train" at least twice elsewhere on campus. In its defense the fraternity argued that "it is common for multiple consensual sexual intercourse to occur in one evening on the university campus approximately one to two times per month." The examiner concluded that if a train occurs with such frequency, then the university must "make an unambiguous statement of the position of the University with respect to the underlying conduct." Such conduct, he said, "can only be viewed as degrading to the participants and observers, both men and women."

> For a fraternity to condone such conduct is to violate the Recognition Policy of the University. The record makes clear that such conduct in a house invites participation by brothers who could otherwise have been expected to conduct themselves differently. It creates a negative environment, precisely contrary to the undertaking in the fraternity's contract with the host educational institution.

The examiner's final decision regarding sanctions was inspired by the fact that the brothers did not share his belief that "seriatim sexual intercourse" is degrading to all participants. The examiner referred to testimony indicating that the "fraternity did in fact consider such multiple seriatim sexual intercourse as 'no problem' or permissible." Whether or not this testimony was credible, the examiner found it most significant that

> nowhere in the record is there an unequivocal statement that today the fraternity considers such an event improper, to be condemned rather than condoned. Under the circumstances no penalty less severe than suspension can be adequate.

The examiner concluded that the fraternity house should be closed promptly and remain closed for a period of six months. He also stated that "no individual who was a member or pledge of the chapter in February, 1983, shall serve as an officer of the chapter."

Thus, in the absence of any criminal offense, the examiner imposed a parietal judgment based on his own conclusions about a proper environment. Although he concluded that no criminal offense had occurred, despite the inadmissibility of certain evidence to the contrary and Laurel's refusal to testify, the examiner took it upon himself to condemn "multiple seriatim sexual intercourse," which the brothers admitted had occurred, by punishing the fraternity for indulging in activities that he, the examiner, believed were degrading to all its participants.

REACTION TO FINAL DECISION

This decision ended all litigation, but it did not satisfy anyone on campus. The top administrators, the president and the provost, who had urged that recognition of the fraternity be completely withdrawn, wrote that they were "disappointed with the sanction." Judge Forer, whose jurisdiction had ended with the agreement that there would be no further review, was also not satisfied. The Assistant District Attorney for Sex Crimes, who testified before the examiner, expressed his outrage at the outcome:

> I don't know why [the decision] was so gentle to the boys involved. I don't know why he made his judgment in the manner he did, but I think it was a slap on the hands. In my humble opinion it was too soft. I would have closed down the house, thrown out the boys, and that would have been the end of it. But, I don't know why he did what he did. I testified as a witness. He said that there was no direct evidence that there was a rape. Well, fine, maybe there wasn't but they asked me, and I certainly concluded that there was.

Certainly, in light of decisions on other campuses in which recognition was suspended for as many as five years or the charter was revoked, the sanction imposed in this case was extraordinarily mild.

Between the time of the party in February 1983 and September 1985, when she resumed her studies at another institution, Laurel successfully overcame addiction to drugs and alcohol. The university reached a settlement with her in which they paid for medical, legal, and educational expenses. The settlement required that the specific terms be kept confidential.

In October 1984, just after the XYZ fraternity reopened its doors, the Director of Fraternity Affairs received a letter from an irate woman claiming that she had been pawed by a man asking her to dance at an XYZ party. This letter was never answered. Later that same school year another woman described abusive remarks shouted at her as she passed the XYZ house with a male friend:

> We walked past the XYZ house where there were ten or so guys hanging out on the steps. It was getting kind of dark out and they were being pretty rowdy, drinking beer and yelling to each other. As we walked by, one of them yelled to John, "Nice hair, homo, do you want to suck my cock?" Another one of them yelled some comment to me that I didn't really understand about how my underwear was probably so dirty he wouldn't fuck me if I begged him. We didn't say anything back; we just ignored it and walked away, but I avoid walking past that house alone after dark when they're all hanging out, it makes me very uncomfortable to be checked out like a piece of meat and given a grade.

CONCLUSION

In their more candid statements to the journalist, Mark Bowden, and me, the XYZ brothers admitted to having had sex with Laurel under questionable circumstances. They also appeared to be aware that their actions that night were not motivated simply by spontaneous sexual desire for Laurel. Their reference to a crazy mood, scenes they witnessed on TV, or stories heard from other fraternities indicate that their desire was motivated by other considerations. These considerations, I suggest, are related not only to issues of social dominance, as Bowden notes, but also to concerns about sexual identity. A confused sexual identity is resolved through casual sex. Using casual sex in this manner means that sexual performance helps insecure men find a place in a status hierarchy that privileges heterosexual males over women and homosexual men.

Related to the quest for social dominance and the concern about sexual identity is another more complicated issue having to do with acting out well-known social scripts. One of these derives from pop versions of Western philosophical thought that represent human nature as having evolved through history from a state of nature (described as wild and untamed) to a state of culture (described as civilized and tamed). Today many people believe that this evolutionary progression is repeated in the task of growing up.

For example, in many of the XYZ house activities there is an opposition between excess and restraint. For instance, compare the excess of
party activities with the restraint and discipline needed to succeed academically and in sports. This opposition is also observable in the brothers' substitution of "sexual service" for "community service" in the letter seeking nominations for the annual fraternity leadership award.

Similar oppositions characterize much of XYZ house behavior. The
binary oppositions posed by Western philosophers to characterize personhood   and   society—body/mind,   flesh/spirit,   instinct/reason,
chaos/order—apply to the XYZ lifestyle more faithfully perhaps than
they apply to behavior in the larger society. Whereas mind, spirit, reason, and order are set forth as the ideals by the larger society, the frat
house revels in behavior that celebrates body, flesh, instinct, and chaos.
What is rejected and frowned upon in adult behavior is acted out in this
fraternity context. Within this kind of discourse gang rapes are called
"gang bangs" and are interpreted as the means by which boys, still in a
state of nature, slough off their natural wildness as they journey toward
civilization and culture.

According to this discourse, women must protect themselves from
the explosive, "wild" nature of male sexuality. If a woman gets into a
situation where she is alone at night with a bunch of drunken men, she
gets what she deserves. She "deserves it" because she has not carried
out her appointed task as regulator of her own and male sexuality. If she
stays, then she serves another function. She helps the brothers discover
the "wild" masculinity that the broader sexual discourse about being
male tells them is supposed to be there. Once they discover it is there
they can then slough it off, as they slough off the women who serve as
their partners in the voyage of discovery.

A cross-cultural examination of sexual customs demonstrates that
there is nothing that is natural in this kind of behavior and a great deal
that reflects and reproduces social customs of power and dominance.
The sexual discourse that defines adolescent male sexual aggression as
prompted by basic biological drives and promotes the notion that
women must protect themselves or else they are "asking for it" is, quite
simply, the sexual counterpart of social male dominance. By blaming
women for provoking male sexual aggression, women are controlled
through the agency of fear. The fear is that a woman who doesn't guard
her behavior runs the risk of becoming the target of uncontrollable male
sexual aggression. Thus, although women are ostensibly the controlling

agent, it is fear of the imagined, explosive nature of male sexuality that ultimately reigns for both sexes. This fear instills an aggressive attitude in men and a passive, fearful attitude in women. It is a consciousness that helps to align social relations of male dominance and female subordination with sexual relations of male aggression and female passivity or masochism.

NOTES

1. The material quoted in this chapter is drawn from a number of sources: *Almanac,* 22 and 29 March and 13 December 1983; *Almanac Supplement,* 20 December 1983; *Almanac Special Bulletin,* 9 February 1984; Deposition Exhibits D–2, D–6, D–9, D–15, D–18, presented in the Court of Common Pleas of Philadelphia County, March term 1983, No. 6300; Memorandum of Understanding of Conference, 5 December 1983; and Bowden 1983.

Four

Other Victims, Other Campuses

Gang rapes like the XYZ Express appear to be part of a widespread sexual pattern found on college campuses throughout the United States. Barry Burkhart, a rape researcher and counselor at Auburn University, estimates that he has talked with two dozen students since 1974 who said they had been gang raped. Claire Walsh, who has conducted seminars at nearly every university in the Southeast as Director of the Sexual Assault Recovery Service, says that gang rape is a regular event on every college campus. Bernice Sandler, Executive Director of the Project on the Status and Education of Women for the Association of American Colleges, has found more than seventy-five documented cases of gang rape on college campuses in the past six years (*Atlanta Constitution*, 7 June 1988). Because a cloak of secrecy usually surrounds the incidence of gang rape on college campuses, the actual incidence may be much higher than reported. The testimony presented to the hearing examiner at U. that "trains" occur approximately once or twice a month gives us some idea as to the actual incidence. The latter testimony as well as the fraternity's reaction to the XYZ incident also demonstrates the belief that "trains" are part of normal sexual behavior.

Information on specific cases is difficult to collect. The case of the XYZ Express is unique because the victim, together with Anna and feminists at U., resisted the brothers' definition of the event and publicly named it rape. But resistance has occurred in other cases as well, and it is now possible to construct a profile of gang rape on college campuses.

This chapter describes three cases from widely different geographic locations of the country. In each case a common pattern is discernible. The incident begins with drinking or drugs and male conspiracy in finding, trapping or coercing, and sharing a "party girl." A vulnerable young woman, one who is seeking acceptance or who is high on drugs or alcohol, is taken to a room. She may or may not agree to have sex with one man. She then passes out, or she is too weak or scared to protest, and a "train" of men have sex with her.

The first case took place at a large midwestern university. This is the only case I know of in which the victim tells her own story. In order to conceal her identity, the name of the university is withheld. The second case took place at a large southern university. The case is reconstructed from police reports and the campus newspaper. Again to conceal the identity of the victim, the name of the university is withheld. The final case considered took place at a large western university. Most of the material gathered on this case was published in the local newspaper or presented in news releases.

FRATS AND TROLLS IN THE MIDWEST

When Amy heard I was working on the XYZ case she contacted me about a similar event that had occurred about the same time, in which she was the victim. At my request Amy and I spent a weekend together talking about the events that led up to the night she was raped after a fraternity party during the summer.

Amy's story displays remarkable insight and honesty. She is aware that she turned to group sex with fraternity brothers in her search for acceptance and power. Her case is important because it clearly illustrates the line between consent and nonconsent. The night that she was raped Amy had agreed to have sex with a fraternity brother she knew. On other occasions she had agreed to have sex with him and another male of his choice. On the night in question, however, after consenting to sex with this brother alone, she passed out on his bed. Before passing out she was dimly aware that guys were coming into the room to have intercourse with her. She tried to resist but didn't have the strength. When she awoke she found a brother on top of her trying to force oral intercourse. Amy pushed him off, went home, and later filed charges against the fraternity.

Amy's story helps us to understand why victims' actions may be interpreted as "willing." Like many of the women who engage in casual sex at fraternities, Amy was young, insecure about her looks, and looking for acceptance. In the following account, she tells us why she turned to sex and drinking. It is important to keep in mind while reading her story that despite one's assessment of the way she met her needs, she drew the line between consenting and nonconsenting sex. The story she tells is one of rape. To keep Amy's identity anonymous the fraternity is given a fictitious name.

AMY'S STORY

"Early one morning, after a late night party at the RST house at the beginning of my junior year, I was raped by I don't know how many guys. I had been going to RST parties since I was a freshman, even though I was warned on the first day of orientation never to go to the house alone.

"The RST guys were known to be a rowdy crew, heavy drinkers and 'partyers.' I started going there in October of my freshman year and went about three times a week during that year. From the first time I went, the brothers were kind of friendly. At least they noticed me. At other fraternities I was treated as a complete nonentity.

"The RST brothers did a lot of weird things. They had this doll they called 'Troll.' It was a plastic blowup doll, about life size. The guys would carry it around. I never really understood the significance of this doll. It seemed as if it represented the girls the brothers picked up, because the doll was always mentioned in connection with a brother who had managed to get laid. The brothers referred to women at the parties as trolls, particularly women they thought less of. If a brother did not manage to pick up a woman at a party, the other brothers would make jokes about him spending the night with this doll, Troll-Ann. It seemed as if the doll got more respect than the women the brothers had sex with.

"Girlfriends were treated with more respect. There were different classes of women associated with RST. In addition to the girlfriends, who didn't go much to the parties, there were the little sisters. A prerequisite to being a little sister was sleeping with the brothers. That was just sort of accepted. The little sisters were never treated too well. But, there was a stratum of women even lower than the little sisters, the stratum I belonged to. This class of women, called Trolls, consisted of those who went to the parties and slept with the brothers but did not demand in return the status of girlfriend or little sister. The difference between the Trolls and the little sisters was that during the week the little sisters could drop by the house on a friendly basis and the Trolls could not.

"The brothers marked women who came to their parties with something called power dots. They were black, red, yellow, white, and blue colored dots that the brothers would stick to a girl's clothing at parties.

"I'm not sure what the dots meant. Someone said that they indicated how good a friend you were to RST. The estimate for how good a friend you were was based on how easy you were to pick up, with white being the most difficult, then yellow, then blue, red, and with black being the easiest. They put blue, sometimes yellow or orange dots on me. I never saw them put black on anyone because that was really pushing it. But they joked about the black dot. They put red on girls who had been there before, girls who were blatantly interested in picking up guys. White was mostly for girls who had never been there before, and who looked really sweet, or who weren't sorority. They weren't interested in sorority women. I think the dots helped to mark women for other men so they would know where to start. For example, if a woman had a white dot, you didn't say really raunchy things to her when you first met her. If she had a red dot you didn't start off by asking her what her major was.

"The parties were for sex and drinking. People would sort of go back and forth between the bedrooms and the party. I first started sleeping with somebody about maybe three weeks after I started going to RST. It was very late and I'd been at the party for hours. At that point I don't think there were even any women left at the party. I felt like I could pick and choose among the guys. Being able to do that made me feel kind of powerful. It seemed like the thing to do, like that was what was expected of me, and it was no big deal.

"After I had slept with a brother the first time, brothers would approach me fairly directly and say, 'Do you want to go to my room with me?' As an incentive they would offer grain punch or pot. If I agreed to go that meant having sex. If I said no, that meant I was saying no to sex. In all, I must have slept with six different RST brothers.

"I only slept with Tim on a regular basis. The other guys I slept with because I wasn't feeling real happy and I thought sex would make me feel better. But Tim was somebody I'd sort of staked out earlier on. Someone I liked and thought was kind of cool. I slept with him for the first time after Christmas break of my freshman year.

"Tim was kind of weird. There were two occasions when he asked somebody else to join us in a sort of ménage à trois situation. At the time I wasn't comfortable with the situation, but because it was Tim, I felt it was okay. It wasn't that bad, but I wasn't that comfortable with the way I looked nude.

"The guys didn't touch each other when we had sex. Usually one of them would just kind of hang out and watch while the other one and I were involved. It was kind of a voyeuristic situation.

"The first time it happened it was with a good friend of Tim's who was not very attractive. I got the feeling that Tim was doing him a favor. Sort of like, 'you can have her for a while.' The other time he had sort of talked to the guy ahead of time. We were sitting around in this other guy's room and we were talking and drinking when Tim started making sexual moves towards me. I was real uncomfortable, because this other man was in the room. Tim said, 'How would you feel about him, you know, kind of joining in?'

"I was like, 'I guess that's okay.'

"But I'm not real sure what was going on there. That particular guy had a reputation at RST for being one of the easy brothers. He was known for being able to pick up good-looking women with no problem. I don't know why Tim arranged for the three of us to have sex.

"The relationship with Tim was real off and on until December of my sophomore year. After that I didn't go there much. I didn't love Tim but I thought he was neat. I prided myself on being the sort who could have a casual relationship. I was also sleeping with other men. Keeping a head count was sort of a point of pride with me. I liked shocking my friends, none of whom were sleeping with anyone. I also wanted to prove to them that I was attractive to men.

"It was the same thing in high school. I lost my virginity in order to shock and impress my friends, all of whom were virgins. It was when I was sixteen, the day after my sixteenth birthday. I wanted to get it over with because I thought that once I had lost my virginity I could move on to bigger and better things. Of course, it didn't really work out that way.

"My friends thought that what I had done was very adult and kind of sophisticated. It shattered an image I had in high school of being kind of intellectual—a bookwormy type of person. I was really getting tired of that image and I needed to shatter it. I got very involved with a guy who made me pregnant. He was a real loser; he was into dealing drugs, and he had been arrested three or four times by the time he was sixteen or so, but I thought he was neat. His whole family found out I was pregnant before he did. I had told his sister and she spilled it to her mother. They were all shocked. After he found out I still saw him but we didn't go out again.

"After that I didn't get involved with anyone for years. I couldn't deal with a romantic relationship because it made me feel really vulnerable and I didn't want to feel that way. So, I guess when I went to college and started going to RST parties I wasn't expecting much from men or from myself. I was willing to please Tim sexually. I didn't get much out of it except a reputation that I felt good about.

"I didn't go to RST so much during my sophomore year. But, I was still sleeping on and off with Tim. I was kind of changing my attitudes toward sex. I didn't want to be quite so casual. For me that meant not going to RST so much. In the eight months before I got raped, I probably went about three times. Once I slept with another brother, not Tim. Tim was real relaxed about the situation. When he saw me at a party he would say, 'Well, you haven't come to the house much.' I would answer, 'Well, I've been sort of busy.'

"During the summer after my sophomore year, I lived in a fraternity, just half a block away from RST. I went to RST parties twice during the summer. They were different than the parties during the year. There were all kinds of people there, not just brothers. But the parties still had this general RST sort of feel in the air, like you didn't know what was going to happen next.

"The morning I was raped, I had started drinking at a party we had at our apartment earlier in the evening. It was just after the first day of classes. One of my friends from another university was up. I went to the RST party with this girl. She was really high on drugs. I was really drunk. Earlier in the evening I had blacked out for an hour at about nine-thirty or ten and the next thing I remembered was that we were eating a sandwich on our way to the fraternity.

"When we got to the frat there was a party in session. They had a nasty purple punch that had grain alcohol in it. I started drinking and lost track of my friend. Some brothers came downstairs where I was and invited me upstairs to the balcony in front of the house. There were about fifteen to twenty people on the balcony, two or three women and the rest brothers and pledges. My friend had met this guy who was a pledge and she went off with him.

"I ran into Tim. He was in high spirits because he had finally graduated. He'd done really well. He was all excited. We chatted and at some point somebody suggested that we eat hoagies in their room. After we had eaten a hoagie, Tim asked if I wanted to go to his room. I agreed, I thought that would be fine.

"We went to his room and talked for a while. We ended up sleeping together. That was kind of okay. He hadn't seen me since about May. Over the summer I'd lost some weight. I was working out every day and I guess I looked really good. Anyway, he kept commenting on how good I looked. His comments made me feel uncomfortable, because he'd never really mentioned how I'd looked before.

"After we had sex I had to use the bathroom. Since he didn't have a robe, I wrapped a bath towel around myself. I didn't feel all that naked. I walked out into the hall. There were probably people in the hall, but I don't really remember. He came to the bathroom with me to watch the door because it didn't lock.

"When we got to the room there was somebody else in the room. He was lying on the bed and I don't think he had any clothes on at the time. Tim told me to go ahead into the room. I didn't remember seeing the guy before and wanted to know who he was. I was kind of confused. I thought maybe this was another one of those situations where Tim wanted a threesome but he hadn't said anything to me. He hadn't introduced me to this guy, which was kind of weird.

"I sat down on the edge of the bed where the guy was lying. The bed was a bunk bed and that was the only place in the room to sit. I wasn't really into standing for any extended period of time. It was beyond my capability. I guess he started kissing me. I was sort of willing. I was sort of passive about it. It didn't really matter.

"Then, Tim left and closed the door behind him. I sat up and said, 'Where did Tim go?'

"And this guy was like, 'Don't worry about Tim now.'

"And I'm like, 'I don't understand what's going on.'

"I'm not even sure what he said. Basically, he said something like, 'You'll understand what's going on,' or 'You'll see.'

"Next, the door opened and some other guys came in. I think maybe two or three came in at that point. Then, I don't know how, but I went from sitting on the edge of the bed to lying down without the towel wrapped around me. Before, I'd been sitting and wearing the towel on the edge of the bed and then I was lying on the bed without the towel and this guy was on top of me, and there was intercourse going on. Then, the other guys in the room would either come over and one would be like touching me while another was having intercourse or whatever. There was somebody leaning on me most of the time, which made me feel like I was being held down. One person sat on the bed and the other person would sit on my chest with their penis in my mouth or something. It was not like they were saying, 'You can't leave,' but I felt like that's what they were saying.

"At various times, I said, 'That hurts, please stop doing it, please leave me alone.'

"All I heard them saying was, 'That doesn't hurt, you like that. You don't want to leave now.'

"At one point there was some anal penetration, which was really painful. I was crying and somebody held my hand. I said, 'This really hurts.'

"And they said, 'Don't worry, it's not with you that long.' So I got the impression that somebody knew that I was not enjoying this. That was only the first twenty minutes. It was about three-thirty in the morning.

"I knew the time because I went into the room at about three. My girlfriend Molly had gone into Pete's room at a little after three. At the time she went into Pete's room I was still eating hoagies with Tim. It was right after we ate hoagies that I went into Tim's room.

"After the first twenty minutes or so I passed out and didn't wake up until about six in the morning, because I got back into my apartment at six-fifteen. When I woke up there was some guy sitting on my chest with his knees on both sides of my head. I told him to get the hell off me. I'd seen him earlier in the evening, and he said, 'What are you doing? I haven't come yet.'

"I said, 'So what, I don't care whether you have. Do you think I have? Get off me.'

"There was another guy in the room. I was staring at him and looking around the room, trying to figure out what I was doing there, what the guy on top of me was doing, and what the other guy was doing in the room. I wondered why I didn't have any clothes on. These guys left the room and I got dressed and went home.

"I felt terrible. I still had my contacts in, which meant that I must have passed out. I always take my contact case with me when I go out at night, because if I sleep with someone I always take my contacts out and put them into the case. I don't think I've ever been so drunk that I didn't take my contacts out if I had the case. When I woke up that morning with them in, my eyes were puffy and swollen, and my face was puffed.

"My eyes were puffy from crying also. My lips were bleeding and my jaws were stiff. I couldn't smile. My mouth hurt and my lips felt raw. My anus and vagina also felt sore.

"I must have blacked out after Tim left the room. For two hours the guys must have been coming in and out. I knew what happened in the beginning and I knew that when I regained contact with reality, there was still somebody sitting on me trying to force his penis in my mouth. At that point I was able to do something. Earlier, I had been too blacked out to protest or even to have more than a vague awareness of what was happening.

"The next morning I knew I had been the victim of a gang bang. At first I thought of it as a gang bang. Sometimes when I was at the house, I had heard the brothers singing a song that went something like, 'When I'm older and turning grey, I'll only gang bang once a day.'

"A pledge told me about a gang bang he had witnessed in his room. It happened while he was asleep on the top bunk in his room during a party. This woman had come in and passed out on the bunk below him. A little later, some brothers just sort of happened into the room. Then a series of them, I don't know how many, more than six, came in and had intercourse with her. They dropped the rubbers on a pile next to the bed. The next morning when she went to get out of bed she stepped in the pile of rubbers.

"You might ask why I slept with guys at RST knowing that I could get gang banged and knowing that the guys there didn't exactly respect the girls they slept with. I guess I was looking for warmth, some points, a feeling of comfort. Or, maybe just reassurance that I was attractive sexually. Maybe also I felt it gave me some power. I thought I could pick and choose whatever man I was going to sleep with and this gave me a feeling of power to be able to say to some guy, 'No, I don't want to sleep with you,' or 'Yes, I do.'

"I also liked to court danger. Being warned against going to RST was the incentive to make me go. There was a certain thrill in going someplace that I knew had a bad reputation, where it was hard to say what was going to happen next. I also liked going someplace where my name was known, where I would be recognized when I walked into the room—even if they were kind of jerks. I wasn't particularly good about looking out for myself at the time. I was drinking a lot, sleeping with people I didn't know. I was just not real responsible for myself. I was also hitchhiking lots for fun. I really like the feeling of facing danger.

"I also wanted to experience danger in order to learn what it was like so that I could help others. I have always wanted to be a social worker. From a very early age I thought that it was important to experience things in order to learn how to help others. In high school I drank a lot because I felt it was important to be an alcoholic in order to help alcoholics. I also felt that I had to experience problematic relationships in order to effectively help someone else deal with them. The first thought I had when I got my positive pregnancy test was, 'Oh, good, in ten years from now, when I'm a social worker, I'll really know how to deal with this one.'

"At the time of the RST incident I was drinking once a week. The night of the incident I drank a lot because my friend was up. I really don't know why I drank so much that night. It had been a long time since I had blacked out.

"The day after the rape I felt real stupid about being in such a vulnerable position. I was very angry at myself for getting drunk. This made me feel that I was somewhat responsible, but I felt that they were also responsible. And so I went to the IFC [Inter-Fraternity Council] in order to tell them about the incident. The council agreed with my definition of the event as rape and the fraternity was thrown off campus."

LITTLE SISTER RUSH

The second incident occurred at a large southern university after a little sister rush party at the MNO fraternity house. The victim was described later by her roommates as basically a "sweet girl," who "wouldn't want to harm anyone," who "was always trying to do things to please other people," but who was "very weak." Another roommate said that "she was a girl who wanted to fit in, who would do anything to fit in." This roommate told the campus police that the night before the MNO incident, during a party at their house, some "guy friends" asked the victim to come into the bedroom and to take off her clothes. Although this was supposed to be a practical joke, the victim undressed. Later, her roommates told her not to try and fit in this way "if you don't like what's going to happen." Her roommates also cautioned her against such behavior during little sister rush because she might get caught up in something like a gang bang.

The victim described the party the next day to the university police. It was a little sister rush party. She rode there with roommates and a friend. They arrived at the house between eight-thirty and nine at night. She was not interested in rushing with the fraternity, but she did want to attend the party. At the party the three girls ignored her and eventually left without her. At around eleven, she began asking for a ride home and a pledge said he would drive her home after he finished cleaning up the house after the party.

Around midnight she was the only girl left in the house. Some of the brothers teased her, saying that if she did not leave soon they would take her upstairs. She was introduced to a brother and was told that he was the house REX, Greek for *king*, which made her think he was the house president, which turned out not to be true. He asked her to come upstairs so that they could get to know one another better. He also told her that she did not have to do anything she did not want to. Although hesitant, she went up the back stairs to a bedroom with two brothers. One of the brothers closed the door and stood blocking it. They started talking about a secret bid, which meant that if you sleep with a member you become a little sister. The victim looked for an escape but the door was still blocked by the second brother. She was told that if she didn't do it she could forget about ever coming back to the house. She was frightened and was afraid they would physically harm her if she tried to get away. She knew there was no one to stop them and she resigned herself to fate.

The bedroom had a loft with beds underneath. She was told to get on top of the loft, while one of the brothers stood guard outside. Feeling afraid and intimidated, she got into the loft. The only light in the room came from a digital clock. She was told to get undressed, which she did. One of the brothers started having sex with her and she then discovered that there were two brothers. When she asked about this they said to her, "We brothers share everything." Then a voice from a bed under the loft said there were three brothers. The three then proceeded to sexually assault her. From then on men kept coming in and out of the room. There were never less than three with her, and sometimes more. They made her perform oral sex on them and then they penetrated her vaginally with their penises. She said that every one of the men followed this routine. This continued until two in the morning.

When she asked to go home, they told her she could go in a little while. Finally everyone left and she locked the door and got dressed, brushed her hair, and fixed her makeup. She then let one of the brothers into the room. He told her not to feel bad, that another girl had been upstairs earlier. He also told her she was prettier than most who came upstairs.

She asked the brother to clear the hallway of people. However, when she exited the room, there were men lined up beside the door and down the hallway. Some of them asked if she was going to be a little sister. The young man who drove her home said he would try to get her in as a little sister. He told her also that the initial brother was not the president but that a high-ranking committee member had been there.

She arrived at her apartment at about two-thirty. Her roommates were awake and the man who was supposed to drive her home was there. That night her roommates had received a phone call saying that the victim had gotten "gang banged." They had also received a call telling the roommates to take care of the victim when she got home because she would probably be upset. The next day, when confronted by her roommates, the victim began crying and admitted what had happened. During the next few days various notes were left on the victim's bed, all signed "MNO." One said, "Hey, slut, how was it?" Another said, "Was eight enough?" Another said, "You were used. But don't worry at least you made us come. Call for more. . . ." There was one drawing left of a girl being held down by a lot of boys who are having sex with her. The roommates said the notes were left by their friends as jokes.

Later the victim took a polygraph test. In the opinion of the examiner the victim was truthful and the assault occurred against her will.

All other testimony from the president of the fraternity and from the victim's roommates claimed that the victim was not drunk and had been a willing participant. The roommates, especially, sought to establish the victim's character as weak and prone to consent to any suggestion of sex. The roommates treated the victim as an outcast, especially after they learned that she had contracted herpes. They asked her to leave and expressed little sympathy for her. Throughout the episode the roommates sided with the fraternity brothers to protect them. The victim accepted her roommates' definition of what had happened. It was the victim's mistake because she had gone up to the bedroom willingly. Her roommates told her, "You know, try and forget it even though it's probably hard. You made a mistake but you'll learn from your mistakes."

Like the XYZ brothers at U., the fraternity was only lightly punished. The university reached an agreement with the fraternity under which the fraternity would be put on probation for two years. The fraternity was also forbidden to participate in some rushing activities and intramural athletic championships and was forced to hire a live-in house-parent at its own expense. Six of the fraternity's members were accused of sexually assaulting the victim, but nine months later, hearings for the individual students had not been held.

PLEDGING A SORORITY

The last case considered illustrates the degree to which women will aid men in the sexual degradation of another woman. This case was reported in the local newspapers and involved an eighteen-year-old sorority pledge at a local university, who said that she attended a week-night fraternity party *as part of her pledge obligations.* At the party she drank a glass of punch she assumed was nonalcoholic, but later felt dizzy and lay down on a bed in a room in the house. After consuming another drink she knew contained alcohol, she "blacked out." Several hours later, she woke up and found a nude male on top of her and three others surrounding the bed. A medical report later said she had been a virgin and had been sexually assaulted.

The fraternity involved denied all charges in a letter to their members and alumni, which portrayed the alleged victim as "flirtatious" and a willing participant. The three-page letter, signed by the president of the fraternity, claimed that during the party, the young woman knew she was consuming alcohol. Like the report prepared by the XYZ brothers responding to the charges brought against them, these brothers admitted no wrongdoing. In their letter they blamed the victim, saying that the woman "had been known to be very flirtatious with men at previous exchanges." The letter also claimed that during the party, the alleged victim had voluntarily joined in a beer-drinking game in a private room of the fraternity house and that the woman had told a sorority sister that she had a high tolerance for alcohol.

A campus hearing board charged with investigating the case questioned forty-five witnesses over a period of twenty-two hours. The board also reviewed documents pertinent to the case. This board concluded that the fraternity was

> guilty of maintaining a reckless environment in the Fraternity house both during and after the party with [the sorority] on November 14. Evidence presented at the hearing compelled the board to reach the conclusion that an 18-year-old sorority pledge became intoxicated, and was thereafter physically abused and taken advantage of sexually by members of the fraternity.[1]

The board charged that the fraternity and its elected officials failed in their collective responsibility "to provide for the safety, well-being, or personal privacy of a woman in an obviously intoxicated state." Because the victim was seen in this condition by a "significant number of officers, members, and pledges of the fraternity," the hearing board found that the victim had been "subjected to humiliation and ridicule." Overall, the hearing board found the fraternity

> guilty as an organization of physical abuse, lewd, indecent, and obscene behavior, abusive behavior and hazing, alcoholic beverage violations (including the failure to provide for the safety of any guest exhibiting intoxication), and obstructing the University's disciplinary process by intentionally destroying evidence related to the incident (University News Release 6 February 1986).

The university expelled the fraternity from campus for a period of *"not less than five years."* The university also asked the National Fraternity Organization to revoke the fraternity's charter and announced that administrative charges would be filed against thirty of its members. Eventually twenty-nine fraternity members were given punishments ranging from reprimands to expulsions (*Chronicle of Higher Education,* 18 June 1986).

The fraternity protested bitterly, blaming the harsh verdict on public pressure. The fraternity threatened legal action and a spokesman for the fraternity said,

> The only rape that occurred here was that the university itself raped [this] chapter. . . . That is the only rape that has ever taken place on this campus since I've been here. They raped us of our existence and I don't think that's fair.

The sorority, which cosponsored the party, was cleared of all charges except a violation of state alcohol laws and was placed on indefinite disciplinary probation. The hearing board pointed out, however, that the sorority "failed to provide for the personal safety of an underage pledge who clearly exhibited signs of intoxication" and observed that the sorority, "as with all fraternities and sororities at . . . University, has an obligation to provide for the safety of any member or guest who exhibits intoxication" (University News Release 6 February 1986). Rather than reject all charges and blame the victim, the sorority president responded by saying that her organization was "pleased to meet the challenges established by the hearing board."

In its protest to the hearing board the fraternity mentioned the police reports, as did the XYZ brothers, and claimed innocence based on the fact that "the district attorney, being fully cognizant of the police reports, declined to prosecute, even in the face of extreme media and public pressure based upon inflammatory and prejudicial remarks." A member of the district attorney's office in the county explained why, after interviewing the young woman involved, they decided not to pursue the case:

> Everybody agrees that there was sexual activity—whether it was consensual or not is at issue. But there was, by her own account, a substantial period of time when, due to the ingestion of alcohol, she has no recollection of what took place. No one believes she is being deceitful. It is just that she cannot testify to that which she does not know or cannot recollect. But we didn't disbelieve her. (*New York Times,* 17 February 1986)

In June 1986 the fraternity sued to overturn its expulsion from the campus. The lawsuit in Superior Court charged that the university had overstepped its authority and denied the fraternity a fair hearing (*Chronicle of Higher Education*, 18 June 1986, 3). A year later, in June 1987, the national organization of the fraternity revoked the charter of its local chapter. The victim in the case sued the state, the university, the fraternity, and the sorority she had been pledging at the time for two and a half million dollars (Warshaw 1988, 146).

CONCLUSION

Young women who seek acceptance at a fraternity party subordinate themselves to the brothers' desire in much the same manner as a pledge. The difference between the pledge and the women who become pawns in the brothers' sexual games lies in the final outcome. The pledge earns full and equal membership in the privileged group. Women who serve the brothers' sexual desire, on the other hand, become at most "little sisters," a position defined in terms of service to the brothers, or else the victims are sloughed off like used condoms. Although both males and females are victimized by the process, in the end men are elevated and women are subordinated.

The events described in this chapter follow a stereotypical pattern. A young woman is identified and marked by the brothers, sometimes with the help of women friends, as a possible participant in group sex. The victim, a woman, is alone, and the perpetrators, men, are in the plural. Because she is a woman, weaker, and in the minority, the woman is triply disadvantaged and completely defenseless. Whether or not the woman agrees, acquiesces out of fear, or passes out, the inescapable fact remains that she is in the minority and the men in the majority. The whole scenario presents the classic case of victim and victimizer.

It is useful to reflect for a moment on the meaning of the word *victim*, which derives from the Latin word *victima*, meaning "beast for sacrifice." Three definitions of victim are given in *Webster's New World Dictionary*: "a person or animal killed as a sacrifice to some god in a religious rite"; "someone or something killed, destroyed, injured, or otherwise harmed by, or suffering from, some act, condition, agency or circumstance: as *victims* of war"; "a person who suffers some loss, especially by being swindled; dupe."

Rene Girard, who has written extensively on the meaning of victimization in ritual sacrifice, provides interesting insights to be considered in an analysis of the sexual victimization of women by groups of men. Girard argues that ritual sacrifice checks and controls intragroup aggression through the mechanism of a surrogate victim. The surrogate victim enables the group to control aggression within the group by serving as a substitute object for the venting of aggression. For the whole system to work the surrogate victim must be vulnerable and unable to retaliate, and there must be unanimity within the group that the victim is the one at fault. This unanimity allows the victim to be treated as a criminal, killed, and expelled, which brings the violence to an end because the group has redirected its aggressions onto a harmless victim who represents the original evil (Girard 1987).

A similar process is at work in incidents of group sex. The group looks for a "willing" woman to play the role of victim. She is a victim for all the reasons mentioned by Girard. She is vulnerable, unable to retaliate, and there is unanimity within the group that she is the one at fault—e.g., "she drank too much"; "she wanted it"; "she was provocative"; "she didn't say no"; and so on. There is also unanimity that in the interest of promulgating group bonds it is acceptable to use a "willing" victim sexually.

Scapegoating the victim—saying that she brought the situation on herself—is necessary for the continued efficacy of the ritual, just as the efficacy of ritual sacrifice once depended on the delusion that the victim was responsible for the sins of the world. Just as in ritual sacrifice the victim was thought to embody the sins of the world, a gang rape is rationalized with the belief that the victim embodies the sexual desire of the men.

The god being served in rituals of group sex is brotherhood, a collective force that enthralls men and subverts individuality to the collective will. The whole scenario expunges male sexual aggression from the group just as intragroup aggression is expunged in ritual sacrifice through the mechanism of scapegoating. Reasonable men who gang up sexually on one woman and honestly believe that she can physically withstand multiple sexual activity with many men are operating under the scapegoat delusion that she is more powerful than they. This projection of sexual power onto the woman allows men to see themselves as passive victims of what is in actuality their own sexual aggression. The ritual reminds the brothers of their sexual dominance of women and at the same time it gives each a heterosexual stamp. The sexual activities have the flavor of a bathhouse orgy, with the difference that multiple sexual activity is directed toward a single female victim rather than turned within the group. However, by sharing the same sexual object, the brothers are having sex with each other as well.

NOTES

1. The material in this section is based on articles that appeared in *The San Diego Union*, 7 February 1986, and *The Tribune*, San Diego, 6 and 7 February 1986, as well as on University News Releases that appeared at this time.

PART II

PHALLOCENTRISM, MALE POWER, AND SILENCING THE FEMININE

Psychologically, highly sexually aggressive men [are] typified by greater hostility toward women which may decrease their sensitivity to the victim's suffering or even encourage further aggression in the face of resistance. Also, sexually aggressive men [are] more likely than less sexually aggressive men to believe that force and coercion are legitimate ways to gain compliance in sexual relationships. Finally, the more serious the self-reported sexual aggression, the more likely that current behavior was characterized by frequent use of alcohol, other drugs, violent and degrading pornography, and involvement in peer groups that reinforce highly sexualized views of women.

> (From a national study of sexual aggression among male college students by Mary P. Koss and Thomas E. Dinero, 1987)

A fraternity does create an unequal situation. Without a female perspective, fraternities become the images of the male fantasy. Women are outsiders, who are brought in to fill a function and then asked to leave so the brothers can fulfill their fraternal responsibilities. This can and has combined with the vices present to create rape-prone situations. However, because the overriding themes of college fun are prevalent, these situations become somewhat justified.

> (Mike, fraternity brother)

Five

"Working a Yes Out"

Fraternity Sexual Discourse

"Sometimes a woman has to resist your advances to show how sincere she is. And so, sometimes you've gotta help them along. You know she means no the first time, but the third time she could say no all night and you know she doesn't mean it."

"Yeah, no always means no at the moment, but there might be other ways of . . ."

"Working a yes out?"

"Yeah!"

"Get her out on the dance floor, give her some drinks, talk to her for awhile."

"Agree to something, sign the papers . . ."

"And give her some more drinks!"

"Ply her with alcohol."

[Laughter]

{Fraternity brothers talking about party sex.)

In this chapter I describe a sexual ideology evident in the conversations of fraternity brothers with male interviewers about various topics related to the XYZ incident. I suggest that this ideology and associated discourse channels sexual expression as these young men attempt to define, understand, and express their sexuality. Because it is focused on their own sexuality and makes sexual conquest the primary goal of sexual expression, this discourse is phallocentric. The discourse re-produces phallocentrism in the sense that it both produces specific meanings associated with sexual behavior and maintains these meanings by keeping them current.

By the term *sexuality* I do not mean genitality, nor do I refer to the expression of a biological drive. I use the term as it is defined by some psychoanalysts to mean a diffuse excitation with multiple objects. Psychoanalyst Juliet Mitchell (1982, 2) defines *sexuality* as "psycho-sexuality, a system of conscious and unconscious human fantasies involving a range of excitations and activities that produce pleasure beyond the satisfaction of any basic physiological need." An individual's sexual expression is formed by at least two sources: his or her personal life experiences and the social molding that defines expected sexual expression for him or her. Both sources define the kinds of excitations and activities that the individual expects will produce pleasure. In the absence of such specific channeling, sexuality is polymorphous. As Mitchell notes, "It arises from various sources, seeks satisfaction in many different ways and makes use of many diverse objects for its aim of achieving pleasure" (ibid.). The reduction of polymorphous sexuality to specific forms of pleasure, that is, to "something which appears to be a unified instinct in which genitality predominates," takes place in sexual discourse and sexual relationships that communicate the sexual mores current in a given society and that the individual chooses to adopt in individual sexual expression.

In this chapter I describe a sexual discourse communicated among fraternity brothers. Through this discourse fraternity brothers focus polymorphous sexuality away from one another and onto women in such a manner that the brothers maintain their positions of dominance and control. In addition to defining sexual expression for the individual, this discourse constructs a masculine subjectivity for some men (see chapter 8.) For example, one brother defined masculinity in terms of sexual conquest:

> When a man has many partners, he is not only admired by other men, but he believes that women will think he is an incredible lover. Many men get bothered if they are having sex with only one woman because it makes them question their attractiveness and masculinity in the eyes of other women.

This brother was so worried about his attractiveness and masculinity that he set quotas for sexual encounters for certain time periods. Once he decided to have intercourse with thirteen new and different girls before the end of the semester. Setting quotas was the means by which he checked and evaluated his masculinity. He explained that the joy of sex was "not just the pleasure derived from the act, but the feeling of acceptance and approval of my masculinity which goes along with having sex with a new person."

A man who sets quotas participates in the hunting-sacrifice mentality. In order to feed the masculine persona he has adopted to clothe the self, he must find, trap, and coerce a victim. He does this either by outright rape or by "working a yes out." As this chapter will show, there is a thin line separating "working a yes out" and rape.

"Working a yes out" refers to encouraging or forcing a woman to consent to sex either through talking her into it or plying her with alcohol. Verbal coercion and the use of alcohol to get women to consent are common practices on college campuses as elsewhere. In their study of 3,187 women on thirty-two college campuses, Koss and her colleagues reported that 44 percent of the women reported that they had been verbally pressured to have sex; 12 percent said that men had attempted sexual intercourse by giving them alcohol or drugs (Koss et al. 1987).

Koss's results are replicated by surveys on individual campuses, many of which use questions from her sexual experiences study (for other studies on date rape see Warshaw 1988). For example, a sexual harassment survey at U. in 1985, employing some of these questions, found that 44 percent of the undergraduate women interviewed had experienced behavior ranging from "unwanted deliberate touching, leaning over, cornering or pinching" to "actual or attempted rape or sexual assault." Surveys conducted at campuses all over the country reveal similar results (Hughes and Sandler 1989).

This chapter reports conversations among fraternity brothers that illuminate the sexual ideology underlying "working a yes out." As mentioned, these conversations do more than reveal an ideology; they also channel sexual expression and communicate expected sexual behavior. In telling one another what to expect, how to interpret sexual signals, and how to act at parties, the brothers encourage one another in what can only be described as rape-prone behavior.

The conversations took place in fraternity houses between male interviewers (trained by me) and fraternity brothers. The conversations were taped and transcribed with the knowledge of the brothers. The subject of the conversations included the XYZ incident, the difference between rape and seduction, homosexuality, pornography, and the relationship between sex and male bonding.

REACTIONS TO THE XYZ INCIDENT

Groups of brothers either showed disgust over what had happened at XYZ or candidly admitted that the XYZ incident could easily have happened in their house. Brothers in one house claimed to have kicked Laurel out from two parties, one occurring a week before the XYZ incident and the other the same night as the incident. These brothers said that Laurel was behaving erratically and destructively. Several people associated with this fraternity claim to have seen Laurel at both parties. All agreed that on the night of the XYZ incident, she was obviously very high on drugs and her behavior was "abnormal." These brothers expressed distaste for mixing sex with alcohol or drugs, but said that it happened in their house often. They felt that the XYZ incident is a product of the sexism reflected in pornography and on MTV. They believe that pornography has a negative effect upon male/female relations and feel that people derive too much of their education about sex from pornography. At least two of them spoke out publicly against showing pornographic films at the university after the XYZ incident.

The attitude expressed in this fraternity is not unique. Another group of brothers claimed that they could never take advantage of a drunk woman who appeared to want sex. They expressed disgust at the idea of engaging in group sex with a semiconscious or unconscious woman. One woman who lived in a fraternity for two summers confirmed this attitude, saying that she had "never seen any rude or sexist behavior toward women in this fraternity."

Other groups of brothers admitted that the XYZ incident could easily have occurred in their house. When asked to describe what happened at XYZ one group of brothers said:

> "I kind of feel responsible for what happened to XYZ because I was there and I could have just as easily picked her up before they did, and I could have brought her back here, and they never would have gang-banged her."
>
> "Yeah, because we would have!"
>
> "No, we wouldn't have, because I would have locked the door and had her myself."

These brothers' definition of a gang bang was group sex with a single woman who "was into it." Talking about the XYZ incident, they claimed that Laurel could have walked out, indeed had ample opportunity to "escape." For example, they noted that she was able to go to the bathroom by herself, saying this proved that she was in control. They did not believe anyone took advantage of her, but their definition of taking advantage was restricted to taking by force. Explaining the meaning of taking advantage, one of them said,

> I don't think taking advantage of a situation is the same as taking advantage of a person. If someone is there with their legs spread it's not the same as if you took advantage of the fact that they can't close them. If they went in there and one guy had one leg each, and you took advantage of the fact that she couldn't close those legs because there was a guy holding each side, you're taking advantage of her. If you take advantage of the situation in which she seemed pretty compliant with whatever you wanted to do, that's not taking advantage of her, per se. And she wasn't unconscious, or at least it didn't seem like that.

These brothers don't see anything wrong with forcing a yes out—an activity they classify as seduction rather than rape. They restrict rape to the use of physical force and anything else, including "working a yes out," comes under the heading of seduction. When asked about the difference between seduction and rape the brothers commented, "With rape she never gives in. . . . With seduction, she might say no for awhile, but then she gives up, and decides that she wants sex too. Physical force is the difference."

According to this system of beliefs it is easy to understand the meaning of the common phrase "a no means yes." A "no" means "maybe" or can be turned into a "yes." A woman "might change her mind." A "no is meaningless" because

> sometimes you get surprised. I'm just saying you can't tell. Well, he's saying that you can tell, by the way they say no, but you can't always tell at all . . . haven't you ever got a surprise like, you thought there was no way that you would get laid, and you did.

To this another brother responded, "Yeah, and then you can't get your hard-on because you're so shocked."

Although these brothers define rape as forcing a woman against her will, they also say that sometimes a woman has to show physical resistance "to show you how sincere she is." Even after she has shown physical resistance, they keep trying—usually, by getting the girl drunk. By getting her drunk they help her to release inhibitions and meet them on their own ground. But, they are adamant that what happens after she gets drunk is her own responsibility. As these brothers said about Laurel,

"She was drugged."
"She drugged herself."
"Yeah, she was responsible for her condition, and that just leaves her wide open . . . so to speak."
[laughter]

It is interesting to note that in the fraternities where brothers state that the XYZ incident could not have happened in their house, nonetheless they defended the behavior of brothers at other houses. Although a few of them said that they would help a girl who might be in trouble, most of them were more concerned about one another. Thus even when brothers follow unwritten rules about what is allowable in their house, the impression is left that the rules are not meant to protect vulnerable women but to protect the house reputation. These brothers expressed a we/they attitude, with women being defined in hostile terms. Although they believed that women are mainly responsible for anything that happens to them in fraternity houses, they at least give some small consideration to the responsibility of the brothers.

In another fraternity the brothers blamed the XYZ victim, saying, "That girl just totally brought everything onto herself." However, they gave the XYZ brothers low marks because "those guys were stupid in not realizing that some way or another, this thing could turn around and get them into a lot of trouble, which is exactly what this girl did." Only one brother of the many interviewed admitted that a rape had occurred. He said, "It was rape because of the fact that they knew that she was fucked up, and they took *total* advantage of her."

A brother from another fraternity who was interviewed alone felt very sure that the XYZ incident could never happen in his house, not because the brothers were particularly moral, but because they were very nerdy type of guys, not shallow, but just kind of narrow minded. But as far as sex is concerned, it just would not be like them to allow any kind of sexual needs to invade someone else's rights, it just could never happen.

Talking about reactions to the XYZ case in his fraternity, this brother continued,

Oh, it was bad, you know, the brothers were like, "This sucks, this makes all the fraternities look bad." I think from what they'd read, and from what they knew about the girl, they probably felt that it was a victim-precipitated type of thing. They felt that she shouldn't have been where she was at the time. I mean, we feel that a girl has to take responsibility for herself. So they probably felt that she did bring it on. You know, if you give someone a gun, and tell them to shoot, they don't have to shoot.

BEING "BLUE BALLED"

Brothers rationalize their desire for casual sex by referring to the explosive, uncontrollable nature of male sexuality. According to them, male sexuality is exploitative, abusive, and demands gratification. Rape is considered to be a result of sexual frustration brought on by pornography. In this state of frustration, a man has to go out and hire a prostitute to keep himself from becoming violent. Or, if a woman "comes on" to him he is powerless to resist and experiences a state called being "blue-balled":

[Being] blue-balled is being led on until your balls are almost blue because they hurt so much because your hard-on is stretching, and then you're shut off like a bucket of cold water.

The relationship between the sexes is described as a relationship between "armed camps" in which each side wants something from the other. The male camp wants sex; the female camp wants companionship. Men fight the war with booze, words, and a "third leg." The "third leg" puts men at an advantage.

"She can say no as long as I can say please. And, I always say please."
"They're not as armed as we are."
"Legged or armed?"
"Third leg."

The allusion to the penis in this exchange as the weapon placing men in a position of superiority in the battle between the sexes illustrates once again the phallocentrism of fraternity life. The brothers admit that they are interested only in sex, not in companionship. If a woman is in a situation where she has to say no several times, they believe she should get herself out of the situation. "If she sticks around, that's your signal that she's not quite ready to do anything, but she's still interested in you, so it's worth trying . . . you know, to keep trying."

The interviewer asked, "But what if she just wants to hang around and talk and dance, or just sit and drink or make out halfway or something?" The brothers replied, "Ridiculous!" "Then you got blue-balled, you didn't play your cards right, you were had."

CONCERNS ABOUT HOMOSEXUALITY

In general the brothers described men as sexually driven creatures with large and fragile egos needing continual feeding and caressing. The male is obsessed with status and the size and hardness of his penis. Like the fighting cocks Balinese men play with, the penis for these men serves metaphorically as a "symbolic expression or magnification of the owner's self" (Geertz 1973). The brothers' concern with sexual potency and social success in the male heterosexual role masks a deep fear, hatred, and fascination with homosexuality. Brothers equate virility with heterosexuality. Some brothers reported that when they were pledges there was pressure on them "to get laid" in order to establish their virility as heterosexual males. Fraternities that don't apply this pressure are seen as encouraging homosexuality.

One interviewer asked, "When you guys were being rushed, did you feel any pressure about virility at all?" They replied:

> "Not so much when you rush but after you've pledged, there's this whole big thing, they're like, yeah, what pledges get laid, because you're freshmen, they want to see if the freshmen can get laid."

"If you were pledging [name of another fraternity] or something, they don't care about virility at *all.*"
"Not in the slightest, in fact, you could bend over and they'd just fuck you up the asshole."
"And then you're in for sure."

The fascination with homosexuality is seen in oblique references to sticking "carrots up the asses" of initiates and in endless joking about oral sex. Fantasies about coercing girls to "give a blowjob" were frequently expressed during the interviews. When asked what kind of sex goes on at their parties, one brother laughed and said, "Right! Like, pushing a girl's head down your pants and teaching her to give you a blowjob!" By saying this he was making fun of the interviewer's apparent desire for sordid tales of fraternity sexual misconduct, and he was also sharing and enjoying the fantasy of coerced oral sex. This kind of fantasy not infrequently blurs into reality in the drunken atmosphere of parties.

Much of the fraternity banter is focused on oral sex. One commonly heard joke is illustrative.

What's the difference between your dog, your wife, the system, and a blowjob? You can beat your dog, you can beat your wife, and sometimes you can beat the system, but you just can't beat a blowjob!

One of the male interviewers, also a fraternity member, reflected on the meaning of the fascination with oral sex both from his own point of view and that of brothers he knew.

There are many reasons why oral sex is so gratifying. A blowjob is significant because the emphasis is so completely on having the woman devote herself to our pleasure. In other words, it is the least mutual form of lovemaking. In posture, sensation and emotional content, a blowjob involves the most subservience to the man's desires. I also think that it is important in frat culture because it is a fantasy which can be easily applied to men and women. In other words, there is more homoerotic potential in sharing a fantasy about a woman performing a blowjob than about having heterosexual intercourse, because the blowjob given by a woman can stand for a blowjob given by a brother, whereas intercourse is more specifically heterosexual. This connection is harder to prove, but for me it ties in with the importance of references to homosexual behavior, especially blowjobs, in the constant stream of put-downs and banter by which we relate to each other all the time. I contend that it is no simple putdown or empty joke when one brother says, "Hey! When are you gonna clean this place up?" and the other responds, "Right after you suck my dick." Such references to blowjobs express and manipulate a variety of themes, including sexual domination, violence, and degradation, as well as a certain amount of real affection and attraction (at least between the males) while also sharing the enjoyment of the shared humor and irony of the references within a normally strictly heterosexual (in practice) environment.

The debasement of women is inculcated by a fraternity environment that builds its cohesiveness, at least in part, on abusive relations. One of the brothers explained that abuse, sexual and otherwise, is a way of breaking down barriers, building trust, and bonding more closely. This brother spoke passionately about the meaning of sexually abusive rituals.

> Did you ever notice in your high school guys took showers in those big, open shower rooms. Girls, or girls I knew anyway, said "Oh my God, How can you do that. I wear my bra into my own stall." It's a breakdown of barriers. One of the few barriers left in this society is sexual barriers. It's cutting down. When you can strip somebody down, and get everything possible out of them, whether it's sexual, sexual parts, sexual this and that, and just say, that's where you are. It knocks down any barrier between people and it makes for a closer bond. I think that's part of the reason behind [sexually abusive initiation rites]. Part of the initiation thing is leaving yourself open to abuse for anything that might have been said about you or done to you.

To this one of the brothers responded somewhat vaguely, "*Suck your . . . ,*" alluding to homosexual behavior.

> Which includes things like that . . . even if I told you what it was it would be hard to explain. It has more to do with being friends with everybody and knowing everybody real well.

MALE SOCIAL AND SEXUAL DOMINANCE

Sexual domination is an ever-present theme and concern. Dominance takes a variety of forms—social, sexual, and fraternal. The brothers are concerned to dominate women socially and sexually. Part of the reason they bond as a group is to achieve the domination that they believe is owed to all males. General agreement was expressed that the male wants to dominate and be the leader and that for this reason it is much more important for a man to perform well in college than it is for a woman to do so. A general consensus emerged from one group of brothers that men are more success-oriented than "girls." Success is a component of sexual attraction for men, but does not contribute to female attractiveness. One brother said, "A girl who is real successful could scare a lot of guys off." Another said, "If some girl who I was thinking of marrying in a couple of years didn't graduate, I'd say, So what? That's all right, I'll support you. But I wouldn't be able to deal with it if she had to support me."

The brothers rationalize sexual dominance of women in a curious fashion. They believe that sexual harassment of women—by which they mean verbal harassment—is necessary for male bonding. Verbal harassment means "making someone look worse than you."

> When you come up with a great comment to put somebody down, it makes you feel good. It's just building your ego at the expense of others, such as verbally abusing a girl at a party. Verbally harassing a girl increases male bonding. I mean, people come back the day after a party and say, "You should have seen me abuse this girl." They're real proud of it in front of everybody.

The image of women that emerged from these discussions is very different from images of men. Women are placed outside of the male status hierarchy and are expected to play a less privileged role and to be available for sex. The status of women is assigned according to the nature of their sexual interactions with men. Women who are entirely unresponsive to sexual advances are called "frigid" and "icicles." Women who permit men to make advances up to a point, after which they refuse more intimacy, are called "tease" or "cocktease." Those who have sex with even a few too many or poorly chosen men are classified as "sluts" or "cunts."

About the only role without negative tags attached is that of someone's girlfriend.

Rendering women sex objects demonstrates the double standard that prevails. Men are expected to engage in casual sex—indeed their status depends on it—while the women who are their partners are "worthless sluts." The XYZ victim is called "an ignorant slut" and condemned for having sex with many men, while the men who had sex with her are not as bad because "at least they only had sex with one girl."

Feminists on campus are condemned because they challenge men and speak out against instances of date rape and gang rape. Feminists who argued against showing pornography on campus because it debases women were labeled "rug-munching dykes." Those working to end sexual harassment were described as "narrow-minded" and as "man haters." People who spoke out publicly against the XYZ brothers, labeling their actions rape, received obscene phone calls and death threats. The death threats and obscene phone calls are frightening because they demonstrate how far some men will go, at least in fantasy, to defend male privilege and power.

SEX, PORNOGRAPHY, AND BROTHERHOOD

Watching pornography together is a frequent pastime of brothers. In the shared enjoyment of pornography lie two ingredients for a "train": shared titillation and a certain amount of distance between the viewer and the sex. There is a thin line between getting off by proxy on the screen and getting off on a surrogate in the house, especially when the pornography specifically urges the brothers to make the fantasy real.

One group of brothers discussed with humor and jokes a photofantasy of a "train" that they had read in a pornographic magazine during one of their house initiation rituals. The featured photofantasy of the September 1984 issue of a magazine called *Velvet* was circulated and discussed. The fantasy was explicitly constructed to train young men in the art of the "gang bang." The headline for the photofantasy stated: "Watch Our Cover Girl Take On Three Guys! Then . . . Use Her To Create Your Own X-Rated Action! Fucked Unconscious!" The body of the fantasy depicted the "cover girl" as unconscious not from pain or abuse but from joy at being "fucked":

> ... And Then She's Fucked Some More By Three Studs ... She was the fuckingest, suckingest chick at the party. In fact, she blew so many of the guests that she passed out! But fortunately for her, the last three party-ers were kind enough to bring her back to semi-consciousness. Now the lucky girl had three more stiff dicks to keep her happy. Judge for yourself how grateful she was! ... As soon as she came to, the party girl was hungry for cock. She sucked all three of them dry and still begged for more!

The photofantasy showed several pages of three young guys, all college-aged, wearing oxford shirts and drinking beers and simultaneously having sex with the cover girl. At the end, "party girl" says to the reader: "Now, *Velvet* readers, you can stick it in me too! YOU Can Join This Action By Creating Your Own Hard-Core!" To facilitate "this action," a set of paper dolls is provided (the cover girl and two of the guys) and the reader is invited to join in the fun by playing with the paper dolls and making himself the third guy. It is suggested that a real woman might be substituted. Indeed, a letter is printed in the same issue that describes how the writer and his "buddies ... had a great time playing the Fuck the Centerspread game" from a previous issue with a "willing girl" who was there with them when they "played on one of the guys' living room floor."

This basic message that guys can have a great time together *if only* they can find a willing girl is repeated over and over in the porno magazines and films that are consumed in quantity by some fraternity brothers. Given the importance they attach to group cohesion and sexual conquest, and the fact that the intoxication/disorientation/confusion of the woman is explicitly represented in the porn fantasy as female sexual desire, the motivation for exploiting a vulnerable woman after a party is very strong indeed.

When asked about the advisability of showing pornography, some of the brothers expressed the same attitude about their right to see pornography as they expressed about their right to take advantage of a drunk, "willing" woman. If a movie is made, they have the right to see it, just as they have the right to have sex with a passive woman regardless of her state of consciousness.

"Once a movie is made, regardless of the circumstances, even if a woman is forced, to tell me that I can't go see it, that's going too far, because that's my decision."
"Yeah, if he wants to see a movie, and the actor and whoever is in there wanted to make the movie, then why does anybody care? I mean, whose business is it?"

The brothers are generally in favor of pornography because of its commercial success. They place considerations of money and the status quo ahead of moral or ethical concerns. If something is financially successful, it must be good. They are not troubled about exploiting a certain kind of sexual need for money. They admit this at the same time they admit that abusive relations and attitudes toward women are in part encouraged by pornography. When asked if they thought "anything bad comes out of showing pornography on campus," the brothers replied,

"No, they make a lot of money."
"It might have bad effects on some people. It definitely sort of promotes some, you could call, bad ideas, but it all depends on who's watching it and what mentality he's watching it with."
"Yeah, but who's going to judge someone else's morality?"
"That's why they should let everyone see that movie who wants to [referring to a controversial movie shown on campus]. If you don't want to see it then stay away from there."

The brothers admit that seeing pornography is something to do before their parties start. They want to learn what it's like to "have a two foot dick" and to have a good time together. They never go alone, always together. They go together in order to have a good time, laugh, and make jokes during the movie. They dissociate themselves from the men who go alone to porno movies downtown and sit in seats "with coats and newspapers spread out over their laps" and "jerk off" during the movie. They believe this is sick, but they don't think "getting off" while reading *Playboy* privately or enacting a porno fantasy in their house is necessarily sick.

Some brothers displayed a more ambivalent attitude toward pornography. They felt that pornography "cuts down on rapes drastically" because it acts as a release, just as seeing violence on TV cuts down on actual violence.

> If they don't have porn movies, then you're just going to go out and buy a *Playboy* magazine, and then, if they didn't have that, and if they eliminated all . . . anything that could be pornographic, I think that's when you're going to increase the rape, cause then someone's not going to be able to turn to the media. . . .

However, these same brothers admitted that after seeing a porno movie, "They want to come home and go to a party and get laid!" One brother felt that seeing a porn movie didn't alleviate sexual frustration, but increased it: "It makes you hornier."

Pornography puts them in the mood for sex but does not, in their opinion, result in forcible rape. If a girl "happens by," if "there's a girl around," they say they would "like to fuck her." In these statements they reduce the women they encounter in real life to the status of the "girls" they see in the porno movies—sex objects to be "fucked."

THE ISSUE OF LOVE

Only once in these discussions with fraternity brothers, which spanned a two-year period, did any group of brothers mention love in connection with sex. In a discussion about sex and drinking, one set of brothers introduced the novel idea that it might be better to have sex when drunk not to loosen the girl up but to keep her from falling in love. These brothers admitted that they did not like "fucking" women who were drunk.

> "It's like sleeping with a stranger."
> "It's not like a mutual thing."
> "You cannot say that we don't like doing that, but you can say that we would much rather do it if we were both sober."
> "That would be much more fulfilling to both parties involved."
> "Provided she can handle it."

To this the interviewer responded, " 'Provided she can handle it.' . . . You sound like you need, like you want someone who's going to be able to handle you or something."

"Exactly. And some of them, you have real sex, intimate, giving, sober sex . . ."

"Not just the old Dorito bang."

"They will either just run away terrified, or they will be so whipped, I mean out of bounds in love with you."

"Apeshit!"

CONCLUSION

In their national study of sexual aggression on college campuses, Koss and her colleagues found that 19 percent of the 2,972 male students interviewed said yes to the question, "Have you engaged in sex play (fondling, kissing or petting, but not intercourse) with a woman when she didn't want to, by overwhelming her with continual arguments and pressures?" Five percent of the men admitted they had attempted sexual intercourse with a woman when she didn't want to by giving her alcohol or drugs, and 4 percent said that they had engaged in sexual intercourse with an unwilling woman by giving her alcohol or drugs (Koss and Dinero 1987). Such statistics demonstrate that by their own admission a small sample of men resort to coercive tactics to have sex with unwilling women. This sample of men, however, does not match the number of women who report that they have been verbally coerced or coerced with alcohol or drugs into having sex when they did not want to. As mentioned in the beginning of this chapter, 44 percent of the women in Koss's study reported that they had been verbally pressured into sexplay, and 12 percent reported that men had attempted sexual intercourse by giving them alcohol. Thus it would seem, from the statistics alone, that fewer men than women are involved in coercive sexual behavior. We might conclude that a minority of men engage in coercive sexual behavior with many women. Another possibility, however, is that many men are not even aware that their sexual behavior is coercive and hence do not report it as such.

In this chapter conversations were reported that illuminate the ideology and discourse that might motivate some men to resort to coercive tactics. "Working a yes out" is the label given to verbal coercion or co-ercion by means of alcohol or drugs. Because they do not see this as co-ercion, but a form of seduction, the brothers quoted above would not classify such actions as rape, an act they defined narrowly as physical coercion. However, there is a very fine line between seduction and rape when men candidly admit that they don't take repeated no's for an an-swer or that they take advantage of a situation in which a young woman's resolve has been weakened by the alcohol or drugs they have given her. In these cases, "working a yes out" is better described as "forcing a yes out." The difference that separates the men who use this approach from the rapist, as rape is defined by the brothers, is primarily a matter of technique and of the latitude given the women to escape. The fraternity brother uses a more sophisticated approach, relying on verbal coercion and giving the woman a chance to flee if she has the ego strength to do so, while the rapist relies only on brute strength and fear and gives the woman no chance to get out of the situation. One forces a consent, the other forces the victim. In intent both are guilty of rape be-cause in both cases the victim consents against her will.

Men who see nothing wrong with "forcing a yes out" demonstrate the same phallocentric behavior seen in party gang rape. The brothers whose conversations were produced here denied all responsibility for their actions. They blamed the woman for anything that happened be-cause it was she who gave consent by drinking the drinks that had been prepared for her or by giving in to repeated demands for sex. The re-sponsibility always belongs to the woman, never to the brothers. These men are passive players on a stage whose props they provide and ma-nipulate. Because they "get laid," it is women, not they, who are the se-ducers. They are passive viewers of pornography made for them, not active seekers of this fare. A man is never responsible for the desire that rises within him.

Such attitudes display an infantile, concrete perception of responsi-bility, because it always lays the blame outside of the self. These men are not reflective; they are primarily reactive—reactive to sexual desire that is aroused in discussions among themselves or by the pornographic movies they seek out. The sexual desire they talk about provides the means and the mechanism to bond among themselves. Women are ob-jects used to bring the brothers together as virile, heterosexual, loyal comrades. The sexual identities they define for themselves are narrowly conceived: the possibilities for being male are few. The brothers can be "virile" (i.e., heterosexual) males; "nerdy" type guys who are "narrow minded" and who do not "allow any sexual needs to invade someone else's rights"; or "faggots." Faced with the consequences of the few choices available, it is no wonder that many young men—insecure and uncertain about their sexual identities and in need of social acceptance from other males—end up harassing women.

A joking kind of sadism characterizes much of the discussion reported in this chapter. Brothers relate to one another affectionately through insults and humorous assaults on each other's sense of pride, integrity, masculinity, and general sense of self-worth. This abusive undertone makes chances for meaningful communication with women slim indeed. As one of the male interviewers, also a fraternity brother, concluded:

> The belief that a "no means a yes" is not necessarily just a notion of convenience to allow us to push for gratification. It is part of the general cycle of abuse and ignoring the needs of others by which we learn to pursue all of our social and sexual goals with other people.

The end result of this cycle of abuse, he felt, is alienation:

> Alienation not only from the women in the pornographic films we see, the women we invite to our parties, not only from the XYZ victim, but also from our mothers and our future wives and daughters, who may in fact be better able to produce a lasting, satisfying, and constructive sense of masculine pride and achievement.

The sexual discourse reported in this chapter constructs as it defines sexual expression for these young men. Although an individual's sexuality is based on polymorphous physical excitations, sexual expression is channeled by discourse and practice in interaction with others. Sexual expression is also intimately connected with an individual's development of engendered subjectivity, that is, taking up a position as a male or female subject in a particular discourse or particular practices. "Working a yes out" is an example of a phallocentric discourse and ideology that positions men as subjects and women as objects in an ideology that defines seduction in terms of behavior bordering on date rape. The idea that a *no* never means no encourages men to feel that they can push as far as they like in sexual encounters. Men see nothing wrong with using alcohol and drugs to "break down resistance." Men see nothing wrong with "pulling train," in which activity they watch each other perform sexual acts and then brag about "getting laid." The ideology inscribed in such beliefs legitimates male dominance by assuming that male social and sexual dominance is not only natural but necessary for masculinity.

Six

The Initiation Ritual

A Model for Life

It is likely that very few young men would elect to take part in a "train" if they felt and thought like autonomous individuals. It is from the group, not as separate individuals, that most brothers find reassurance in a college environment that they frequently perceive as hostile to their needs. Bound emotionally to one another in the group, they consider group values and traditions to be significant guides for behavior. These values and traditions are inculcated during the pledging period and in the initiation rituals. In these rituals, pledges endure verbal and physical abuse as a condition for membership. The abusive behavior strips the pledge of his individual identity so that he is ready to accept a group-defined identity.

The victimization of pledges is part of a process designed to bring about a transformation of consciousness so that group identity and attitudes becomes personalized. The process includes a symbolic sacrifice of the self (or some part of the self) to a superior body that represents the communal identity of the house. The sacrifice acts to seal a covenant between the individual pledge and the fraternal organization. Reinforced by a vow of secrecy, the covenant promises masculinity and superior power. By yielding himself to the group in this way, the pledge gains a new self, complete with a set of goals, values, concerns, visions, and ready-made discourses that are designed to help him negotiate the academic, social, and sexual contexts of undergraduate life from a position of power and status. In other words, he becomes a subject in a fraternally defined discourse.

Long before college, many young boys experience "breaking-in" as a condition for membership in an all-male group. Sean, who describes his fraternity initiation ritual in this chapter, experienced the "breaking-in" process in almost every activity that he can remember—in school, sports, and Boy Scouts. All the secret male clubs Sean joined prior to college worked in more or less the same way: the males who were insiders would make the outsider feel like a loser until he was admitted into the group. Once in, the new member would join with the group to find someone else and make him feel like a loser. By the time Sean got to college, the pattern of being hazed and hazing others was not only familiar to him; it seemed absolutely natural. Since nobody ever fitted in perfectly right away, Sean said,

> a few pieces usually had to get knocked off to make the fit right. Part of it is getting the new guy to see things our way, to have a shared viewpoint and some basic things that we all agree on. Real individuality, and the arguments that go with it, never looked as attractive as the shared, seemingly revolutionary creed that we could all champion as a group, supporting each other as we inflicted our rowdy common self on the world and its stuffy sensibilities.

Sean's fraternity initiation ritual at college also knocked a few pieces off in order to mold him to the group image. Indeed, according to Sean's description of this ritual, he was provided with a ready-made self, one he easily adopted as a means of coping with his experience of anxiety and fear in the college environment. The experiences he endured provide powerful evidence for the suggestion that personhood, in this case defined in terms of *the brotherhood*, is socially constructed.

SEAN'S STORY

Sean joined a fraternity during the second semester of his freshman year. He joined to alleviate the anxiety he felt in the college environment. Coupled with general anxiety about his ability to achieve social and academic success in the new environment was his rebellious attitude toward all authority figures. Joining a fraternity provided a ready solution to both problems. The fraternity provided him with a predetermined role.

Probably because of his experiences with hazing as a boy, when Sean entered college, fraternities seemed like the natural way to deal with anxiety. For Sean and his buddies, most of whom arrived at school bewildered, out of touch with their feelings, and carrying patterns of unresolved emotional problems with their parents and females, the role of "rowdy, inconsiderate and misogynist frat brother" seemed compelling and meaningful. Like Richard Ford, who wrote in *Esquire* (June 1986) about his experience as a brother, Sean thinks of himself as "a go-along guy, who wanted friends. A guy with feelings he couldn't understand." For Sean and boys like him, "conformity was a godsend."

Sean did not place much value on his own individuality. He was not assertive, nor did he shape situations or relationships. By his own account, he was "the kind of boy who was willing to mold and deform myself to fit into something that was already out there." He was uncertain about his own worth and his emotional strength. He was looking for situations where he could "just sort of fit in without making too much fuss, without having people look at [him] too hard."

> The fraternity seemed to offer just that. They were easygoing guys. They joked around a lot, but they were always open and friendly, and it seemed that I was accepted without question from the very start. A ready-made group of guys who were actively trying to get me to join! It made me very happy to play hard-to-get for a change.

Sean recognized that fraternity life also offered a "new family" to compensate for the loss he felt at leaving his own family. Although it is a "transitional family," he knew that it would always provide him with a haven in which he could cope with anxiety and work out his sense of adolescent rebellion.

> When I left home I was both glad and scared to be independent of my parents. I felt sick and tired of their control over and constant involvement in my life, but I had never known any other way. Although I was noisily proclaiming and celebrating my new life as a free agent, I needed a family substitute, a tight social situation where I could count on emotional support. The fraternity provided me that support. Since I wasn't very aware of my emotional needs, I didn't go on a conscious search for a healthy support group. Instead, I thought I just needed a "cool place to hang out" and a regular group of friends. Since I and my friends were dealing with heavy sexual and academic tensions at the same time, it seemed natural to find a noisy group of guys where we could laugh and forget about all these complications of life. In the fraternity, we could deal with many of these problems, or at least escape from them: we could laugh off the expectations we felt from our par-

ents and from society in general to be responsible, mature people. Together, we could deal with sexual and social frustration. When we were together, we could laugh at all the things that made us feel alone and powerless. As a group we could deal aggressively with the issues, and sometimes the people, that made us feel insecure inside. Of course, the way we dealt with our insecurities was not exactly calculated to make anyone else feel better. Thus, while we felt like we were just having some laughs, we were thumbing our noses at (or giving the finger to) social responsibility and parental values. Thinking back now, I realize that our responses to anxiety about the blacks around here were too racist and our responses to sexual frustration and lack of friendship with campus women were too sexist. At the time, we felt like we were just responding to a new environment that seem hostile and humorless.

Most young men are not able to articulate their reasons for joining a fraternity with the same degree of insight. Another, less reflective brother, explained his motivation for joining a fraternity in terms of the "mystical tendency" for men to form bonds with other men. This young man was attracted by the "feeling of love" he had for the brothers and by the "love" they displayed for one another. In a less idealistic, more pragmatic vein, he also pointed out that a strong incentive was the desire to be one of the select few whose residence in a fraternity placed him at the hub of social life. He relished the sensational central location of the house he chose to join. The house was located in the middle of campus on Fraternity Row, and the prospect of living and dining at this house with the future brothers of his pledge class was a major incentive for joining that house.

Clearly the sense of self-esteem that comes from being one of the chosen few is an important incentive for joining a fraternity. In psychological terms the "mystic tendency" can be understood as the exhilaration of moving from adolescent dependency to the first stage of male dominance and control. The attraction of fraternal bonding is that it confers a status identity on adolescent males who cannot stand on their own. The depth of the emotional bond men feel for their fraternity is explained by the degree to which this bond helps to compensate feelings of inferiority and powerlessness in a society that privileges male bonding. Fraternity brothers do not become friends or teammates or colleagues; they become *brothers*. As Sean explains,

Brother is not an empty term. In my house, brothers travel thousands of miles every year to get together and to help initiate the new members, and commitments to the brotherhood clearly rank in their lives with family and professional commitments.

Brotherhood helped to reassure Sean about his sexual prowess, a continual source of personal worry and sense of inferiority. Sexual joking among the brothers relieved his anxiety and gave him a sense of mastery. Sexual joking, he explains, made the brothers feel good together.

Any sexual experience was shared with the group. A brother would jokingly thank the rest of us for "helping" him to get laid, either by recruiting a woman for him or by putting on a good party. His success was our success and we would joke about sharing the conquest directly. "Well, now that you've loosened her up for the rest of us . . . ," and we'd all laugh. The humorous references to group sex were always well received. Since some of us were marching band members, the favorite road-trip song, "Gang Bang," was heard regularly. We also liked to share ridiculously exaggerated sexual boasting, such as our mythical "Sixteen Kilometer Flesh-Weapon," and double-entendre plays on sexual performance. Example: "How was the exam this morning? *Much too long!* Yeah, that's what *she* said!" Even when this got embarrassingly out of hand (such as when we sent party invitations to alumni, promising to supply imported women "with big breasts and small brains"), it was always fun to laugh over this stuff together. By including me in this perpetual, hysterical banter and sharing laughter with me, they showed their affection for me. I felt happy, confident, and loved. This really helped my feelings of loneliness and my fear of being sexually unappealing. We managed to give ourselves a satisfying substitute for sexual relations. We acted out all of the sexual tensions between us as brothers on a verbal level. *Women, women* everywhere, feminists, homosexuality, etc., all provided the material for the jokes.

After a few months of interacting with the brothers of his fraternity house, Sean found that it became difficult to have a good time with other friends, especially with women, because the special secret under-

standing was missing and he did not feel comfortable conducting a relationship on any other basis than the one he became accustomed to in
the house. By choosing to interact mainly with his brothers, Sean realized that he gave up the possibility of gaining adult autonomy and developing his unique individuality. Instead, he was increasingly molded
to the frat-house personality type. Although he chose the fraternity as a
stand-in family, in fact the frat-house culture taught him to reject the
tenderness and compassion he had learned at home.

SEAN'S INITIATION

Sean's description of his initiation reveals the cycle of praise, condem-
nation, sacrifice, and agreement that stripped his individuality and
made him into a brother. This cycle is not unlike that described by anthropologists for male initiation rites elsewhere. Generally speaking,
these rites separate boys from psychological and social bonding to their
mothers and forge new bonds centered around men. This process is accomplished by a symbolic death of the old and rebirth of the new. Because the separation, death, and rebirth must be psychologically meaningful as well as socially marked, the rites include techniques for alter-
ing consciousness.

According to anthropologists, within ritual "what we find is primarily manipulation of consciousness, of, by, and for actors, through
symbolic objects, constructions and arrangements." These objects and
arrangements embody cultural meaning "conveyed to actors over the
course of their participation, and realized by actors as they achieve appropriate structures of consciousness." The intent of ritual is "to affect
psychological states" so that there is a "restructuring of meaning." Psychological states are affected by "a variety of well-established dissociation-inducing mechanisms—music, dance, rhythmic chant, verbal repetition, incense, and the like" (Ortner 1978, 5).

Sean's initiation can be analyzed on several levels, following the anthropological approach to ritual. First, we can discuss the symbolic objects, constructions, and arrangements deployed to fuse Sean's identity
with the group-mind of the house. Second, there are the "dissociation-
inducing mechanisms" employed to affect and control his state of mind
so that he experiences a genuine alteration of consciousness. Finally,

there is the question of *what the ritual says*—the sexual meanings it both illuminates and transmits—that might help the reader to understand better the cycle of sexual abuse of women that is the subject of this book.

THE RITUAL PROCESS

The ritual reported below is based on tapes made of several rituals and Sean's memory of his own initiation. A similar ritual takes place at all chapters and has been conducted in more or less the fashion reported for over one hundred years. Thus, what is presented below should not be taken as an idiosyncratic set of events but as part of a more or less standardized ritual passed down from one generation of brothers to the next. The ritual took place on a large, urban campus.

Sean's initiation proceeds from a ritual death along with the usual contract vowing secrecy to a ritual rebirth. During pledging Sean learned the songs and history of the house, but at the time none of this held any particular emotional meaning for him. The emotional engagement came during the initiation ritual, when he was taught the secrets of the fraternity in a ritualized atmosphere full of mystery and verbal abuse designed to induce disorientation and trauma.

The first evening of the initiation he was blindfolded, spun around, and lifted up. He was shown a tombstone in a darkened room, lit by candlelight. On the tombstone were the dates of the fraternity's founding and the name of the founder. He was forced to read these inscriptions repeatedly in a loud voice. The room was filled with figures shrouded in white robes and hoods. He felt disoriented but very excited. He craved an explanation of the bizarre ritual and decided to go through with the initiation because he wanted to share the mystery with the brothers.

> I didn't want to be left on the wrong side of the blindfold. I wanted to be on the other side, with them, sharing the silliness and the mystery as an insider. If it was all a joke, then I wanted to be in on it. If it was serious, then I wanted to be in on that, too.

The following week he was ordered to appear at the back door of the house at night. He was taken blindfolded down a cold, damp passageway and into a warm space filled with incense. He was pressed to his knees and when his blindfold was removed he was kneeling in front of the president and the secretary, who sat at a table. On the table lay an iron dagger with a contract. The president pointed to the contract with the dagger. By signing the contract, Sean swore never to reveal any of the fraternity's secrets. Sean's reaction to these events exhibits the success of the dissociation-inducing mechanisms.

> I was excited by the mysterious tone of the ritual, and the incense and the solemn silences and costumes. This ritual, like the first, made me want to join by making me feel like an outsider. The silences and the blindfold and the obligations all made me feel different from the brothers. They had no blindfolds, they weren't on their knees, and they weren't being given the silent treatment. It was very clear that there was a big difference between a brother and a pledge, and to be a pledge was to be weak and dependent and submissive and ignorant. By contrast, the brothers shared strength and power and knowledge, and I wanted to be one of them.

After these preliminary events, Sean concluded that he had been given a taste of the "bizarre, dark side of the brotherhood," and he understood that these events were supposed to affect him emotionally. He also knew that if the initiation was to be successful in its emotional impact, "these themes would have to be developed and explained and celebrated."

The next event occurred soon after, when he was taken on a long drive and was guided, blindfolded, to a small hut in the woods. He felt excited because he thought "a walk in the woods was a great thing to include in an initiation." The inside of the hut was lighted by candlelight and the brothers were again dressed in white sheets and hoods. In the hut he was again sworn to secrecy and was instructed in the meaning of the symbols on the society's emblem. Later, back at the house, he listened to a speech from an alumnus.

> He spoke about the opportunity initiation provided for personal growth, and said that the process would demand a lot from us, and that we had better be serious about joining. His deep, powerful voice boomed and echoed around the small hot room. I felt overwhelmed and helpless and thoroughly intimidated. The blindfold disoriented and confused me. The room seemed to sway under my chair, and I was

fighting to sit up straight. I blurted out a response to one of his questions, but I felt so lost and confused that I made no sense at all. The voice gravely warned me, "You'd better be careful about speaking with nothing to say, or you'll surely hang yourself that way in the morning." I really felt stupid after that. I had made a fool of myself, and these important men knew it. They were going to be watching me to see if I really was that stupid. Maybe I am!

Throughout the initiation Sean was alternately humiliated and praised, supported and abandoned, until he felt like a "thoroughly confused and very insecure little person." The goal, he was told, was to reduce him and all of the pledges "to a whimpering, blindfolded form whose every feeling was completely under the control of the brothers." He felt miserable whenever it looked as if he would not get enough votes to be accepted, because he believed that his admittance depended on his behavior during the initiation ritual. During a period of intense questioning of the pledges by the brothers in which Sean felt progressively broken down and stripped of self-esteem, he desperately offered himself to the society. He said to the brothers:

> There is nothing that I own, nothing material that I can give that the society could not find somewhere else, that they can't find in other people, that they can't buy a dog for, or a cat, and have them as a member of the society. There's nothing I can give. The most important and the most valuable thing I can offer is *myself*, and that's what I've offered to you! That's why I'm saying, Here! I'm willing to make the dedication, the devotion, and make that step and come and give myself to the society. That's the most valuable thing that I have to offer!

Thus, Sean's self-esteem, and his sense of self, came to depend on being admitted to the fraternity. The initiation process made him feel that on his own he was worthless and that his success was dependent on the brothers. He sought to restore his identity by embracing the very group that had taken it away. In this way his identity was "fused bit by bit with the common identity of the fraternity." This sense of being fused with the common identity of the group was aided by the ruse of making him think that he owed his admission not to his own efforts but to his big brother's efforts on his behalf. Sean was accused of breaking the secrecy vows, and it was his big brother who saved him:

I had demonstrated the secret handshake to an alumnus who wasn't wearing his key at the time. When this fact was discovered, suddenly everyone was enraged with me. All was lost! My big brother was shouting at the alumni to reconsider, saying that I had been tricked, but it was no use. I had sealed my own fate with one foolish move. In desperation, my big brother tore off his key and put it in my hand, saying, "Here! This is yours now! And don't let anyone take it from you!" He dashed out of the room and everyone was quiet. "Do you know how serious this is?" someone asked. "He has given up his place in the society for you." That really devastated me. Now my big brother had sacrificed himself for me. Once again my good fortune had come from the fraternity, just when I had ruined everything. The message was hammered home. On my own I was a weak, ineffectual person in a hostile, capricious environment, but with the fraternity, I was *great*.

Just when he believed that all was lost because he had violated the oath of secrecy, Sean learned that he had been admitted to the fraternity and that he had been a member throughout the event. His blindfold was removed and he found his big brother standing beside him and he saw all of the other pledges with their big brothers. Everyone was shouting and laughing and slapping backs. Sean's big brother hugged him, saying, "It was all bullshit!! The whole thing was total bullshit!!"

In a long speech, the secretary then explained to the pledges what had happened. In this speech the secretary described the fraternity worldview and how the pledges are remade in the image of this worldview.

The shackles of sense have been burst once again, and, like the great sun rising majestically from a certain coffin, our proud tradition has renewed itself tonight, and all in this room are awed and privileged to bear witness thereof. I salute you, our newly found, for indeed you have all proven yourselves today. You have proven yourselves by your intelligence, you have proven yourselves by your prudence, and, occasionally, you have proven yourselves by your complete lack of intelligence and prudence. Paradoxical as it may seem, one's own faults are an integral part of the initiation, for they are as much a part of one as are the determination and commitment that helped you endure a full day of insanity. [Laughter] And now, having honored us by showing us something of your inner selves, you are welcome with true love

and affection into the starry band, the court of our beloved Queen.
[Cheering, applause] And, what you began last night, in the darkness
and confusion of the nocturnal world, alone and cold you wandered
in your quest for the golden key. . . . You were in such inner turmoil last
night that you hardly slept at all!

As you gamely tried to make order out of chaos during the day, you
were introduced to rites and rituals seen by only a chosen few. . . . In
particular, a secret handshake was taught you, and it shall be the measure of your identity for the remainder of your days. Back in your room,
however, rewards were not so easy. You were berated and praised and
a pattern emerged. You found yourself at the height of ecstasy one moment, and in the valley of despair the next, in ever-widening oscilla-
tions. For one day, your mind was miraculously transformed into a yo-
yo!

Thus, the vacillation between ecstasy and despair that Sean experienced was deliberately manipulated by the brothers through positive and negative reinforcement. This form of manipulation is
known as the "swing" and is meant to instill the kinds of oscillating
psychological states believed to reflect reality as the pledges will
come to experience it as adults. The secretary explains to the pledges
that their

> mood shifts were no accident of fate. They were controlled from sec-
> ond to second with the minutest accuracy. This is at the heart of initia-
> tion. When the thumb is oriented up, your every word is as manna
> from heaven, a pearl of wisdom that blesses you, its maker. But when
> the thumb is pointed down, toward Hades, your every utterance is
> flatulence!

The pledges are meant to feel the "thrill of victory and the agony of de-
feat." The initiation process is designed so that they beat their heads
"against a brick wall" as the brothers stand and watch "fascinated."
Having endured this ordeal, when the day is over, "without apparent
cause," they find themselves "admitted into the society." The whole
procedure is arbitrary; its stress is on finding a group-defined "right answer" that admits the pledges into the brotherhood. As the secretary explains, the whole thing is a "paradigm of life."

Just as in life, the easy answer is not necessarily the correct one. The wrong answer means that you fall from the grace of [name of mythical Queen, symbol of the fraternity identity] into the misery, loneliness, wretchedness, despair, and acute malaise of [the uninitiated].

The secretary calls initiation the "swing." He explains to the pledges that some see the swing as

a paradigm of life, preparing one for the trials and tribulations of the real world. Others see the swing as merely a unique and beloved initiatory experience. All are in agreement, however, that the swing is a deeply personal, enriching experience for all who go through it. That, at the very least, is what you will take with you as you leave here today. Look around you, newly found. Everyone you see here has been in the hot seat before, and this evening, we are inducting you into our society, because you have earned our respect, and because we are ecstatic to be able to call you by that name that signifies the eternal bond of [name of fraternity].

After the secretary's speech the initiates are taught the meaning of the symbols engraved on the house key and in the constitution. When it was all over, Sean felt tremendous relief.

We all laughed and screamed and shook hands, hugging one another hysterically. Suddenly the whole day of abuse had turned into a shared joke, something that we had experienced together and could laugh about together. It was all incredibly funny, because now it wasn't just a matter of having been hurt by criticism, and having to deal with my hurt pride by myself. Now it was a group experience, and it turned into another way for us to get close to each other. The central fact that was repeated over and over by the other brothers was that: *it was the same for us.* We all acted the same way. We all fell for it. We all dissolved under the abuse. We all felt worthless, *but now we're all together and we feel good.* I felt exhilarated. I kept saying, "Oh, wow!" and hugging my big brother and shaking hands with everybody. I was incredibly happy. I was made to feel worthless by the fraternity as an individual, and now that it was all over, I was made to feel wonderful by the fraternity as a brother. My worth was celebrated by the same process that had previously denied it, because of the change that it had effected within me. I now saw myself as a *brother,* and what may feel terrible to an individual confronted by brothers feels tremendous to an individual who *is* a brother.

WHAT THE RITUAL SAYS AND MEANS

Sean's initiation ritual provides a training ground for fraternal social dominance. First and foremost, the ritual teaches young men how to control experience and manipulate consciousness. This is done through the mechanism of the swing. The brothers use the swing to dramatize the humiliation of life for the individual outside of the fraternity and as a means to forge the group self. This created self is protected by the goddess of friendship, who represents fraternal identity. Basking in the light of an astral female deity makes each brother feel good in a complete and perfect way that was never possible before he entered into the fraternity with its secret wisdom.

The swing punishes the brothers for their sensitivity and emotional accessibility. It kills the vulnerable in them and leaves them with an inverted view of what has actually happened to them. They are made to believe that it is in the outside world that they are punished for their sensitivity, not in the fraternity, and that only within the fraternity can true love and friendship flourish without fear of abuse. In reality, of course, it is the fraternity that abuses their sensitivity. Instead of protesting against the group's attempt to break down his self-esteem, Sean actually assisted in the process. This is an important point because it helps us to understand why fraternity brothers blame the victims of gang rape. Sean implies that because pledges willingly undergo victimization in initiation, in exchange for entrance into the fraternity, victims of gang rape may endure victimization in exchange for interaction with the brothers.

> We blame the victim because we fraternity brothers facilitate and ask for our own victimization. The initiation battered away at my weaknesses, and I acted as if a basic unworthiness I had been trying to conceal had at last been discovered. The fact that I was being set up to take a fall didn't really matter. Even though I was blindfolded in a smoky room with perhaps a dozen men at a time quizzing and ridiculing me,

the main point was that they were actually succeeding. If I had any real strength, they wouldn't be able to get to me. By asking me questions about myself and continually pulling apart my answers, it felt like they were peeling away my brave but ridiculous manlike facade to reveal the raw, weak, and agony-ridden little child that still lived inside. It didn't feel like I was just being hurt, which would have raised my anger. It felt like I was being discovered. They said, in friendly tones, that they just wanted to get to know me, and that they were assuming that I would turn out to be a fine person. Instead, they were finding hollowness and bullshit everywhere they probed, and there was nothing I could do or say to change their impression because it was all true. I couldn't stand up and get angry, because I had nothing to stand on. I had no basis for resentment, because I felt like there was no defense. They had uncovered me, and I had provided the tools and the information. The rest was just what would happen if anybody bothered to look closely enough. It felt terrible, but it seemed like it felt so bad only because such a group of intelligent men had never looked at me so closely before.

By manipulating the initiate's psychological states and bringing him through the ordeal, the brothers seize control of a power that parents or sexually and emotionally unresponsive girlfriends may once have had over them. The pledges conspire in this process because by exposing their vulnerability to the group they prepare the way for rebirth as powerful brothers. Power and dominance are both enacted and transmitted during the initiation process. Without the fraternity there is no power—there is certainly no power that accrues to the individual male. It is for this reason that brothers do not value individuality. The emotional manipulation of initiation tricks the pledges into exposing their weakness to one another—something many of them will never allow to happen again outside of the fraternal context. Weaknesses are sacrificed to the house in exchange for the power that comes from fraternal identity. As Sean puts it,

We felt that salvation is achieved through brotherhood, and nothing else (certainly not our individuality) mattered at all. When the initiation was over we all shared stories and jokes about how we had reacted and how we had fallen apart, how we had cried, and how foolishly we had acted. We were laughing together about our common weakness as individuals, because we were building bonds that were transforming us into something larger and, hopefully, stronger. We had to laugh about it, because we needed to talk about the pain, but we had to do it in a way that made it seem more distant from ourselves, because we were really talking about our "selves" in the past tense. We were collectively celebrating the death of our individuality.

The death of our individuality is seen in the initiation symbolism of the sun rising over a coffin, indicating the rebirth of our perfect spiritual selves after we have cast off our mortal existence by joining the society. The deeper meaning, which is never explicitly expressed, is that we have each participated in the punishment and execution of our fragile individuality in order to be reborn through the brotherhood in a collective birth as a new collective being. We were celebrating the fact that we had survived the painful process of killing off the sensitive, vulnerable, separate selves in order to give birth to the powerful, unified self of the brotherhood.

The celebration of their newfound, fraternally-identified social power is a ubiquitous part of fraternity life everywhere and takes many forms. As Richard Ford reports in *Esquire* (June 1986) about his fraternity,

> We called ourselves by animal names. . . . We put people's heads in toilets. We lighted our farts. We dropped our trousers in public. We drank and pissed on things. We danced. We shouted. We groped. We gave the finger. We got sick. We wore coats and ties. We were men and knew no bottom line.

Knowing no bottom line means having social power. Degrading initiation rituals celebrate the bottom line and announce to the world that the fraternity is irreverent towards society's bottom lines of decency, kindness, and fairness. The fraternity determines its own values; the brothers construct a social milieu in which they can be as unkind and as unfair as they wish.

Taking charge of values and exposing vulnerability has a sadistic side to it, a side that Sean recognizes:

> Everyone and everything was open to ridicule, all people and all standards became vulnerable, because we had powerfully felt our own

vulnerability. That was our deepest kept secret, the thing that really separated us from the world outside: we knew how insignificant people can feel when they are really up against the wall—how insignificant we felt during initiation. We had ventured into the dark, terrified heart of humanity: We finally understood that the real meaning of Conrad's *Heart of Darkness* lay in every man's soul. We had staggered through hell, and came out to look at the world with the jaded, contemptuous eyes of the combat veteran. Our initiation experiences and new knowledge constituted the deepest insight and a sacred revelation. It gave us a secret weapon and invisible armor. It made us special, and it united us against the world. Now we could be masters of life, because we knew its tiny, black, hollow core. Since we had learned the inner structure of life, we could toy with it and watch with amusement as everyone else staggered blindly through it, vainly trying to fight the cycles of pain and pleasure. We were *privileged* not only economically but in our souls as well. Whenever we chose we could bring yet another into the circle, mold and manipulate him as we retraced our steps and took him on the special journey to our bottom line.

There is a central paradox in this tale of boys transforming themselves into privileged men who know and control the innermost secrets of life. The heart of their identity is cast in the form of an astral goddess. The brothers maintain that the secrets of the brotherhood were first given them by a Greek goddess, and it is to the astral plane of this goddess that they claim they ascend in becoming a brother. Given the group's frequent debasement of women, it is curious that they turn to goddess imagery in their rites. The brothers kill one type of femininity—the type that makes them feel helpless—in order to rise to another, male-constructed and controlled form of the feminine.

In this death and resurrection lies one of the psychological secrets of fraternal bonding. A sense of powerlessness, loss, and fear of separation is instilled in the brothers so that they will welcome the brotherhood as a source of protection and power. Sean and his brothers fuse themselves to a symbolically constructed image of the all-powerful female and substitute brotherly love where familial attachments once existed. In their new family the brothers control their own emotions and those of the pledges by adopting the swing as a model for life. Unfortunately this newfound design for living can never compensate for the real problems they face and is thus fake. Because it is fake they must constantly reassure one another that it is real. Sean finally came to understand this. After leaving college and reflecting back on his fraternity life, he realized that its sexism and racism were ways the brothers hid from themselves the knowledge of their powerlessness.

> When women and minorities see us abusing our privileged position as traditionally powerful white males, they don't understand that we are more concerned with our own very real feelings of powerlessness and disappointment, and our desire is to have a good time in spite of the hostile environment we perceive ourselves to be in. So, in our new home away from home, we create a daily environment that addresses our feeling of powerlessness and our anxieties. The result, in the eyes of others, is a pattern of serious irresponsibility, sexism, racism, and homophobia, all of which may seem to serve our immediate emotional needs as brothers, but which also tends to decrease the possibility of meaningful interaction with nonbrothers and promotes the mutual mistrust and frequent incidents of sexual and racial violence that occur at this university.

CONCLUSION

By joining a fraternity, Sean, a privileged young man who felt powerless, acquired an all-powerful, male-defined self. The ritual acts he endured helped him find strength where he felt vulnerable. He learned how to grapple with a part of himself he would thereafter deny—that tiny, infant self who cries out for physical love and attention, the self that "wants it." Sean's experience and his honesty provide powerful evidence for the argument that masculine identity is socially negotiated outside the family. Fraternity initiation rituals provide a forum for adolescent males to solidify an identity. The fact that this identity intertwines brotherhood, misogyny, and phallocentrism is disquieting because of the realization that initiates acquire these characteristics not as a subtle part of early family socialization but as an important part of their education at college.

Seven

The Law of the Brothers

In this chapter two initiation rituals are described that took place in separate fraternities during the mid-1980s on two large, urban eastern campuses. The fraternities are well-known and exist nationwide. Sexual abuse and gang rape have occurred in both fraternities. This is not surprising in view of the fact that admission to these fraternities makes abuse, sexism, and homophobia part of masculinity and brotherhood.

All the steps seen in Sean's initiation ritual are repeated in the rituals described below: death of the old self, exposing and stripping the initiate's vulnerabilities, a covenant of power, and creation of a new self. One difference in these rituals, not seen in Sean's initiation, is their portrayal of the old self as being fragmented and of shifting sexual identity. The pledges are treated as polluted and despised women and as "pansies." Becoming a brother is synonymous with becoming a man. To this end the rituals "cleanse" the "pussy," "nerd sin," and "faggot" from the bodies and minds of the pledges. The rituals also force the pledges to declare their loyalty to the fraternity in "trust tests." In one case the test requires a symbolic sacrifice of the left testicle to a superior power representing the communal identity of the house. This sacrifice seals the covenant between the individual pledge and the fraternal organization. Like the covenant struck by Abraham with Yaweh, the sacrifice confers power.

These rituals stamp the pledge with two collective images: one image is of the cleansed and purified "manly" self bonded to the brotherhood; the second image is of the despised and dirty feminine, "nerdy," and "faggot" self bonded to the mother. Thus the process of becoming a man and a brother relies on negation and humiliation as a ritual device in order to break social and psychological bonds to the family in establishing new bonds to the brotherhood. The traumatic means employed to achieve these goals induces a state of consciousness that makes the abuse of women a repetition of cleansing the self of the inner, despised female as brothers renew their fraternal bonds. The overwhelming conclusion must be that these rituals re-produce an abusive social order and construct a misogynist subjectivity. As with Sean's initiation ritual, these rituals provide a model for life and have been followed by generations of brothers in chapters all over the country.

ATTRACTION OF BROTHERHOOD: BREAKING AWAY FROM MOM

The rituals are described by two male students who participated in them, one as a brother and the other as a close friend of the brothers. One of these young men believes that joining a fraternity is a way of escaping the influence of the mother. Bob believes that life for most boys is uncomplicated until they graduate from high school. Boys are used to living at home, and the majority of their parental contact has probably been with their mothers. According to Bob, mothers are still the homemakers and fathers the breadwinners.

> Although recently there has been a trend for women to occupy more and more of the outer, or working world, a "popular conception" of a mother is still of one who stays home and raises her children. Even in families with mothers who do work, mothers are usually more involved in family life and the raising of children, as society generally regards this to be the role of the mother rather than the role of the father. From birth, then, until the beginning of college, the young male is most closely bonded to and identified with his mother.

Like Sean, Bob stresses the degree of confusion boys feel upon reaching college.

> At first the world appears to be turned upside down. High school friends are away at different colleges, and the young male feels alone and secluded. No one is looked down upon more than a male freshman. The male upperclassmen generally choose not to associate themselves with these freshmen, and the female freshmen often have their eyes set on the older males. The male then perceives himself lost in a sea of confusion—alone, helpless, and sometimes worthless.

His first longings are to be back home with his family, and he realizes how stable and comfortable life was in the past, but that is an im-
possibility, as he is now a college student. He longs to be with his old
friends, yet they are away at other schools and are of no help to him.
He then tries to find ways to fit in with college life and to find a sense
of self worth. Various school clubs and organizations are possibilities,
as are college athletic teams. Joining a fraternity is another possibility.

For those who choose the path of brotherhood, fraternities stand for
a number of things—a place of belonging, friendship, support, and,
last but not least, the fraternity is associated with good times, coed
parties, and access to women. It may be difficult to tell how brothers
will act in a one-on-one setting with a date. At a fraternity party, however, there is a strong tendency for brothers to denigrate, demean, and
dehumanize women. In the minds of the brothers, women are reduced
to pieces of meat whose sole function is to be exploited.

Bob observed the following ritual many times as a member of the
fraternity. He agreed to described the ritual because of his belief that the
ritual acts were harmful to the pledges and created a rape-prone atmosphere in the house. The ritual process he describes presents a classic, textbook case of what Karen Horney (1967) calls "dread of women."
During the ritual the pledge is forced into the mold of the infant male
child as conceived by this group of brothers—girlish, filthy, and sexually inadequate.

Upon arriving at the frat house for their final initiation ceremony,
the pledges are hosed down with buckets of red, sticky liquid. Their status as infants is signified by the fact that they are made to wear diapers.
They are then physically and verbally abused and are reduced to the
status of females. While the pledges are clothed in diapers, one of the
brothers says to them,

> Look at you all, you're nothing but a bunch of girls . . . pussies! All
> your life you've been pampered. There's not a man among you. Since
> the first time we saw you you've made us sick. This is our house, not
> a place for a bunch of pansies. You don't belong here. If you girls
> want to stay, fine, but do something useful and clean up all this shit,
> the house is a mess! But do it quietly. We don't need to hear any
> bitching.

As the pledges cleaned the brothers made more and more mess for them to clean. This continued for several hours, and then they were forced to do push-ups until they could do no more. Next they were told to remove their diapers and expose their genitals. The brothers then ridiculed their genitals. Those who tried to cover themselves with their hands were made to do more push-ups. Their diapers were then re-placed, and makeup and perfume were applied to the pledges, result-ing in more laughter and embarrassment. One brother spoke:

> Now your insides match your outside. Look at these jokers, a bunch of baby girls, and they want to become [name of fraternity]? Well, I doubt it, not this bunch if I have any say! Here, why don't you have some milk and slop!

The pledges were given glasses of milk and jars of baby food to drink and eat. Those who refused the food were pelted with eggs, and finally everyone drank and ate the food. The brothers then began to shout loud and fast, "Shit, shit, shit. . . ." And then a brother spoke:

> Look at you all, you're all shit. As babies you were nurtured and pam-pered, given milk and diapers, and you became soiled inside and out. You're all mama's boys. Outside you look like a bunch of girls, and in-side you rot like dead fish. Now get back into the showers and wash off that makeup.

The pledges did so, and then buckets of feces mixed with water were thrown onto them. Some proceeded to vomit, while others just stood there horrified. Others vomited in response to seeing and smelling the vomit, but two pledges held back and didn't vomit. These pledges were given glasses of milk with hydrogen peroxide in them. They were forced to drink the mixture and quickly began to vomit. Three brothers then entered the shower room and threw the pledges to the ground, forcing them to lie in their own vomit. One brother then spoke:

> Look at you! Weak wretched creatures—Shitheads, all of you! Look at that mess you made. This house is sacred, now clean it up! [Name of fraternity] is no place for scum like you!

The pledges then cleaned up the vomit and feces. As they did so, they vomited more and more, but finally they got the showers cleaned. It was obvious that they were becoming enraged and fed up with the brothers. The brothers, however, all enjoyed the misery of the pledges. One brother spoke:

> We can't have you like this. You'll never become men, so you must die! You will die! It must be known who killed you, so we will leave our mark on your carcasses for everyone to see.

The pledges were gagged and their hands and feet were bound. Hot wax was dripped from a candle onto their backs. They were then carried to the basement (where they had never before been permitted to go). The brothers began to open multiple doors hidden within the floor, and caskets were raised to the floor level. Bound, gagged, and helpless, the pledges were forced into the caskets, and the lids were closed. The caskets were lowered, and the brothers then threw handfuls of sand over them. Screams and moans could be heard from within the caskets, as well as sounds of pounding as the pledges thrashed around inside. These noises were quickly drowned out by brothers loudly chanting, "Die pussies die, die pussies die" as they walked upstairs. They left the pledges buried for about thirty minutes.

Finally they were let out. All were covered with perspiration, and a few had urinated on themselves. They were all reprimanded for their fears and their mistrust of the brothers, and then the pledges were sent back to the showers and given time to clean themselves with soap and water. When they finished they were given black robes to wear and were escorted to a large room. They found themselves encircled by the brothers, who were all dressed in white robes, bearing lit torches in one hand and large swords in the other. One brother spoke:

> You have all died. Weakness and fear have been removed from your bodies and minds. What remains is strength. You are left with the ability to become men, but you are not yet complete. Now you see before you brothers as we really are. Look at us! Powerful, strong, and fearless. One group unified by the strength of brotherhood, loyalty to the fraternity, and trust in our fellow brothers. If you want, you may become one of us, one with us, and one with the fraternity. If not, you are free to go, but you may never return.

One pledge stood up and began to walk out of the circle. He was immediately thrown to the ground by a couple of the brothers. One placed his sword at the throat of the pledge, and the other placed his sword at the pledge's crotch. A third brother walked over to this pledge and said:

> Do you want to die? Trust is the word, pledge, trust. Do you trust me not to kill you? I'm going to drop this sword across your chest. Do you trust that I won't kill you?

The pledge nodded his head yes, and the sword came crashing down on his chest. As it did the pledges screamed and turned to look away. When the sword hit him, it broke into pieces, as it was made from wood. The brother continued to speak:

> You see! Trust kept you alive. The only people you have to trust is us. The fraternity will never fail you. It will always be here to protect you, to feed you, to house you, it will always welcome you. You may not be able to run to your parents or to your other friends, but you will never be turned away from this house. Remember that, always. It could save your life. You, in return, must show the fraternity that it can trust you, that you are loyal to it. You must be willing to die for it. By force we removed the woman in you. We killed it and buried it. Now you must be willing to kill the man in you to show your loyalty to [name of fraternity]. [Name of fraternity] must know that you will protect it and die for it. If you reveal the secrets of this house you will kill it, and then you will die as it does. Turn around, then, and prove yourselves.

As they turned around, they saw before them a noose for each pledge hanging from a pipe. Below it the brothers placed a platform. The pledges were helped onto the platform and examined the nooses. Their heads were then covered with pillow cases, and music began to blast from the house stereo. The pledges were unaware that the brothers had untied the knots of the nooses, and the brothers then placed the nooses around the heads of the pledges. The platform was tipped, and the pledges fell to the ground. The pillow cases were removed from their heads and the brothers all chanted the name of the fraternity.

The pledges were then reassembled, facing the brothers, who were still holding swords and torches. One brother spoke:

You have shown trust in the fraternity and trust in the brothers. We know we can trust you now. A bond has been formed between us. No one has experienced the hell you have except us and the brothers before us. Bonded by strength, loyalty, and trust, we are one. Cleansed of weakness and filth, we are men. As men we stand tall. As men we stand for the fraternity, and [name of fraternity] stands for us.

White robes were handed out to all of the pledges. They put them on, and they were given swords and torches of their own. One brother spoke: "Welcome, new life. Welcome, new men. Welcome new brothers, welcome." Then the name of the fraternity was chanted repeatedly, and the rest of the house joined in on the chant.

THE SECOND RITUAL: RICK'S STORY

The second initiation ritual, which took place at another university in another city, repeats in even more graphic detail many of the same ritual themes. The ritual is described by a young man who lived at home while attending college and spent much of his time at the fraternity house. He participated in the following ritual as would a full-fledged brother. The details he provides are based on memory. The speeches he cites may not be completely verbatim. Although there might be some minor errors in the chronological ordering of some minor events, he believes that the major events are in their correct sequence. To the best of his knowledge and memory, the following account is complete and accurate. Like Bob, Rick begins by describing the ritualized reduction of the pledges to the status of polluted women.

The pledges arrived at the house at nine in the evening. As they had been previously instructed to do, they arrived with firewood, bananas, maxipads, two rolls of tape, one basting brush, towels, and hand-crafted paddles that each pledge had made for a brother of the house. All of the pledges were wearing everyday attire, except for the fact that each was wearing a jock strap instead of underwear, and each wore an old sport jacket. When the pledges knocked on the back door of the house, they were startled by the cries, screams, and moans that came from within the house. Three brothers emerged on the roof bearing lit torches. Three more brothers appeared behind the pledges, bearing lit torches. All of the brothers looked as if they had been covered with blood, and their faces were painted so elaborately with various colors that it was almost impossible to identify any one brother. All of the brothers began screaming at the pledges simultaneously, and only a few words were clearly audible: "scum, wimps, fairies, shitheads, worthless, die."

The pledges were being verbally assaulted from every direction. Some panicked and tried to run away, but brothers emerged seemingly from out of nowhere and forced the pledges into a circle. At this point, one brother emerged from the house. He stood with the skull of some recently killed animal impaled upon a wooden staff. This he held up and thrust into the face of each pledge. As the animal head was still dripping with blood, pledges became spattered with the blood. While this was happening, some other brothers took the large crates containing the objects the pledges had brought inside the house. Then three brothers came outside. Two of them were holding the crafted paddles, and the third one spoke:

> You worthless pieces of shit! Do you call these paddles? Do we look like a bunch of pussies you can pan these paddles off on? Well, they suck! [Turning to the brothers behind him, he continued,] Somebody better get these women out of here before I puke or I'll have to kill them all. God damn pussies, all of them!

This brother then knocked the paddles out of his brothers' hands and kicked them towards the pledges. He then went inside. All of the brothers followed him inside. The pledges tried to enter the house, but they found the door locked. One brother came from the side of the house and spoke to the pledges:

> Well, looks like you pledges screwed up again. These guys are really pissed! What a weak effort! Look at those paddles, they really do suck, don't they? Right now we're not sure that you're ready to go through this, so we'll talk it over for a while.

He started walking toward the door. When he got there he turned around to look at the pledges. They all looked heartbroken and humiliated. Before he walked inside, he said,

By the way, while we're talking this over, you girls may as well do something constructive. You've got one minute to get to the phone on [names street]. Answer it by the third ring or initiation is canceled. Stop crying and move it!

This was the beginning of a long and exhausting phone run. Each time they answered the phone they were given a new location to run to. Their phone run took them all over the city, with countless stops along the way to answer the phones. Three carloads of brothers followed them on their run to make sure nobody slacked off, to make them do pushups and sit-ups, and to throw eggs at them while they ran. Two and a half hours later, when the pledges answered the phone on the fourth ring, the brother on the line spoke: "Fourth ring, losers! Initiation's just been canceled. See you around sometime."

The pledge hung up the phone and said, "It's over guys, we didn't make it." They all looked at each other, and then most fell to the ground, exhausted and broken. A couple of the pledges began to cry, some cursed, and some just lay on the ground trying to catch their breath. The phone rang again, and a pledge answered it. A brother spoke: "What are you girls waiting for, a formal invitation? Back to the house, and fast!"

They arrived back at the house sore, exhausted, and breathless, barely able to stand. The back door was open and the inside of the house was dark. As the first pledge entered the house he was instantly thrown to the floor. The brothers began to scream, "Crawl, crawl," and one brother alone screamed at them,

Nobody waltzes their way into this house. You want to be brothers? Then crawl, vermin, crawl! Slither on your stomachs! You're not men, you're rotten, dying flesh. Maggot meat! Crawl, maggots, crawl.

One by one the pledges entered the house and one by one they were thrown to the ground and forced to crawl through a gauntlet of brothers' legs. As they did, they were spit on, kicked, and stomped on. Once inside, they felt the intense heat of the house, as all of the thermostats had been turned up and all of the fireplaces had been roaring. Perspiration was dripping from both brothers and pledges.

The pledges were then taken to a large room in the house and were blindfolded with maxipads and tape, so that none could see. They remained blindfolded until the end of the initiation. They were told to strip and all of their clothes were fed into the fireplaces. They were told to drop their jock straps to the floor, and as they did they were all laughed at and humiliated. One brother said, "Look at the pin-dicks . . . pussies . . . fags. . . . Between all of them they don't even have one penis. . . . They're all a bunch of girls, it's amazing they don't have tits."

The brothers then all joined in on a chant, "Cleanse them, cleanse them . . . ," and one brother spoke to the pledges:

> Listen up, girls. We're going to cleanse you, and it's for your own good. We're going to cleanse you of your "nerd sin." All your life you've been a bunch of nerds. You always went home from school to your mom, and she cooked for you, did your wash, made your beds, and told you what to wear. All you've ever done is be dependent, parasitic leeches, but now it's time to grow up, and you'll do it real soon, and real fast. We're going to cleanse the weak, dependent, pussy out of you, and maybe then you won't look so wretched.

All of the pledges were told to drop their jock straps to their knees and were assembled in a line. One brother held a bowl of Ben-Gay in one hand and a basting brush in the other. One after another, he painted the scrotum of each pledge with the balm, and their jock straps were replaced. Thirty seconds later all of the pledges were writhing on the floor, holding their genitalia, screaming in pain as the balm burned into the sensitive skin. Meanwhile, all of the brothers were cheering, stomping, and screaming at the pledges in their agony. About ten minutes later they were forced to their feet and one brother spoke to them: "Sorry we had to do that, but we had to cleanse you of your 'nerd sin,' but now we'll do something for you that will make you forget about the pain."

They were then paddle-whipped on their rumps with the paddles they had made for the brothers. All of their hind ends were red, chafed, and sore, but the pain of the cleansing did not let up. The pledges were angry, burned, sore, exhausted, and numb at the same time, and all looked like they would pass out at any moment. They were then taken into a bathroom, where one by one they were thrown into a tub filled with water and ice cubes and submerged multiple times. The freezing water did not help the pain of the cleansing; rather, it enhanced it. They were then dried off, had new maxipads taped over their eyes, and listened while one brother spoke to them:

> Your outside has now been cleansed. You don't look like a bunch of
> wimps anymore. You sure as hell don't look like men, like us, but at
> least you don't look like a bunch of fags. But inside you're still just as
> filthy and disgusting as you ever were. Think about it. All your lives,
> depending on your parents, nursed through life by your mothers.
> You've become weak and spoiled. You're all spineless, and we can't accept you like this. It's not your fault but it has to be changed. You are
> going to drink the potion that will remove all filth in you, and you will
> become clean, and pure, like us.

They were given a concoction of sour milk, hot peppers, and rotten squid to drink. Each pledge was forced to drink a pint of this solution. Each sip brought with it gut-wrenching vomit, and each pledge finished his pint and vomited multiple times. They had now been cleansed inside and out by the potion and the Ben-Gay balm. They were then taken out to the back porch and hosed off, and then taken back inside to the showers and given soap, shampoo, and towels. They were given a short time to shower, and when they were finished they were given sweat pants and t-shirts to wear. Again they were blindfolded and taken to a room where they listened to a brother speak:

> Well, I'm sure that each and every one of you is pretty upset with us,
> but when you think back on it, you'll realize it all had to be done. Now,
> the worst is surely over. Of course, you don't believe me, since you've
> been given no reason to trust me. You have been lied to, deceived,
> tricked, humiliated, weakened, and injured. So, why should you trust
> me? Because I'm a brother, and brothers are the only people you can
> really trust. You must show us, as well as the house, that we can trust
> you. You must be loyal and selfless with regard to the brothers and the
> fraternity. Now is the time to show that trust.

They were taken through a series of trust tests, in which the pledges had to show the brothers that they trusted them to harm them no longer. They were first placed on top of a chair and made to listen to the rattling of broken glass in a box. They were told to jump down from the chair and that the glass would not cut their bare feet. Each jumped down and landed instead on a box of corn flakes.

Next they were walked up a flight of stairs and turned around at the top. They were told to let themselves fall face first down the stairs and that they would not be hurt. As each pledge fell, he was caught in the arms of brothers.

They were then taken to a room with a fireplace and told that one of their testicles must be burned off, as a sacrifice to the house. They were told to trust that the brothers would not hurt them as they burned the testicle. The brothers lifted a red-hot poker near their noses and burned some squid with it, and they told the pledges that they were smelling human flesh. Next they touched a cool stick to the crotch of the pledges, which startled them but left them unharmed.

After this they were taken into a bathroom and told to eat some feces out of a toilet and to trust that they would not become sick from it. As they reached in, they picked up some soft matter and ate it, realizing that it was actually a banana and that the toilet was lined with a plastic bag.

After passing these trust tests they were again assembled in the large room where they were cleansed with the balm. The room still smelled of menthol, and one brother spoke:

> So far, you have been cleansed of your filth, of your sins, of your evil. You have shown the house that you trust it, and us that you trust the brothers. We have seen that we can trust you, for you were willing to obey our commands that could have caused you more harm. We are now all bonded by purity, trust, and loyalty. You will soon be brothers. But we must be sure that you are men enough to join us. We are going to have a test of strength and endurance. You will choose one among you to compete against any one of us that you choose in a push-up competition. If you win, you will be brothers, but if we do then we'll know that you are still full of filth, sin, and weakness, and we'll be forced to recleanse you.

The pledges chose the strongest among them to compete against the weakest brother for the competition. Because the pledges were thoroughly weakened and exhausted through the process of initiation, they still lost. The brothers then all joined in another chant of "Cleanse them, cleanse them." Finally everyone became silent. One brother then began to whisper the name of the fraternity. More and more brothers joined in, and they all quickly raised this to a loud and quick chant. The brothers then removed the blindfolds from the pledges, and one brother spoke:

> You were not supposed to win the competition. Not only were you too tired, but older brothers have more power. Power that comes from being [a member of this fraternity], it accumulates over time. Soon, you will accumulate this power and strength as you live in the house, under its guidance and direction. Just remember, never reveal the secrets of pledging, initiation, or brotherhood. If you do, it will cost you your life. Welcome, brothers, welcome to [this fraternity] and congratulations. You are now a brother of [this fraternity] and you will always be a brother. [This fraternity] will be your guide, it will protect you, support you, and keep you from the filth of the world.

Everyone in the house then joined in chanting the name of the fraternity.

CONCLUSION

The initiation rituals described in this chapter are rife with sexual meanings. The acts, images, and discourse of the rituals not only provide templates for a masculine identity; they force this identity on the pledges through the use of mind-altering techniques. Power and manhood are conferred on the subject—the pledge—in exchange for lifelong loyalty to the brotherhood. The subject is first defined as powerless and as tied to his mother. Brotherhood and manhood are achieved simultaneously by first killing the inner woman and then the inner man. A masculine subjectivity is thus constructed by first stressing sexual differences and then representing these differences as hierarchical: part of the same psychic process, manhood and brotherhood are represented as infinitely superior to the despised and dirty feminine. The ritual inducts pledges into the brotherhood by first producing and then resolving anxiety about masculinity. The ritual produces anxiety by representing the feminine to the pledge as both dirty and as part of his subjectivity. The ritual then resolves the anxiety by cleansing the pledge of his supposed feminine identification and promising him a lifelong position in a purified male social order.

The brothers are not just concerned with establishing their social and sexual identity; they are also concerned with social power. It is a power that transcends not just their mothers but also their fathers, adults in general, and even themselves. In their group rituals they seek to re-produce the power of fraternity, a power that supports their purified male social order. The purification process requires them to abuse pledges in order to break bonds to one family and to break down gendered subjectivity that developed in this two-sexed family of father and mother. Having resorted to abuse as a means to establish their bond to the brotherhood, the newly confirmed brothers resort to abusing others—new generations of pledges and party women—to uphold the original contract and renew their sense of the autonomous power of the brotherhood.

Abusive initiation rituals that stamp insecure boys in the image of the heroic sadist can be compared with the social contract instituting a fraternal patriarchy described by Carole Pateman (1988, 113), in which men "share a common interest in upholding the original contract which legitimizes masculine right and allows them to gain material and psychological benefit from women's subjection." Affiliation with a fraternal patriarchy answers the need certain men have to assume social authority by breaking with the authority of the paternal generation and asserting their authority as a united male group. The bond these men forge by abusing others glosses over the competition and hostility that exists within the group. As Pateman points out, "If brothers do not share a common bond, they are often in competition or hostile to one another" (ibid., 114).

The bond males forge with one another in physically and psychologically abusive rituals can be compared with the bond they experience when they banter about "working a yes out" or watch pornography together. Susan Griffin (1981) argues that watching pornography together helps men silence vulnerability in themselves. The pornographic image represents men as being in charge of a female sexuality that knows no bottom line. In the pornographic scenario men represent women as responding to their every desire, their every demand. In this scenario men represent themselves as indisputable sexual masters.

The concern for social mastery displayed by vulnerable, anxious men is explained by some psychologists as a natural outgrowth of the boy child's early dependence on maternal physical and psychological nurturing. Such explanations of what is called "protest masculinity" usually lead to the conclusion that male social dominance is necessary for building a separated masculine identity. It is true that some form of dependence on maternal nurturing is part of the human condition. However, male dominance is not necessarily the logical consequence. There are many societies of the world in which the male role is not based on negating the feminine and mothering is not conceived as engulfing young boys. On college campuses there are many men who do not turn to fraternal social rituals in their search for manhood.

Parodies of the negative influence of the mother on masculine development are best seen as strategies that rationalize and give legitimacy to a male-dominated social order. By deploying such strategies fraternity brothers construct a bridge between a *hypothetical* psychic state and an *artificial* social order. Cleansing the feminine in the pledge neither alleviates anxiety nor produces a secure masculinity. Such acts are best interpreted as constructing or reinforcing the misogynist subjectivity necessary for the survival of the fraternal patriarchy.

Eight

Constructing a Sexist Subjectivity

The subject is . . . perpetually in the process of construction, thrown into crisis by alterations in language and in the social formation, capable of change. And in the fact that the subject is a *process* lies the possibility of transformation.

—Catherine Belsey

When young men arrive at college, many find joining a fraternity an attractive possibility. Some have been led to believe that membership in a socially prestigious fraternity is a good way to begin to build a network of connections that can be useful in their later careers. To others fraternities offer a reassuring base from which to explore the risky and uncertain business of proving to themselves their adequacy as heterosexual males now on the threshold of developing relations with young women that will lead to marriage. As Sean explained, the fraternity offers an easy solution to anxious young men in a society that expects successful individuals to display a unified, heterosexual self. The initiation ritual helps construct this new self by "killing off the sensitive, vulnerable, separate self in order to give birth to the powerful, *unified self* of brotherhood." As in other brainwashing experiences, the new self is constructed by holding up a mirror through which the pledge can see himself as a particular kind of subject, with particular thoughts, feelings, and desires. The pledges come to "recognize" themselves by the way in which the ritual addresses them as subjects and defines their status as brothers. By willingly adopting the subject-positions necessary to their participation in the fraternity, the pledges do not, in reality, achieve autonomy or wholeness. Rather, they become subjected beings who not only submit their autonomy to the authority of the fraternity but mold their identity to fit mythologies of masculinity.

One of the more obvious mythologies, associated with fraternity rituals such as described in the last chapter, is the mystique of the polluting woman and the demanding, engulfing mother. This myth is firmly entrenched in American popular thought, especially as it relates to popular views of masculine development. This myth motivates fraternity initiation rituals that stress the primordial tie between a boy and his mother and the importance of breaking this tie to achieve independence in a competitive society. Such rituals force impressionable young men to define themselves in terms of acts and images that are in opposition to traits associated with the female and the mother.

Regardless of his prior experience of a masculine identity, telling the pledge that he is psychically female is likely to produce anxiety about masculinity where it didn't exist before. For pledges who actually feel this anxiety, the ritual brings their experience into the realm of language and behavior. For these pledges and those more certain about their gender identity, the ritual promotes regressive psychological states compelling brothers to resolve anxiety in acts of male bonding. In sum, the ritual *produces* the very confusion it supposedly aims to resolve by *forcing* pledges to make the transition from a ritually *constructed* anxiety to a fraternally *defined* sense of self.

Related to the myth of the dominating mother is an analogous cultural myth that assumes the ubiquity of male adolescent rebellion against male authority figures. This myth is evident in the first ritual described in the last chapter. After the pledges were cleansed of their identification with their mothers, after weakness and fear had been removed from their bodies and minds, after they had been threatened with castration, they were told,

> You, in return, must show the fraternity that it can trust you, that you are loyal to it. You must be willing to die for it. By force we removed the woman in you. We killed it and buried it. Now you must be willing *to kill the man in you* to show your loyalty to [name of the fraternity] (emphasis mine).

The reference to "killing the man" suggests that all prior identifications with male figures must be expunged from the pledge's masculine subjectivity, including identification with the father.

The reference to killing the man along with the references to removing the woman is reminiscent of psychoanalytic discussions of the role of the Oedipus complex in masculine psychosexual development. In the terms of psychoanalytic theory, the resolution of the Oedipus complex occurs when the male child gives up his love for his mother and identifies with his father. Because the mother provides the infant with his or her first experience of satisfaction, the separation of the child from the mother means that other sources of satisfaction will be sought as substitutes. The infant child resolves the loss of satisfaction, that is, the loss of the mother, by using "his or her first words to establish, in fantasy, control over the loss of the object which gave satisfaction" (Henriques et al. 1984, 215). The fusion with the mother is broken by the father who instills castration anxiety, which prompts the boy to give up the mother and identify with the father. According to the oedipal model described by Lacan, the loss of the mother brings about an attempt to replace her, which Lacan says brings into being the dimension of desire.

Applying Lacan's discussion to the initiation rituals described in the previous chapter, one can note that whereas it is the father who is the main agent separating an infant from his mother, it is the brothers who play this role in the initiation ritual. Just as the father separates the infant from the mother by means of the threat of castration, so the brothers threaten the pledges with castration. The rituals deploy symbols and acts referring to castration: a sword crashes down on the crotch of the pledge who threatens to leave the ceremony; the blood-dripping head of a newly killed animal is brandished about by the brothers; pledges who cannot withstand the horrors of the trust tests are consigned forever to the status identity of "wimp," "fag," or "girl." It is only by accepting the "Law of the Brothers" that pledges can find admission to the masculine social order.

Lacan's model of the Oedipus complex (see Lemaire 1977, 84) includes two important stages that are also seen in the initiation ritual: the forbidden and the sacrifice. In Lacanian terms the forbidden refers to the prohibition of incest with the mother, and the sacrifice is realized through the symbolic castration. The child sacrifices his forbidden desire for his mother and enters into the social order, which Lacan calls the Law of the Father. In terms of the acts of the initiation ritual, the forbidden is evident in the expulsion of the pledge's supposed feminine identification. The forbidden is also evident in the exhortation against disclosing fraternity secrets. The sacrifice is evident in the symbolism of death of the old self and resurrection of the new, fraternally-defined self. Sacrifice is also implied when the brothers kill and drink the blood of an animal. The sacrifice of the left testicle, evident in one of the rituals, marks the maleness of the whole process. The sacrifice of the testicle—the container of life-producing sperm—also signifies a generative and sexual fusion of the self with the fraternal body. The boy will help the fraternal body to grow and reproduce by virtue of sacrifice and loyalty.

Having noted the similarity between the dynamic of the initiation ritual and the oedipal dynamic posited by psychoanalytic theory, one might well conclude that the brothers are operating as ritual psychoanalysts for the pledges—giving them the sense of masculinity they might otherwise acquire on the couch. However, initiation rituals such as described in the last chapter were probably conducted long before Freud or Lacan wrote about the Oedipus complex. Another conclusion might be that the similarity between these two initiation rituals and psychoanalytic theory is due to universal unconscious processes in male psychosexual development.

From an anthropological perspective I reach a different conclusion. I suggest that the social expression of the oedipal dynamic, such as seen in some fraternity initiation rituals, is nothing more than a social manifestation of the ideology necessary to legitimize male social dominance. Acts reminiscent of what Freud referred to as the oedipal drama provide a logical social mechanism for introducing males to a purified male social order within a system that extols masculine power. Freudian theory attributes universal psychological and social importance to the bond between mother and child. To grow up male one must break this bond. I don't dispute this fact. All men are born of women, but not all men, in a complex society such as ours, seek to dominate women by means of the power they derive by virtue of their membership in a privileged and purified male social order. Additionally, there is considerable variation cross-culturally in the extension of political power to male solidarity groups. In societies where such groups exist and membership in them confers political power and grants a competitive edge, it is logical that some men will treat early ties to the mother as inherently problematic. In such cases it is logical also that some adult males—members of the purified masculine group—will stand outside of the mother-child dyad as representatives of that group. Given this state of social affairs we can agree that the father (or the brotherhood in the case of the fraternal patriarchy) "stands in the position of the third term that *must* break the asocial dyadic unit of mother and child" (Mitchell 1982, 23).

In the case of the fraternity initiation rituals that have been described, it is not the father but the brothers, as a collective body, who stand in the position of the third term that breaks the tie of the mother and child. Thus, the fraternity provides an example of a social order that constructs the mother-child relationship as asocial and problematic as a ritual device for inserting the law of the brothers and displacing emotional ties from one family to another, the family of the brothers. However, by fusing the pledge to the fraternal body as a condition for manhood, the brotherhood does not so much make *men as mother brothers.*

Parallels with the psychoanalytic position are limited, however. While psychoanalytic theory and practice prescribe psychosexual *development,* fraternity initiation rituals encourage psychosexual *regression.* Lacan argues that once separated from the mother, infants will engage in behavior by which they seek to compensate for the original lost object, namely the mother. Once the separation takes place, the child "enters into a quest for objects which are further and further removed from the initial object of his desire" (Lemaire 1977, 87). According to Lacan the child "names his desire and renounces it" (ibid.). However, in the case of fraternities, although brothers may name their desire, as when they admit their ties to their families, they do not seek a substitute that transforms this desire; they simply deflect their desire onto each other or onto party women.

Like the child who uses his first words to establish, in fantasy, control over the loss of the object that gave him satisfaction (Henriques et al. 1984, 215), the brothers use their rituals, other brothers, and women to gain control over infantile desires. They do not sublimate or transform this desire; they indulge it in an institutional context that reproduces the desire as a condition for membership. In reality the supposed emotional identification with the mother is not transformed; it is simply displaced and split into its physical and sexual components. The physical bond is reserved for brothers, the sexual bond for "party girls." The sexual relationship with these girls is disparaged just as the tie with the mother was disparaged because it, too, cannot interfere with the bonding of brotherhood.

The displacement of maternal dependency onto brothers and party girls ensures that fraternal bonds resonate psychologically at the most infantile and primordial levels. This displacement is seen in the other regressive, infantile forms of fraternal bonding described in previous chapters. For example, there is the circle dance—described as unconscious of the individual—that physically fuses the brothers in one incoherent mass of brotherhood. In the gang rape of Laurel the same concern with bodily fusion is evident. Additionally, there are the remarks of a brother who spoke nostalgically about being naked in the shower with his buddies as a way of "breaking down barriers." Fusion is also evident in the experience of suffering abuse during initiation. As one brother said, abuse has "more to do with being friends with everybody and knowing everybody real well" (see chapter 5). One can also mention the importance brothers attach to alcohol and drunkenness.

As mentioned, I do not mean to underestimate the role of the mother in the development of masculine subjectivity. However, in constructing a masculine identity, neither in this society nor in others do all men enter a privileged male social order, negate the feminine, or seek to gain material or psychological advantage from women's subjugation. Although these social strategies have a long history in Western thought and society (see Sanday 1988; Lerner 1986), other social templates for masculinity exist, and not all men in Western society make use of sexist strategies. While some men derive power from their association with sexist viewpoints, other men consciously seek to avoid sexism in their own psychosexual development. An important issue for future research will be the situational and psychological determinants of male choice in these matters.

SOME SITUATIONAL DETERMINANTS OF SEXIST BEHAVIOR

In United States society there are people who manage cross-sex interaction easily, without undue emotional conflict or anxiety, and there are those who don't. What the factors are that contribute to this difference is a matter for future research. One hypothesis, yielded by a study of four kindergarten classes in the United States, concerns the degree to which there is continuity of cross-gender relations from early childhood into adulthood, especially among peer-group males and females, that allow for companionship, play, mutual dependency, and friendship. One of a series of classroom ethnographies in different societies, this study (published in Spindler and Spindler 1987, 409—-44) examined in depth the interaction among male and female kindergartners in four separate classes. One of the four groups showed extremely sexist behavior, one was mildly sexist, and the other two were not sexist at all. The sexist group was marked by exaggerated male bonding and dominance behaviors, rejection of dependency, devaluation of things female, and repression of female input. These features were largely absent in the non-sexist groups, which displayed egalitarian, nurturing interaction between males and females. The characteristic most sharply distinguishing the groups was the discontinuity of relationships between boys and girls between their preschool years and kindergarten in the most sexist group and the continuity of such relationships in the two nonsexist groups.

Throughout childhood, adolescence, and young adulthood, boys may turn to male bonding as a device to seek a position of advantage not only in relation to girls but also in relation to other boys against whom they compete. Young boys of kindergarten age are already facing problems associated with the shift away from identification with their mothers and toward conceptualization of themselves as males. At this time they may exhibit great interest in heroic exemplars of maleness such as are represented by space and war toys and by *Star Wars* and similar motion pictures or TV programs. In a society where cultural myths devalue and negate the feminine, this process of identity change may make boys conflicted about who and what they are, especially as they try to sort out how to relate to females as males rather than as fellow persons or as dependent sons.

In the kindergarten groups where there was continuity of relationships with girls, established prior to entering kindergarten, cross-sex interaction was egalitarian, being relatively unaffected by the problem of relating as males to strange girls. The sexist group, by contrast, was one in which such continuity had been broken. A few boys who knew one another were faced with establishing relationships with girls and other boys who were strangers. Trying to relate as males to females and feeling unsure of themselves, this small group bonded and excluded the girls as a way of managing their insecurity. Having established a position of power and social advantage, they dismissed protest by the girls on the grounds that what girls think and feel doesn't matter anyway. This strategy is much like that used by men in Highland New Guinea societies in relation to wives who come into their husbands' home community as outsiders and strangers (Poole 1981).

When they enter college, young males, with the heightened sexuality of their late teens, may also feel anxious about how to relate to their female peers and to other males in the new and unfamiliar setting. Fraternities provide institutionalized mechanisms for male bonding by which these males can gain a position of social advantage. The initiation ritual provides a ready-made self for confronting anxiety about successful performance in the new environment. Depending on the initiation rituals undergone and the house culture encountered, this new self may include sexist attitudes as a means for coping with feelings of powerlessness.

There are many young men who see the rowdy, misogynist behavior of fraternity brothers for what it is and rate the perpetrators as a bunch of jerks. A major question for future research is how to account for the adoption of sexist behaviors on the part of some boys and not others. The study of the four kindergarten classes suggests the role of continuity and discontinuity of cross-gender relations from early childhood into young adulthood as a factor in sorting out those who exhibit extreme sexist behavior from those who do not.

Another question to be considered concerns the degree to which male bonding exacerbates sexism and negative views of women. Can such bonding occur without sexism and under what conditions? Related to this is the question of whether sexism is likely to be absent in the absence of institutionalized male bonding. If there were no fraternities with their ritual apparatus of initiation, for example, would most young college men find nonsexist ways to manage the uncertainties of the college environment? Finally, we must also ask whether institutionalized male bonding is made more sexist than it might otherwise be by virtue of its being privileged by larger societal institutions such as universities.

THE SOCIAL DEPLOYMENT OF
SEXIST STRATEGIES CROSS-CULTURALLY

As already mentioned, a sexist mentality cannot be explained in terms of universal unconscious processes in men. In many societies, demeaning women and negating the feminine in boys are not evident in the larger social ideology, nor are they strategies for male bonding. For example, the most salient social bond for the matrifocal Minangkabau of West Sumatra (Indonesia) is the bond with the mother. The social ideology of the Minangkabau legitimizes the mother-child relationship and the bond between brothers and sisters. During early childhood, boy and girl infants are closely tied to their mothers. In the transition to masculinity, this bond is celebrated, not demeaned. It is celebrated in a fashion enabling a boy to break psychological dependence on his mother while upholding the social importance of the bond. Traditionally, young men were expected to leave their homes and villages in order to prove their worth and leave their sisters and mothers securely in charge of matrilineal property. This was done so as not to introduce any element of competition between boys and their mothers and sisters. Later, boys came back to the village to get married to a wife selected by their mothers and maternal uncles (Sanday 1986, 1990a).

Thus, as is the case in patri-centered societies, the maturation of Minangkabau males involves physical and emotional separation from the maternal; however, there are no rituals that either display male dominance of the maternal or demean the feminine in the man or, for that matter, the masculine in the woman. Silencing the feminine is not necessary for becoming a proud and independent male in Minangkabau society. Indeed, the main feature that defines adult male and female behavior is expressed in terms of "good deeds and kindheartedness." Thus, autonomy and independence from the mother do not have the same psychosocial relevance as found in American society. Minangkabau men are separated from the domain of the feminine as part of the masculinization process, but they do not kill vulnerability in themselves by flexing their muscles vis-à-vis women. There is no theory of the mother-child bond as being oppressive to masculine development. There is no symbol system by which males define their gender identity as the antithesis of the feminine. For the Minangkabau the dominant social image is not the exclusively male social group, but the family of mother and children and the bond among siblings. Not surprisingly, the Minangkabau do not exhibit the sexual abuse and aggression seen in societies where the fraternal patriarchy is synonymous with the public domain (Sanday 1986).

Another well-known anthropological case study illustrates the contrasting social processes associated with a fraternal patriarchy. As described by the Murphys (1974), the Mundurucu of the tropical forest of South America display a sexist ideology. Men in this society engage in gang rape, using the penis as a weapon to dominate women. Male dominance in this case is motivated by the desire to control the reproductive powers of women, which gives men male-defined social power.

An important aspect of Mundurucu life affecting psychosexual development for males and females is the existence of a purified male social group into which all boys are introduced. There are three major structures in which the Mundurucu live their lives. The men's house, Nadelson (1981, 267) says, is the key institution structuring Mundurucu life in general. Its totally male character and the fact that it is the primary residence for men reinforces the extreme separation of the sexes. The second structure for living is the dwelling where the women live and where men go to have sex with their wives. The area of Mundurucu life that balances the homosocial nature of the men's house is the shed where village women collectively prepare the staple food. This seeming balance is offset by the fact that the most important items of ritual, believed to be the source of reproductive power, are guarded in the inner sanctuary of the men's house.

Sequestered in a concealed, closed chamber attached to the men's house are the sacred trumpets that women may not see under penalty of gang rape. The trumpets are believed to contain the spirits of the ancestors who demand ritual offerings of meat. The trumpets must be properly played and "fed" with meat from the hunt to please the ancestor spirits that dwell within the trumpets and to ensure the fertility of humans and animals. The symbolism of the trumpets suggests that they are like reproductive cavities, the source of all fertility. The trumpet complex involves men in the emulation of female reproductive functions. The uterine-phallic nature of the trumpets (they are long and hollow, yet contain spirits within them) and the idea that animal and human fertility depends on their being properly fed with meat hunted by men suggests that the trumpets are bisexual symbols of the wellspring of life.

Thus, the symbolic apparatus supporting Mundurucu maleness is modeled on female reproduction and male hunting. The threat of gang rape should women see the trumpets can now be understood. Men fear that women will steal the trumpets to reclaim what was originally theirs. Men believe that women once owned the trumpets but were forced by men to give them up because only men could hunt the meat demanded as ritual offerings by the trumpet spirits. Men feed the trumpets, the source of all fertility, just as women feed babies. This is much more than womb envy. It is male dependency on the feminine reproductive model for their masculine sense of self, power, and control. Men rape women when they are threatened with the loss of their culturally constructed maleness, represented by their control of the trumpets. However, because women are the real source of fertility, men's control of the trumpets and male status is insecure—largely a symbolic device to create a balance between female and male power. As Nadelson (1981, 270) says about the Mundurucu,

> The assertion of male homosexual reproductive capacity, protected as it is by ritual secrecy, equalizes the capacities of men and women. If men and women both reproduce, each in their own way, there is nothing of *importance* that a woman can do that a man cannot.

The threat of gang rape is men's way of reminding themselves and others that they have power.

The similarity between the Mundurucu trumpet complex and the fraternity initiation rituals is seen in the concern on the part of men in both societies to build an all-male segregated order in which women play no role. Mundurucu male control of feminine reproductive cavities, as represented by the trumpets, is the social building block of male dominance.

In the case of the fraternity ritual, male disparagement of feminine qualities in themselves builds the phallocentric social order of the brotherhood. In both cases male dominance is based on the idea that men must separate boys from their mothers by turning women into objects that men control. In both cases, also, men engage in infantile practices that displace rather than resolve maternal dependency.

An obvious question at this point might be, Why do some societies develop matrifocal social processes and others exhibit the social processes related to a fraternal patriarchy? Considerable discussion appears in the anthropological literature concerning the question of universal male dominance. Several hypotheses have been elaborated, and scholars are more or less split between those who argue for the universal subordination of women and those who disagree and argue that cross-sex interaction is socially constructed and dependent on social context.[1]

Recent anthropological research concludes that it is misleading to assume that one gender template—such as male dominance, matrifocality, or sexual equality—necessarily characterizes all male-female interaction in any one society. Referring to fieldwork in several societies, anthropologists point out that a multiplicity of gender templates may actually exist and that the major focus of study should be on how gender constructions define everyday events for both sexes (Lederman 1990; see also Meigs 1990 and Gottlieb 1990). Other anthropologists point out that there may be an overarching gender ideology, despite contradictory gender templates exhibited in given contexts (Schlegel 1990; Lepowsky 1990). These points are well taken and can be applied to American society, where one finds a multiplicity of gender templates. For example, I have already noted that both accommodating and sexist behaviors can be found in the primary school and college contexts of American life. However, an overarching gender ideology that encourages sexism and has the effect of excluding women from the public domain also exists. As many studies conducted on college campuses report, the majority of female students have experienced unwanted sexual attention.[2] In addition to being burdened by these and other displays of sexism such as described in previous chapters, young women are burdened by a dominant sex-role ideology that makes it very difficult for them to achieve public positions of power and authority, as is discussed below.

RESPONSES TO SEXISM

Responses to sexism manifested by female college students include wariness and decreased spontaneity and participation, as well as an unwillingness to speak up in the presence of male peers (Lewis and Simon 1986). After over twenty years of college teaching, I am very familiar with this response. It would seem that women students, in many cases, are silenced and intimidated by sexism as well as by the usual feelings of anxiety and insecurity many students feel in the college setting.

Not all women respond with silence in the face of sexism. A vocal number of them turn to feminism and find there the strength to identify and resist the instances of exploitative male dominance they may encounter. Others cope with whatever anxieties or insecurities they feel by committing themselves to campus activities that are far removed from issues of sexual hierarchy or harassment. Environmental issues, political activities, and sports and outing club memberships appeal to both female and male students and can provide arenas of heterosexual activity and opportunities for belonging that may be largely free of sexism. Joining a sorority may serve the same function, providing a safe and self-sufficient feminine environment for some women (although this may be illusory if the sorority bonds with a particular fraternity at the cost of accepting second-class status).

A significant number of women students reject the phallo-centric discourse of the fraternities either explicitly, by challenging it over key issues, or implicitly, by choosing alternative lifestyle commitments that disdain the alcohol-party-sex compulsions of the brothers. What of the women who attach themselves to fraternities in the ways described in this book—particularly by Alice (chapter 2), Anna (chapter 2), and Amy (chapter 4)? By accepting fraternal social life on its own terms and attempting to live up to these terms as equal players and partners, these women found an outlet for their sense of adventure. In doing so they tried to accommodate themselves to the ideology of male dominance they encountered. However, when confronted with sexual victimization, they resisted the brotherhood and challenged its treatment of women.

Alice drank with the brothers and Amy and Anna had sex with the brothers. The three women chose sex and alcohol to establish their prowess, much like the brothers establish theirs. The three of them adopted a "male-identified attitude," as Anna perceptively noted about herself. In their sexual behavior Anna and Amy hoped to find the same kind of power and adventure experienced by the brothers in their sexual exploits. In the end both of them were victimized by the game of male bonding and then rejected. The thin line separating Anna and Alice's experience from that of Amy was Anna's sobriety and the care Alice took to protect herself. Anna narrowly missed a possible gang rape because she managed to stay sober and awake. Alice kicked a male party guest who made "a sexual move on her." When Anna and Amy were confronted with the brothers' victimizing they spoke out against it, as did Laurel. The resistance of these women required enormous courage because not only were they rejected by the fraternal social order thereafter; they were also harassed and threatened by anonymous men throughout their remaining years on campus.

Other women append themselves to the phallocentric social order of the fraternities by playing the roles of "suppliers" and "protectors." Women who send pledges or their female acquaintances to fraternity parties are "suppliers," akin to female pimps in a barely concealed game of female sexual slavery (see Barry's 1984 analysis of another kind of female sexual slavery). In return for their "pimping" these women achieve social acceptance from the brothers. Protectors excuse the brother's sexual abuse and do not report incidents of date rape or gang rape. Although protectors may be afraid of reprisal from the brothers, they also know that by condoning specific instances of group sexual behavior, they will be accepted into the status hierarchy. The "boys will be boys" attitude of protectors admits them into the joking comradery of the phallocentric discourse.

Finally, there are the women who submit to the brothers' sexual demands. Their identification is not with the active aggressivity of the brothers, such as was the case with Alice, Anna, and Amy, but with passive submission. Feminine subjectivity for these women is defined in terms of passivity, and their social status depends almost completely on being accepted by men. As Beauvoir (1952, 717) wrote, "When woman gives herself completely to her idol, she hopes that he will give her at once possession of herself and of the universe he represents." Women who resign themselves to victimization can be compared to pledges whose victimization is the condition of entrance into the fraternal order. However, while the victimization that pledges endure admits them to the fraternal order on an equal basis, female victims are always expected to take a backstage role.

There are many societies of the world in which it would be inconceivable for a woman to seek possession of herself by becoming an appendage of a man in order to gain entrance into the public social order. In these societies women are autonomous and effective social actors separate from their ties to men. While marriage and children may be prerequisites for a public, adult social status, the same is true of men, and there may be ways to achieve this status other than through a lifelong, heterosexual union (Kopytoff 1990). Completeness as a woman in these societies does not conflict with engaging in significant public activity. Thus, a woman who engages in significant market activity, such as the African "free woman" or a woman who becomes a head of state, as is the case in several Asian countries today, are not automatically seen as nonfeminine, as they would be seen in the United States. In the United States women are greatly constrained by the heavily loaded expectations of "what women are in their being," which burdens and handicaps them in their move out from the domestic world—and certainly limits their access to positions of power. The culturally dominant conception of womanhood is based on a number of supposedly essential features—what a woman must do in order to realize her "inner [i.e., feminine] self." The demands on a woman's time and energy imposed by such expectations make taking on political or entrepreneurial roles extremely difficult. By contrast the conception of womanhood in many Asian and African countries allows women more room for negotiation and delegation of tasks without risk of losing their social identities as women (Kopytoff 1990).

The cross-cultural perspective suggests that American conceptions of the female role severely limit social possibilities for women. Given these limitations, freedom and excitement for young women means that they must wander into the behavioral possibilities traditionally open primarily to men. If they are aggressive and sure in their manner, young women are in danger of being called "intimidating"; if they are active sexually or dress as they please, they risk being called "sluts." Retaining a feminine identification in the sexist, homophobic social order means that women must find their position along a continuum defined by two extremes: housewife or sexual slave. A professional woman who wishes to maintain a feminine identification in the sexist social order must be first a woman—housewife, mother, or sexual slave—and then an actor in the professional world. Achieving a position of equality under such circumstances is next to impossible because it means deviating from the social norm and risking the loss of social acceptance.

CONCLUSION

Whatever a young man's subjective or ethical position might be upon entering college, if he joins a fraternity he may experience during initiation or in house activities a radical alteration of consciousness that shapes his masculine subjectivity and attitudes toward women. In exchange for brotherhood and power some pledges are molded by the group mind of the fraternity that casts them in the role of "rowdy, misogynist male." Individuals in these groups are truly subjected to a profound alteration in their mental activity—a characteristic Freud claimed was true of all groups (1959, 20). The misogyny evident in some fraternity group rituals raises the question of the legal status of groups of men on campus who train incoming students to demean and disparage their female peers, attitudes that may well lead to breaking the law in cases of gang rape or date rape. The silencing effect of sexist practices and institutions on a college campus also places their legality in question because by blocking women's achievement they deny women equality of educational opportunity.

Abusive behavior toward women is not necessary to male development. Viewed cross-culturally, it can be demonstrated that many societies are free of sexual assault while others are rape-prone (Sanday 1986). Social ideologies, not human nature, prepare men to abuse women. Whatever the underlying psychological and biological needs might be, cultural templates will change and alter these tendencies. Numerous studies indicate that culture is a powerful force in channeling the human sex drive. It is interesting to note that my informants in West Sumatra were as adamant about the role of culture in establishing a rape-free society as comparable informants in the United States were adamant about the role of biology in establishing a rape-prone society. Minangkabau informants claimed that rape was impossible in their society because custom, law, and religion forbade rape. American informants, on the other hand, emphasized the role of biology to explain the prevalence of sexual assault. Both explanations are ideologies because both act to promote certain social behaviors and not others.

The popular Western view that man (i.e., the male) is basically an animal who evolved by virtue of his dominance over women and nature rationalizes the "boys will be boys" mentality. Another cultural myth depicts male sexuality as inherently explosive and likely to erupt in acts of rape when teased by provocative women. Along with the myth of the emasculating woman, these are ideologies that legitimize male dominance and encourage insecure men to seek sexual solutions in a society that inundates men with images of physically powerful and sexually active men. One might well ask why the image of the cooperative, tender male does not occupy the same mythical status in American culture as the image of the heroic sadist. Sexism is an unavoidable byproduct of a cultural fascination with the virile, sexually powerful hero who dominates everyone, male and female alike.

NOTES

1. Elsewhere, I discuss the sources of disagreement and summarize some of the current viewpoints (see Sanday 1988, 1990b). Lepowsky (1990) provides an extended case study of an egalitarian society in which she comments from the perspective of her fieldwork on many of the central issues.

In my own work, I emphasize the importance of examining the historical and ecological foundations of any given social system (Sanday 1981a). I suggest that primordial male attachments in exclusively male sodalities develop when societies are formed of a mixture of shreds and patches of other cultures, and when ancient power symbols have been drained of their efficacy. Tracing the effects of depletion in food resources, population expansion, and migration in a number of societies, I show how a people's orientation to nature and their sacred symbols result in different solutions to stress. Overarching patriarchal symbols will develop in some contexts, and nurturant, strong female figures in others.

For example, I suggest that the patriarchal Judeo-Christian god arose from the lesser figure of Yahweh during a time when pluralism threatened the social identity of the Hebrews. To defend against this threat the Hebrew fathers expanded Yahweh's domain in order to preserve the social and political integrity of the Hebrew people. In all likelihood, Canaanite goddess worship posed a significant threat at the time to the fledgling identity of the Hebrews in their new land. By raising Yahweh on high to control men, who in turn were charged with controlling women, the Hebrews reminded themselves that their mission in the new land was one of dominion and not of participation in the surrounding cultural pleasures (1981a, 10).

Matrifocal societies, on the other hand, do not display the same history of disruptive forces. In the case of the Minangkabau, for example, while there is evidence of migrations into the traditional territory of the Minangkabau people, there is no evidence that this movement significantly disrupted the Minangkabau system of customary law. Minangkabau history projects a picture of a population settled in a relatively fertile territory for a long period. When a group of Minangkabau migrated to Negri Sembilan in Malaysia, it seems they were able to establish their customary law there relatively intact. Additionally, there is evidence that the Minangkabau matrilineal system of property inheritance provided continuity during times of historical change. In the Minangkabau case one finds an overarching, female figure who serves as an important culture heroine revered by men and women (Sanday 1990a).

An interesting analysis of the role of the sexes in human evolution suggests that a matrifocal model for human social processes was in all probability the model followed by early humans (Tanner 1981). This analysis is sharply critical of older models positing the importance of male bonding and hunting.

2. Some of these statistics are cited in a report issued by the Project on the Status and Education of Women, Association of American Colleges, 1818 R Street, NW, Washington, D.C. 20009. Entitled "Peer Harassment, Hassles for Women on Campus," this study reports the results of surveys conducted on a number of college campuses. For example, in 1986, Cornell University surveyed women students and found that 78 percent of those responding had experienced sexist comments and 68 percent had received unwelcome attention from their male peers. In another study, at the Massachusetts Institute of Technology, 92 percent of the women (as compared with 57 percent of the men) had experienced at least one form of unwanted sexual attention and had reacted negatively to it. At the University of Rhode Island, 70 percent of the women surveyed reported having been sexually insulted by a man (Hughes and Sandler 1989).

Afterword

2006—Has Anything Changed?

College campuses host large concentrations of young women who are at greater risk for rape and other forms of sexual assault than women in the general population or in a comparable age group . . . many women do not characterize their sexual victimizations as a crime for a number of reasons (such as embarrassment, not clearly understanding the legal definition of rape, or not wanting to define someone they know who victimized them as a rapist) or because they blame themselves for their sexual assault.

> —Julie E. Samuels, Acting Director, National Institute of Justice, and Jan M. Chaiken, Director, Bureau of Justice Statistics, 2000

A quick answer to the question "Has anything changed?" is yes and no. "The more things change the more they stay the same" is an apt assessment of the sexual victimization of college women in 2006, twenty-three years after the XYZ Express. Change is obvious in the policies instituted on many campuses since 1990 to respond to the problem of rape and other forms of sexual assault. Victim support services, preventative education, codes defining rape, and policies for responding to allegations were instituted in response to the growing pressure from the anti-rape movement. "Rape Awareness Weeks," often organized by students, with "Take Back the Night" marches inviting women and men to speak out publicly about their rape experiences, are now part of a nationwide preventative public discourse. The diffusion of this discourse to campuses across the country makes the anti-rape movement—of which *Fraternity Gang Rape* was a part—a major new sexual revolution, one that understands the relationship between being sexual and social values.

Another important change is the widespread media coverage of high-profile cases, airing public attitudes as well as providing information. While in 1990 the subject of campus date and gang rape was virtually unknown, this is no longer the case. The nationwide coverage of the forcible rape allegations and subsequent indictments of members of Duke University's lacrosse team in the spring of 2006 exemplify both the degree to which information is now disseminated and the ongoing debate it inspires. The debate shows a split between those who continue to blame the victim and those who are more likely to hold institutions and individuals accountable.[1]

Unfortunately, neither the measures taken on campus nor the media coverage has made a difference if we take the most recent campus statistics as a measure. The tension between two trends—one associated with college policies and the discourse of the anti-rape movement promoting a rape-free consciousness, the other associated with the old rape-prone culture of predatory sexual behavior—is the subject of this Afterword.

THE CAMPUS ANTI-RAPE MOVEMENT

The University of Pennsylvania was an early leader in the campus anti-rape movement. In response to a four-day anti-rape sit-in in 1973, the administration founded the Penn Women's Center (PWC), one of the earliest of its kind. Students, faculty, and staff organized the sit-in in the aftermath of a series of rapes on and around campus, including an off-campus gang rape of nursing students. The anger fueling the sit-in came in response to the manner in which the then public safety director "blamed the victim." The four-day sit-in, which included over two hundred women, took place in College Hall, the location of the president's office. Male allies delivered food and kept the line of communication open between the sit-in leaders and the media.

The university eventually agreed to a number of actions, which included hiring a female police officer. Most important was the creation of PWC as a safe space for women to gather, report harassment and rape, and talk about issues of concern without fear of being ignored or blamed. The center provided free self-defense classes and support services for women students, faculty, staff, and the community. It opened its doors in October 1973. According to Elena M. Di Lapi, who was appointed director of PWC in 1985, the center has become an important campus focal point for women in its mission to ensure that the university "is responsive to women's concerns in any activity and at all levels" (personal communication, April 2006).

With this background, it was logical for Penn to become one of the early leaders in the development of anti-rape campus policies and education about acquaintance rape. The latter initiative came in response to the uproar over the XYZ Express. Student activism, pressure from PWC, concerned faculty, and my research all played a role. Institutionalized changes began when a few female students backed by male friends and supported by administrators organized to create a prevention education program using student peers. Their efforts led to the creation of a campuswide Acquaintance Rape Task Force, which met from 1990 to 1995. The student initiative developed into a peer education program called Students Together Against Acquaintance Rape (STAAR). This group founded the National Student Conference on Campus Sexual Violence. After its debut year at Penn in 1992, the conference was sponsored by campus organizations at colleges and universities on both coasts, generating a national movement devoted to rape-free sexual practices based on consent, communication, and sexual health (see Gold and Villari 2000).[2]

In April 1990, the campus newspaper reported that Penn's president, Sheldon Hackney, signed the report of the Committee to Diversify Locust Walk, the infamous walk down the center of campus past the fraternities. Hackney explained that although the campus grew up around fraternities it was time for a greater women's presence on the Walk (*Daily Pennsylvanian*, Feb. 15, 2005.) In the same month that *Fraternity Gang Rape* was published, September 1990, four top university officials released a statement condemning sexual violence on campus as part of a new campaign to combat acquaintance rape at the university. The statement was signed by the president, the vice provost for University Life, the provost, and a senior vice president. The latter individual explained further that one of the reasons that date and acquaintance rape is a continuing problem on college campuses is that students are unaware of the problem (DP, Sept. 11, 1990).

In 1994, when one of the fraternities vacated its house on the Walk, the Penn Women's Center was moved onto the heart of campus from its isolated closet in Houston Hall, the Student Center. Although this move along with the increasing presence of other non-Greek buildings makes the center of campus less dominantly Greek, women students still complain sometimes of being scored as they walk past the fraternity houses. In February 1995, Elena M. Di Lapi acknowledged the many positive changes but emphasized that there was still work to be done. In an interview with the school newspaper she said: "The issues are still there. . . . They just don't manifest themselves in the same way."

At Penn and elsewhere, including Duke University, the campus anti-rape movement developed campus programs founded on a "pro-pleasure principle" in which students were taught that sexual behavior, including safe-sex considerations, is to be negotiated between consenting sexual partners. The peer education component of the new policies put the problem in the hands of students. The idea was that fraternity brothers, athletes, and sorority sisters would join with students from the general student population to conduct rape awareness workshops on the importance and meaning of sexual consent. Many of these programs developed because of particular incidents that came to the attention of students but were ignored by administrators. These efforts coincided with national and international conferences devoted to bringing "individuals, campus organizations, schools, government agencies, and community institutions together . . . to reduce the insult and effects of sexual assault and harassment."[3] Affirmative verbal consent, freely given agreement, and sexual communication are the operative words of the new sexual paradigm discussed at these conferences.

In some circles these developments closed the door on two hundred years of stereotyping female sexuality. Under the new mores, women are not expected to resist—saying No is enough. Nor is their alleged sexiness, desire, inebriation, or silence translated as a yes. The underlying sexual paradigm is based on the assumption of an equal rather than an asymmetric sexual partnership in which both women and men are frank about their desire, and women are not presumed to be primarily servers of male desire. Everyone is held equally to the verbal consent standard and to the principle of safe sex. This standard is the twenty-first century version of the one-sex model insofar as both sexes are believed to be endowed with equal sexual rights and needs. Understanding the ethical, health, and legal significance of standards promoting sexual and social equality is crucial for educating those who don't get the message.

WHAT DO THE MOST RECENT STATISTICS SUGGEST?

That many do not yet get the message is suggested in the results of a national study of male attitudes on seven campuses around the country conducted between 1999 and 2003. Although most males (83 percent) in this study said they respect their partner's wishes about sexual activity, only 74 percent said they would intervene to prevent a sexual assault.[4] This means that one-quarter (26 percent) were either not concerned, did not comprehend the tell-tale signs of potential sexual assault, or kept silent in a show of support, which comes perilously close to abetting rape-prone behavior.

This finding is consistent with the description in *Fraternity Gang Rape* showing that brothers often set the stage for sex by getting a girl drunk. While these same males understand the necessity of peer oversight to prevent fights and drunk driving, their ignorance of the consequences of sex and binge drinking and their sense of entitlement to sex at the end of an evening's activities actively promotes if not abets nonconsensual sexual behavior. One can only imagine that this was the goal of the Duke lacrosse team party attended by forty-one members of the team and two exotic dancers. The dehumanization of women as sex objects was amply on display in the email written after the Duke incident by one of the lacrosse players present at the party: *tomorrow night, after tonight's show, ive [sic] decided to have some strippers over* [dorm room.] *all are welcome . . . however there will be no nudity. i plan on killing the bitches as soon as they walk in and proceeding [sic] to cut their skin off while cumming in my duke issue spandex . . . all in besides arch and tack please respond. 41*

This email was signed by 41, the jersey number for a member of the Duke lacrosse team (Probable Cause Affidavit: Attachment for Application for Search Warrant, Durham, 2006).

The continuation of the male-dominated, binge-drinking, casual-sex, party culture together with the continuing tendency for women students not to report nonconsensual sex explains why the nationwide statistics of rape on campus remain more or less the same. Several studies illustrate the extent of the continuing problem. Based on data pertaining to the school year 1996–97, a study conducted by the National Institute of Justice and the Bureau of Justice Statistics, entitled "The Sexual Victimization of College Women," estimated that "nearly 5 percent (4.9 percent) of college women are victimized in any given calendar year. Over the course of a college career—which now lasts an average

of 5 years—the percentage of completed or attempted rape victimization among women in higher educational institutions might climb to
between one-fifth and one-quarter" (Fisher, Cullen, and Turner
2000:10).

These results are similar to a study on the relationship between alcohol and rape. Based on data gathered in the years 1997, 1999, and 2001
by the Harvard School of Public Health, this study surveyed students at
119 schools representing a national cross section of students enrolled at
four-year colleges. Between 6,900 and 8,000 women students were sam-
pled each year of the study (a total of 23,980 students.) Looking at the
totals for the three samples, roughly one in twenty, or 5 percent of the
women, reported being raped since the beginning of the school year.
Seventy-two percent of these women experienced rape while intoxicated. The factors the authors found to be most associated with a
woman's experience of rape while intoxicated were troubling because
of the implication that campuses are not enforcing alcohol policies. The
women who experienced rape while intoxicated tended to be under
twenty-one, white, resided in sorority houses, used illicit drugs, drank
heavily in high school, and attended colleges with high rates of heavy
episodic (binge) drinking. Women on the higher binge drinking campuses were more likely to be raped compared to women on the lower
binge drinking campuses independently of the other factors (Mohler-
Kuo, Dowdall, and Koss 2004:37).

The linkage between alcohol and rape in the Greek context is evident in a study conducted at Penn by two students in 2005. This study
demonstrates the ways in which male bonding through sex continues.
The old practices are evident in the binge drinking, hooking-up culture
described by these students. The complicity of sororities is more evident now than before. Strippers and "hoes" don't need to be hired;
these roles are now assigned to pledges. At Greek mixers in which
drinking and drugs are plentiful and sex is the goal, the line between
consensual and nonconsensual sex is blurred in what is called "the
blacked-out hook-up."

THE HOOK-UP SEXUAL CULTURE AT PENN IN 2005

In the spring semester of 2005, two women students, Natalie and Claire
(pseudonyms), approached me about doing a restudy of the Greek

party scene after they read *Fraternity Gang Rape* in the fall. Throughout the spring semester they conducted qualitative one-on-one, in-depth interviews with cooperative fraternity brothers and sorority sisters at the same time as they became participant observers of the party scene. Their goal, as they put it, "was to determine if changes had occurred (and if yes, to what degree) in regard to the issues of sex, brotherhood, and privilege."

Their findings are based on interviews with males in five fraternities and with females in four sororities, along with participant observation of parties during their years at Penn and Natalie's experience as a sorority member until she deactivated. The interviews shed light on student experiences and perceptions regarding sex, rape, drugs, alcohol abuse, and hazing. Although their findings cannot be taken either as conclusive or representative of the entire Greek system, their observations are troubling.

Date rape is common but rarely reported. Campus policies regarding drinking, drugs, and hazing are routinely ignored. Perhaps the most significant finding was the evidence of the degree to which some sororities are complicit in preparing their pledges for the "hooking-up" culture. This is evident in Natalie's account of her pledging, hazing, and party experiences in one of Penn's popular sororities.

Pledging a Sorority

Natalie had spent little time on the East Coast before entering Penn. As is true of other West Coast students, she felt at somewhat of a social disadvantage because so many of the first-year East Coast students had friends and acquaintances from high school or summer camp in the entering class or classes above. Upon arriving at Penn from the West, Natalie noticed differences between West and East Coast dress, dialogue, and attitudes. For instance, she was surprised at the amount of time girls devoted to "primping," starting at 6 P.M. on a Friday night to leave around 10:30 P.M. for a fraternity party; the importance attached to designer purses; and the way in which family money was flaunted.

"Rush" began after returning from winter break in January of Natalie's first year. She had no idea what to expect except that business casual dress was required and name tags were to be worn at all times. She described how rush operated:

Lining up outside the sorority houses in the middle of winter in high-heeled black boots, long black wool coats, Burberry scarves and designer purses stood the herds of freshman girls anticipating their future inclusion in a Greek house. Each "rush round" seemed more intense and more fake . . . like receiving an oral pop quiz on Penn social life from the most "competitive" houses. On bid day, it seemed like every freshman girl I had met during first semester was crowded into Houston Hall awaiting their white envelope containing their future Greek house. I had mixed feelings and I remember being more overwhelmed than nervous, just hoping that I would get something in my envelope and not walk away from the rush experience empty handed. Sure enough, in my envelope was an invitation to join the so-called most exclusive house. As I left to walk outside and see what all the screaming crowds of girls with balloons, flowers, signs, and posters were gallivanting around for, I walked past several hysterical girls who either did not get into a sorority or got their second choice.

I remember thinking that I was one of the chosen ones and proud that I made it through the rush experience and had gotten into the house that so many girls wanted . . . however, I had no idea what was to come.

At least half of the "No Hazing" rules were broken in the first month of pledging, which no one reported to the appropriate administrative office for fear of retaliation from older sisters. Hooking-up was always encouraged and talked about—the best (usually, the most public) stories were shared during weekly meetings. The pledges had to bang on fraternity doors to gather girls sleeping in different beds or have the cell phone numbers of all the boys each girl could be hooking up with so that we could find her in the middle of a night for a line up. Hooking-up was common at fraternity mixers, which are held either at fraternity houses or off campus because sororities are banned from having parties or mixers at their on-campus houses.

Our sorority's fraternity mixers usually consisted of drinking (top shelf liquors), smoking pot, and using a variety of other on-demand drugs in the upstairs rooms. Obviously, not all 50 pledges or older girls would participate in all drinking and drug use, but I never remember anyone sitting in the corner complaining. The most infamous mixer occurred a week after pledging began. The event was called "Anything for $1" and it was an annual party dedicated to introducing the "hot" new 50 pledges to a certain fraternity. The pledges were told to wear lingerie (or less) and the fraternity provided whipped cream and whatever props they felt necessary. As soon as the pledges arrived, their jackets and sweats were taken and stored in a bedroom (since it was still snowing outside) and they were taken into bedrooms to begin drinking 100-proof alcohol and tequila shots with the boys. Soon, girls were giving lap dances and licking whip cream off of the fraternity brothers on command. Scandalous pictures were taken with digital cameras and posted online the following day. To avoid anyone in the administration or in the National Sorority from finding the pictures, the sorority asked the fraternity to take down the Web site.

At all mixers, it was typical for male and female pledge classes to dress up to the theme of male sexual dominance. The boys dressed as "pimps" or CEOs and girls dressed for the role of "hoes" or secretaries. Playing these parts was also expected. From the start, pledges were informed that they would be "on display" and would need to uphold the sorority's image, which Natalie summed up as stressing "promiscuity, drug use, and 'holier than thou' attitudes."

A few weeks into pledging, Natalie told her mom that she felt she had made a mistake and joined a cult. The older sisters would dress in long black cloaks and carry candles, and the pledges were forced to drink mixed wines and other substances she couldn't identify, chant songs, and stand in ordered lines, typically blindfolded for the majority of the event. When the blindfolds were removed, the pledges would find that they had been led either to an off-campus house, for what appeared to be some sort of séance, or to the basement of the sorority house. The long hours of such events took a toll on the health and schoolwork of the pledges. She noted that it was typical for girls to cry or faint at events due to stress, dehydration, or dizziness.

After more of these kinds of events, the pledges went through initiation, a seven-hour event starting at 8:30 P.M. at an off-campus location. They wore a white T-shirt and carried a blindfold. Upon arrival, each pledge was asked if she was allergic to food/drinks/spices. As Natalie described it:

Blindfolds were placed tightly over our eyes and we were led into a damp, pitch-black basement. We were arranged in a corner, forced to sit up on our knees, and a raw egg was placed in our mouths. We were instructed to keep our mouths open wide around the egg, and if the egg broke or fell out we would be punished. We had to stay sitting up with our hands behind our back in silence while the rest of our pledge class arrived and joined us on the cold cement floor. After over an hour of sitting up in silence, the seniors began quizzing individuals on the sorority's history. . . . Unless we were being directly addressed, we had to keep the egg in our mouth. The oral quizzing continued for at least another hour. We were then asked to stand up and arrange ourselves in two circles. Two huge plastic buckets full of a horrid-smelling substance were placed in the middle of each circle. The buckets smelled of raw seafood, spoiled milk, tomatoes, eggs, mustard, ketchup, and muddled spices—to this day, I still wonder what we consumed. Each group had to pass the bucket around, from girl to girl, until it was completely empty. The basement reeked of vomit after the buckets had been consumed, and two girls fainted during the event and were taken outside for water. Next, we were led single-file up three flights of stairs and led into dark bedrooms, where we were instructed to stand still while older sisters wrote everything they didn't like about us or what we needed to change about ourselves on our T-shirts in permanent pens. (When we were finally out of the house, hours later, we read our shirts to find out they said "welcome to . . ." and "we love you.") Next, we were led into bathrooms and thrown into showers. Once we were all dripping wet, we were escorted blindfolded downstairs again and by this time it was around 3 A.M. . . . and I honestly don't remember what else happened or if we were just allowed to leave.

Natalie hated living in the sorority house. She said that the personalities and competitiveness of the girls in the house clashed on a daily basis and the house was divided into cliques. Mealtime was something of a nightmare in being

a show of competitive restraint—bulimia, the Atkin's diet, and anorexia. The second-floor bathroom needed to have toilet plumbing pipes replaced due to the amount of stomach acid subsiding inside. Everyone knew who would purge after a meal, but it was never a topic of discussion.

Although it was considered to be one of the most popular houses, within weeks after initiation a few girls deactivated their membership. Natalie followed suit with two friends in her junior year. During that year, half of her pledge class of fifty deactivated.

Natalie and Claire believe that there is a connection between the increasing rate of students engaging in high-risk behaviors and the "masochistic process of rush and hazing in the Greek system and other similar societies." They suggest that both are coping mechanisms for dealing with

> fears of academic and social pressures and the debilitating effects of low self-esteem that arise in the unfamiliar and often unsupportive atmosphere of college life. Whether in a group of drunken friends or the temporary comfort of a brief sexual encounter, students derive a sense of belonging from these actions and sharing the stories that follow. These sorts of coping mechanisms have become accepted methods of socialization and have become so pervasive that they are perceived as the norm. Although stress, insecurity, or the anxiety of choosing a direction for life after college may not be behind high-risk behavior for all students, it is possible that many participate in these behaviors whether or not he or she is aware of the reasons for their actions.

Hazing in Fraternities

In their interviews with fraternity brothers, Natalie and Claire were told that hazing is common in fraternities as well. According to the Anti-hazing Law of Pennsylvania, the term "hazing"

> shall include but not be limited to, any brutality of a physical nature, such as whipping, beating, branding, forced calisthenics, exposure to the elements, forced consumption of any food, liquor, drug or other substance, or any other forced physical activity which could adversely affect the physical health and safety of the individual, and shall include any activity which would subject the individual to extreme mental stress, such as sleep deprivation, forced exclusion from social contact, forced conduct which could result in extreme embarrassment, or any other forced activity, which could adversely affect the mental health and dignity of the individual, or any willful destruction or removal of public or private property.

Brothers rationalized hazing as necessary for bonding. One brother said that the "worst part of pledging is physical sickness from alcohol or forced consumption of seven cups of prune juice" and eating a "butterdog—a stick of butter in a hot dog bun, verbal and physical degradation . . . , and threats of punishment for not memorizing chapter material or missing an event." In one fraternity house, hazing included sexual behavior with the fraternity's dog. All of the brothers emphasized that the lifelong bond of brotherhood was worth whatever pledging and hazing rituals they had to get through in order to be part of the organization. Their comments were not unlike those I heard in 1983.

- The abusive stuff done to pledges is because they have to go through a rite of passage. You have to earn your place in the fraternity. I mean being a brother is, I mean people think it's really easy but it's actually a lot of work, and you want kids to prove they want to be in a house . . . if you're nice to them, there's really nothing. . . . When you pledge kids you realize that events can't be that hard if you're nice to them. You can't say, "Drink this till you puke" and be nice to them. You can't really make anyone do anything that bad if you're nice to them. . . . They have to do certain things while you're screaming at them. Otherwise it's just easy, and you can't have easy pledging.–White male senior
- It's definitely forced bonding . . . in virtually every fraternity that I'm aware of, pledges have to do disgusting and horrible things, and I hated pledging. A little later on, I sort of agreed with it and understood the purpose. . . . If you go through all that shit to get into the fraternity, you will value your fraternity membership more. . . . Houses in which they don't haze the pledges and just make them run a lot—they are a bunch of dorks, and not worth it. . . . No one is going to go through hell to get into those kinds of houses.–Hispanic male senior

The Hooking-up Sexual Culture

While no one talked to them about incidents of "pulling train," Natalie and Claire found that "riffing" on women—getting sex in exchange for alcohol, drugs, and a good time—is still quite common.

They described the sexual culture in which they operated during their early years at Penn as "one of binge drinking, drug experimentation, and casual sex." What they first thought of as the freedom so touted in the 1970s, they now understand involved "risk of dangerous and destructive consequences." "In spite of these dangers," they said, "the freedom of college still induces a lust for all three."

Although their peers used *hooking-up* as the most common term for a casual sexual encounter, Natalie and Claire found little agreement on what it actually meant.

> To some students, *hooking-up* can be anything from kissing to sexual intercourse. To others, it implies sexual intercourse automatically. Others said *hooking-up* only happened after the making-out stages, and some suggested there needed to be lying down involved. One student provided the condition that it "had no long-term implications." He said, "Like you don't 'hook-up' with your girlfriend. 'Hook-up' is more of a promiscuous, no-strings-attached kinda thing." It looks like Bill Clinton wasn't the only one confused by the word *sex*.

Hooking-up at Mixers

A mixer between a fraternity and a sorority is an exclusive party, on or off-campus, which introduces the new pledge class. Often the mixers involve costumes that hypersexualize the female pledges. Male fraternity members act as hosts providing alcohol, and often drugs. The consumption of alcohol, with the males acting as pimps and the females dressed up as hoes, burlesques male sexual dominance and female sexual subservience. A number of fraternity brothers and sorority sisters representing different organizations described the goals of mixers they had attended.

- The point of a mixer is really to hook up. You meet people and that's part of it, but you get two groups of people together who wanna hook up. I mean, if you look at the themes it's pretty obvious. CEO's and Executive Hoes.—White male senior
- A mixer theme just means that girls dress very slutty—like Pimps and Hoes or CEO's and their secretaries. . . . It's always

implied that the guys play dominant roles and girls dress like hookers.—White female senior

- Often there is some theme which highly sexualizes the female party . . . there's alcohol; it's basically an opportunity for sorority girls to dress up in questionable outfits, like Halloween, the guys just dress like themselves. Drugs are always available— there are certain houses that are more known for drug use. The lines between sexual harassment are blurred during these events because it's sexualized. Girls know how to take care of themselves, if they put themselves in those positions.—Black female senior
- From a fraternity standpoint, the point of a mixer is so that people can hook up without the pressure of being at a party and not knowing who's with whom and what's what, you go into a mixer with certain expectations. . . . Usually themes are sexual, like pimps and hoes, and centered around alcohol in some way. . . . Males play into the dominant stereotypes.—Black male senior
- The point is just to hang out with girls. Themes? Golf pros and tennis hoes—golfers with sweaters, and girls have short skirts. Usually they just involve girls dressing very promiscuous and that's about it.—White male senior
- Fraternities are very masculine organizations, devoted to beer, sex, and pot.—White male senior
- The point of mixers is to hook up with scantily clad women. Fraternity houses are places of porn, kegs, and dialogue between brothers which could be perceived as racist, sexist, and homophobic.—White female senior

Watching Porn and Videotaping Sexual Activity

Watching porn is common even though some brothers admit that "it could definitely change the way you think about women." As one said, "College males who watch porn are more likely to act out the sexual aggression they saw on porn on a girl. . . . The guy who thinks it's cool is the one who is going to try that stuff on a girl. It's also used as a learning tool."

Like the "ledging" and "beaching" described in this book, brothers admitted that "there are some fraternity rituals which include busting in on a couple hooking up." As one said, "Members burst open a brother's door while he is having sex with someone and run in yelling and cheering for them."

In another fraternity, Natalie and Claire were told about a video-tape that a brother made during his freshman year that depicted him having sex with another freshman. The tape was viewed by the entire pledge class. The girl who was videotaped never knew that the tape exists or that twenty male seniors have watched it.

If hooking up remains the crux of the Greek scene in some contexts, sharing stories afterwards is also an essential aspect of bonding.

> Weekend hookup confessions typically start with the phrase "I was so drunk that I. . . ." Stories like these are frequently shared in dorms, apartments, and Greek chapter houses. Unless they were involved in a serious relationship, both men and women admitted to sharing hook up stories with friends. Sometimes the storytelling amounts to bragging.

One fraternity member said that his fraternity has a chart with its "greatest sluts." The chart consists of "a network drawn on a poster board with girls' names who had hooked up with several guys." In this fraternity they use as their password "a slutty girl's name who had hooked up with lots of guys in the house." Chapter meetings in this house include talking about girls who have hooked up with someone. A brother in this fraternity suggested that "it is guys who are less confident who tend to gloat and want to share things." Gossiping about sex isn't restricted to fraternities and occurs commonly in some sororities.

Date Rape

Not surprisingly, date rape is common in this atmosphere. Some women who wake up with a guy and have no idea what happened to them don't call it date rape. They call it "the blacked-out hook-up." Like Karen Zailacks, author of *Smashed*, some of these girls don't want to know what happened after they got drunk and passed out. As Zailacks says, "If you can't remember, you hope you never remember. You indulge your selective amnesia. You operate under the philosophy I don't think, therefore I am."[5] This is truly a startling admission in a campus

context where thinking is an essential part of preparing for a future oc-
cupation as an adult member of society.

Claire admitted that she felt similarly after she realized that she had
been the victim of a date-rape drug administered by a guy she didn't
like. She told herself that it didn't matter because nothing harmful had
come of it. Yet, she admitted that "something inside of me was clearly
damaged and I was indeed resentful. I know because I haven't spoken
to or even looked directly at this guy since that day." She neither reported the incident nor confronted him about it. She didn't think what
happened was nonconsensual until three years later, after reading this
book. Other students with whom Claire and Natalie talked did consider
nonconsensual sex rape, but for various reasons they did not report it
because they wanted to forget it happened. Many of the women interviewed had either been raped or knew someone who had. One inter-
viewee described the abortion she had to seek out alone in the aftermath of party sex. One student explained why she thinks the Penn sexual culture is rape-prone.

> Drinking and drugs and stress are such problems here and girls who
> don't have self-respect for themselves are vulnerable and susceptible
> to violence and I'm not saying it's their fault, but there's such a small
> support system for women on this campus that they feel belittled by
> the institution and the men to begin with, so they don't realize that
> they deserve more than being harassed or assaulted. This is a large
> university which is high stress, and oppressive people take out their
> frustration by controlling others. Every week or two, a new friend,
> tells me of their experience. Most incidents go unreported because of
> shame, no one wants to deal with it, some people are afraid to admit
> that they were actually abused. . . . One-fourth of my friends have been
> raped, assaulted, violated in some way. I think there's a stigma in so-
> ciety towards therapy and I don't think people are aware of the re-
> sources at the Penn women's center.—White female junior

Peer group oversight to stop a potential sexual offense is uncommon. At parties, fraternity brothers look out for one another, not for
their women guests. One brother had this to say on the subject of
whether he would stop an inebriated brother from hooking up with a
drunken woman:

I mean people are just always drunk when they hook up, so I mean I wouldn't stop [two drunken people going upstairs.] If it was one of my good friends and the girl clearly wouldn't hook up with them except in this state, then I'd probably be like, "that's not the right thing to do," but I don't think I'd intervene forcefully because that girl got that drunk on her own, like I wouldn't condone any raping, but if the girl wants to hook up with him in whatever state she's in, she got herself into that state and probably the guy's drunk too and maybe wouldn't have hooked up with her. That's sort of an unwritten agreement that people have when they get wasted.—You might hook up with someone.–White male senior

Conclusion

Natalie and Claire concluded that there is a difference between expectations and reality with regard to sexual assault, racism, and pledging on Penn's campus.

> While not every fraternity house is rape-prone nor does every sorority promote promiscuity, there are several issues that need to be addressed. Although we didn't hear of any incidents of "pulling train," there have been dozens of sexual assault cases.

Natalie and Claire named "the sexualization of females" by fraternity members and what they called "the problem of the 'casualization' of sex" as being pervasive.

> Particular to our generation is a vagueness that permeates throughout our vernacular, and spreads into the way we relate to other people. Terms such as *whatever, like, ya know,* and *random,* have transformed existing words into place-holders without universally known meanings.

This was their way of describing the party culture in which there are no standards for behavior. If you get drunk there is no right or wrong in sexual matters. If something happens, you live with it. You don't report it. Emotion is superficial and so is moral commitment.

The trivialization Natalie and Claire find in their peer culture is displayed in student responses to a recently published popular book in which the "anything goes" attitude about acceptable sexual behavior is prominently displayed. Written by Tucker Max, *I Hope They Serve Beer in Hell* began circulating in the fraternity scene in January 2006. The book is a prime example not only of the "casualization" of sex but of the dehumanization of sexual partners as well. "Any woman will do" is the attitude expressed on the front cover with a picture of the author alongside a faceless female. Tucker Max, a University of Chicago graduate, proudly admits that he is "an asshole." To catch the eye of the browsing book buyer on the jacket he lists the norms he breaks:

> I get excessively drunk at inappropriate times, disregard social norms, indulge every whim, ignore the consequences of my actions, mock idiots and posers, sleep with more women than is safe or reasonable, and just generally act like a raging dickhead. (Max 2006)

After he promoted his book at one of Penn's fraternity houses, there was an outpouring of excited commentary and approbation in the school newspaper.

- "Tucker Max is brilliant and his stories are hilarious, and I've read all of them and I'm really excited that he's doing this."—Male business major
- "I aspire to be like him."—Male engineering sophomore
- "Your first impulse is probably to judge his behavior, wondering how anyone could ever be so dumb as to waste an education like his. After all we are Penn students. Our idea of success involves commanding a business empire from a fancy corner office on Wall Street, a salary in the high six figures and a Fifth Avenue penthouse apartment. We work hard in class and pack our resumes with extracurriculars so we can get hired for prestigious summer internships, which will, at the end of four years, hopefully guarantee us this fantasy lifestyle. . . . After judging his career choice [to write books like this one] it is also a natural impulse to be offended by his behavior. After all, promiscuity and alcoholism are things we've been trained to look down on. But no matter how despicable a human being you may find him, maybe there are lessons the most staunch conservatives can take from Tucker Max. He lives his life for his own personal fulfillment, and makes no apologies for who he is: "I do not write fiction, and I do not make anything up. Good or bad, this is my

life." . . . Maybe Tucker Max can show us that we should find paths in life that make *us* happy and make no apologies for who we choose to become. . . . We are all smart enough to find success after graduation, and how we do so is of no concern to anyone else."—Female English major (DP, Jan. 30, 2006.)

The response to Tucker Max is an example of what Natalie and Claire mean in extending the notion of "casualization" to what they call the "*casualization of dialogue, sex, and racism.*" Being cool trumps all else. The goal is to be whoever you fantasize being regardless of the consequences. Projected onto the campus sexual culture in the Greek scene they studied, casualization means that words such as rape don't have a meaning because acquaintance rape is still not on the radar screen of the don'ts. In response to the furor that would be created if someone reported a date rape, including the hassle and trauma the young woman would face in an environment where "scoring" trumps caring, living one's life with the attitude that abuse "happens" is a way of forgetting. Getting by under the *whatever* philosophy flattens the trauma. Making abuse casual is the alternative to standing up and fighting.

According to Natalie and Claire, responding casually to sexual and racial abuse "is consistent in all of the issues that we have investigated."

> We named this problem "casualization" because students have become accustomed to the ambiguity that is now so common in both language and interpersonal relationships. Activism in the form of condemning racist language or speaking out against sexual assault is intimidating to a generation with distaste for commitment. This socio-cultural trend of accepting ambiguity motivates students who have been victimized to choose silence over action against their perpetrators. Therefore, the informal and often careless use of racist and homophobic jokes and slang in fraternity male dialogue, and the common occurrence of sexual assault in the hookup culture are signifiers of our generation's lackadaisical attitudes toward activism and toward issues which must be discussed and addressed.

One year later, thinking back on their years at Penn, Natalie and Claire expressed regret for the time they lost due to the distractions of those aspects of student culture they do not now admire. Natalie wrote that she now treasures her time at Penn—not the time pledging or belonging to a sorority, but the time spent "living with non-Greek friends and getting out of the sorority bubble of social aristocracy and materialism." As she put it:

> It is the air of privilege and a sense of entitlement that overwhelms and dilutes the undergraduate experience. When binge drinking, date rape, casualization of racism, and degradation of women become shared activities among groups of male fraternity brothers, incidences of violence, abuse, and overdosing will rampantly continue in a vicious cycle as each new pledge class becomes inducted. College is essentially about experience—trying new things, meeting new people, and most of all learning to be an individual and live independently.

Claire had similar thoughts, but was more critical about the atmosphere of privilege and entitlement of the Greek system. A year after graduation she wrote:

> All of my alumni colleagues currently kick themselves for losing and abusing four years at the University of Pennsylvania and for most of the people in the Greek system, doing so FOR FREE! What they once thought was the beginning of reckless freedom [was] in fact the last breath before capitalistic enslavement. This book, in addition to identifying important gender-power-relationships, and female disillusionment, hopefully will capture and communicate the worrisome wealth of missed opportunities and wasted money. Personally, I think Penn should dissolve the Greek community and start accepting hard workers and people who want to make every day of their education count.

Claire also indicated that the rebellion of drinking too much might be in itself a rite of passage, which should be recognized and dealt with. As she put it,

> People need to have their hard lessons learned. I would just hope they were around safe people who could take care of them—and not left in the bottom of a frat house to choke on their own vomit.

I think that *casualization* is encouraged by many sources. In the student culture, the ills of society—racism, the poverty that confronts students on a daily basis in the inner city, the social inequity on campus separating students of color, and the degradation of women students—are made meaningless through joking. With respect to racial joking, one student explained it away: "If he really meant it, he wouldn't joke about it." She was surprised at my response, which was to say that he meant every word of it. I pointed out that students who tell racist jokes simultaneously demean the problem of racism and ensure its continuation by injecting it into the common discourse. Those who hear the joke can call him on it or pass it off as being cool. The first response is that of an activist, the second of someone who wants to be accepted.

The price female students pay for their passive acceptance of the inhumanity of casualization is an even greater sense of low self-esteem. As Claire suggested, what women students think of as reckless freedom is in reality acceptance of the gender inequality inherent in the Greek system. The same inequality will also greet them in the work world.

Claire's mention of students learning to accept "capitalistic enslavement" is interesting from other angles as well. In the campus social economy, racist joking, hitting on women, and primping is the price paid for acceptance and having a good time. Primping four hours before going to a party is flight from authenticity in the expenditure of capital to sell the self through the body. It hangs selfhood on superficial appearance. Girls can't be who they are but must cast themselves in the image of a poster face made up with a product. They appear clad in the latest fashion, the latest brand, the latest logo, the latest pair of lips, breast, nose, and so on. Life is a constant struggle *to be made in the image of someone else*—in other words, *to become* rather than *to be*. Girls buy the face and give the sex in order to put themselves into the social economy.

Guys can't be who they are but must cast themselves in the image of the sexually successful male who "scores." They run the sexual economy by preparing the girls to hook up by putting out the money for alcohol and drugs and then boasting to one another in the following days about the payoff they received at the end of the evening. Both the guys and the girls gain status in this sexual economy—not exactly an equal status, but status nonetheless.

Everyone, including the university administrators who look the other way, is responsible for the high-risk behavior encouraged in this atmosphere and its deadly consequences. Although the self-indulgence of binge drinking and thoughtless sex may increase one's status temporarily, like the high one gets from drugs it only lowers self-respect for both the women and men and the sense of being a functioning, responsible human being. Gross sexual inequality in the form of sexual abuse flows into the vacuum created by the absence of responsibility.

The frittering away of sexual pleasure on the altar of sexual commodification acted out through porno-inspired mixers strikes me as promoting rape as "cool." When sororities dress their pledges as hoes, they should think about the young women around the world who are sold in order to become hoes in some faraway land. When brothers get off on being a pimp they should ask themselves how they would feel if their daughters or sisters were treated as fodder for some male's sexual appetite. "I don't think, therefore I am" is behind this kind of behavior at many levels.

When sororities buy into the male-defined sexual culture by presenting their pledges as lustful partners, as interested in hooking up as any male, they revert to the old two-sex model of the nineteenth century with one difference. Privileged women no longer play the role of the virgin on the pedestal but are brought in to play the working-class hoes of the past. Just in case the young women do not embrace this role with ease, the males make drugs and alcohol readily available to "loosen up inhibitions." In this environment the line between consensual and nonconsensual sex is blurred in "the blacked out" hook-up.

Much of the casual sex Natalie and Claire describe is acquaintance rape, an act punishable by expulsion from college and/or a jail term if tried and convicted. It is Penn's responsibility and that of every campus administration to convey the legal and moral consequences of nonconsensual sex to students in no uncertain terms. It is not just women students who need to be protected from the rape-prone sexual culture. Since many of the male students I have interviewed do not necessarily enter college with rape-prone attitudes, they need to understand the consequences of the "scoring" sexual status system. What they may see as raising their social status among male peers may possibly get them a jail sentence or expulsion, despite the high-price lawyers their families can afford.

There are now clearly defined guidelines for understanding rape on many college campuses and in the courts as well. For example, clarity defines the well-known standards stressing verbal consent developed by Antioch College in Ohio in the early 1990s. If students think the Antioch standards are too restrictive, they should at least understand the legal consequences of their acts by studying rape statutes and selected courtroom decisions. One notable decision is a New Jersey Supreme Court decision that provides clear guidelines for determining when sexual behavior is nonconsensual. These guidelines should be posted in residence halls and in fraternities and sororities around the country. Affirmative verbal consent is the watchword of this more responsible sexual culture.

AFFIRMATIVE VERBAL CONSENT: ANTIOCH'S SEXUAL OFFENSE PREVENTION POLICY

The imperative of affirmative verbal consent is now widely taught in peer-education workshops on college campuses and in secondary schools on the grounds that verbal discussion is not just necessary for consent but crucial for safe sex. How many abortions and cases of sexually transmitted diseases could be avoided if people talked before jumping into sex? The concept of verbal consent first garnered nationwide attention at Antioch College in Ohio in 1991. Although Antioch's emphasis on verbal consent was at first lambasted by the news media as being "puritanical" and "prudish," the logic of this standard is now widely recognized, if not accepted.

Antioch's policy illustrates the rebirth of the one-sex model with the addition of a revolutionary stress on responsible sexual freedom defined in terms of affirmative verbal consent, sex rights, protection, and gender equality. The policy developed in response to a group known as the "Womyn of Antioch," who in 1991 began a campaign to challenge the culture of sexual violence at Antioch. Their concern arose from the school's response to a date rape in which the offender was allowed to remain on campus during the hearing procedure and subsequently received no punishment. Eventually, a policy was hammered out by administrators, faculty, and students.

In an interview in 1994 with anthropologist Melinda Kanner, who was teaching a human sexuality course at the time the policy was developed, she indicated that the students involved didn't talk about sexual freedom per se; rather, they talked about choice and the appropriate exercise of sex rights. According to Kanner, the sexual offense policy was designed "not to restrict freedom, but to make some kind of accord so that freedom could be enjoyed and rights exercised."[6] The resulting policy, labeled "The Antioch College Sexual Offense Policy," was adopted in 1993.

At that time the policy defined consent as "the act of willingly and verbally agreeing to engage in specific sexual contact or conduct." This basic definition did not change in the revised policy that became effective on January 1, 2006, labeled the Sexual Offense Prevention Policy. As before, verbal consent was to be obtained "each and every time there is sexual activity." In the new policy, the nature of consent was clarified in such a way as to apply "equally to all types of sexualities, gender identities and gender expression." It was also written to cover group sex. The following expectations are listed in the current policy:

- All parties must have a clear and accurate understanding of the sexual activity.
- The person(s) who initiate(s) the sexual activity is responsible for asking for consent.
- The person(s) who are asked are responsible for verbally responding.
- Each new level of sexual activity requires consent.
- Use of agreed-upon forms of communications such as gestures or safe words is acceptable, but must be discussed and verbally agreed to by all parties before sexual activity occurs.
- Consent is required regardless of the parties' relationship, prior sexual history, or current activity (e.g., grinding on the dance floor is not consent for further sexual activity).
- At any and all times when consent is withdrawn or not verbally agreed to, the sexual activity must stop immediately.
- Silence is not consent.
- Body movements and non-verbal responses such as moans are not consent.
- A person can not give consent while sleeping.
- All parties must have unimpaired judgment (examples that may cause impairment include but are not limited to alcohol, drugs, mental health conditions, physical health conditions).
- All parties must use safer sex practices.
- All parties must disclose personal risk factors and any known STIs. Individuals are responsible for maintaining awareness of their sexual health.

These requirements have no restrictions on sexual partners, the type of sexual activity, the props/toys/tools used, the number of persons involved, or the gender(s) or gender expression of persons involved.[7]

It was not the intent of Antioch's Sexual Offense Prevention Policy to replace existing laws, or even to emulate the local legal tradition. The college recognized that while it existed within a larger society governed by existing laws, it understood its mission as striving "for the betterment of both the individual and society." Thus, it claimed "our standards for behavior may be broader than currently exist under state and federal laws." Antioch saw such community standards as part of its educational mission, to be dealt with through on-campus administrative means "as part of the educational process." Thus, community members were expected "to protect and uphold these standards."[8] In its assumption that sexual offenses are not just a violation of an individual but a violation of community standards and thereby a violation of the Antioch community, Antioch is the first to take the focus off subjective sexual desire and place it into a community context in which gender equality and mutual respect are valued as community norms. As such, it was the first policy to seek a rape-free campus community.

A LEGAL VERSION OF AFFIRMATIVE CONSENT: THE 1992 NEW JERSEY SUPREME COURT DECISION

The philosophy behind affirmative consent was argued in a precedent-setting 1992 New Jersey Supreme Court decision. The principles enunciated in this decision and increasingly reflected in campus debates were as important for releasing women from male sexual domination in the late twentieth century as the call for "free love" in the late nineteenth century that released women from Victorian sexual restraint. Like the Antioch policy, the New Jersey Supreme Court decision went much farther by interjecting the dimension of responsibility into the freedom of free love. It is unfortunate that it took a century to accomplish this end.

The New Jersey case involved a juvenile who was found delinquent and convicted for committing a sexual assault in 1990. The Superior Court Appellate Division reversed the conviction in 1991 on the grounds that there was no physical force. The state then appealed to the Supreme Court of New Jersey, which reinstated the original conviction for delinquency in 1992. The case involved a fifteen-year-old girl, C.G., and a seventeen-year-old boy, M.T.S., who testified that he got on top of the girl while they were kissing and "stuck it in" and "did it three times." He said that "the fourth time [he] stuck it in . . . [she] pulled [him] off of her." He also testified that when she said, "Stop, get off," he "hopped off right away."[9]

The case revolved around the meaning of "physical force or coercion." The New Jersey law defines "sexual assault" as the commission of "an act of sexual penetration with another person" accomplished by any one of a number of circumstances, among which is the use of "physical force or coercion." At the original trial, the court interpreted "physical force" as meaning "sexual penetration of the victim without her consent." The Appellate Division reversed the conviction on the grounds that the statute "requires some amount of force more than that necessary to accomplish the penetration" to establish sexual assault.[10]

The original trial court concluded that C.G. had consented to the kissing and heavy petting but not to the actual sex act. The Supreme Court agreed that the trial court had proven second-degree sexual assault "beyond a reasonable doubt." In its decision, it disagreed with the appellate division's finding that "non-consensual penetration does not constitute sexual assault unless it is accompanied by some level of force more than that necessary to accomplish the penetration." According to the Supreme Court's decision, *"physical force in excess of that inherent in the act of sexual penetration is not required for such penetration to be unlawful."*[11]

The Supreme Court drew a parallel between sexual assault and other forms of assault and battery. As would be true in any other kind of assault, the Court argued, the victim is not required to resist and claimed that how he or she responded upon being assaulted is immaterial. Therefore, the Court concluded:

We are thus satisfied that an interpretation of the statutory crime of sexual assault to require physical force in addition to that entailed in an act of involuntary or unwanted sexual penetration would be fundamentally inconsistent with the legislative purpose to eliminate any consideration of whether the victim resisted or expressed non-consent.

The court stated that the definition of "physical force" is satisfied under New Jersey's law *"if the defendant applies any amount of force against another person in the absence of what a reasonable person would believe to be affirmative and freely-given permission to the act of sexual penetration."* Based on this reasoning, the Court concluded that *"any act of sexual penetration engaged in by the defendant without the affirmative and freely-given permission of the victim to the specific act of penetration constitutes the offense of sexual assault."*[12]

The New Jersey Court's precedent-setting decision was cited during a well-known gang-rape case tried in the early 1990s, involving middle-class defendants. The defendants were four high school athletes in the New Jersey town of Glen Ridge who were tried and convicted of gang raping a mentally retarded schoolmate with a broom and a baseball bat.

In 1989 the young woman was lured by jocks she admired into a basement with thirteen young men, who were described as "the princes of the playing field" and "the pride of Glen Ridge High" by Bernard Lefkowitz in his book on the case (1997:13,20). Feeling uncomfortable with what was about to transpire, six of the young men left. Seven stayed behind, six high school seniors and one junior. Four of them assaulted her while the others watched. One stuck his penis into her mouth. Another used a broom to penetrate her; another a baseball bat. When it was all over, they swore the young woman to secrecy, convincing her that she would get kicked out of school if she revealed their secret. Standing in a circle, they clasped one hand on top of the other, "all their hands together, like a basketball team on the sidelines at the end of a time-out."[13]

The case came to trial in 1992 and ended in 1993 with four convictions. In closing arguments, Glenn Goldberg, one of the prosecutors, said that the jury could find the four young men guilty even if they concluded that the young woman did not actively resist the alleged sexual assault. According to Goldberg, "the victim does not have to say no." Nor does she have to resist. "If she just lies there and says nothing, if she doesn't give affirmative consent, you can find them guilty."[14] After eight days of deliberations the jury convicted three of the defendants on counts of first-degree aggravated sexual assault, which under New Jersey law is synonymous with rape. The fourth defendant was convicted of third-degree conspiracy.[15]

The New Jersey Supreme Court decision in the case of M.T.S. is not alone in holding that a showing of affirmative consent is required. This requirement exists in other states as well. In 1980, the Wisconsin Supreme Court upheld a conviction for sexual assault despite the defendant's contention that parties can enter into consensual sexual relationships without showing "freely given consent in words or acts." The Wisconsin sexual assault law defines consent as "words or overt actions by a person who is competent to give informed consent indicating a freely given agreement to have sexual intercourse or sexual contact."[16]

The Illinois sexual assault law defines consent as words or actions indicating "a freely given agreement to the act of sexual penetration or sexual conduct in question." The Illinois statute explicitly states that "lack of verbal or physical resistance or submission by the victim resulting from the use of force . . . shall not constitute consent." Nor will the "manner of dress of the victim at the time of the offense."[17] Another state stressing affirmative consent is Washington. According to its revised code, "Consent means that at the time of the act of sexual intercourse or sexual contact there are actual words or conduct indicating freely given agreement to have sexual intercourse or sexual contact."[18]

An important difference between these statutes and the Antioch policy is that the affirmative consent is not required to be verbal. According to the New Jersey Court, for example, permission can be "indicated through physical actions rather than words." The New Jersey court claimed that permission would be determined "when the evidence, in whatever form, is sufficient to demonstrate that a reasonable person would have believed that the alleged victim had affirmatively and freely given authorization to the act." Since this approach raises a host of questions regarding the definition of a "reasonable person" and of "freely given authorization," the Antioch policy requiring affirmative verbal consent seems more reasonable. As lawyer and author Susan Estrich (1987:98) has indicated, "reasonable" could mean either the assumption that no means yes and anything goes, or, the assumption that "no means no." According to Estrich, "Extortion for sex is no more justifiable than extortion for money."[19]

As long as the old stereotypes continue to remain current, the safest approach in sex education would be to emphasize verbal consent. In an article written for the University of Pennsylvania Law Review, Lani Anne Remick argues persuasively for verbal consent as a way to solve the interpretation and intent problems. She argues that a man "who has not established the willing participation of his partner by obtaining her verbal consent" must shoulder the risk of punishment if it should turn out that she was not consenting. Remick comes to this conclusion by weighing the relative value of two interests: her sexual autonomy on the one hand, and his freedom "not to trouble himself with inquiring as to his partner's consent" on the other. Remick argues persuasively that a woman's interest in sexual autonomy is much greater than a man's interest in engaging in nonconsensual sexual activity. Given the legal implications involved, obtaining verbal consent is obviously "the clearest and most unambiguous form of consent." In addition, there is the question of harm to the rape victim. As one set of commentators quoted by Remick states: "Given the severity of the harm and pain that rape victims experience, the obligation positively to inquire so that unequivocal consent is obtained seems a minimal requirement indeed" (Remick 1993:1133–38).

CONSTRUCTING A RAPE-FREE FRATERNITY

In light of the old stereotypes naming acquaintance and gang rape as "boys will be boys" along with the sexually addictive discourse of Internet pornography and the still continuing use of drugs and alcohol on college campuses, there is not much hope for a transition from rape-prone to rape-free values in the absence of a concerted effort over time on the part of administrators, faculty, and both male and female students. College males will be the ones to change the rape-prone ways in their social environments. In this effort they must be both encouraged and held accountable by campus administrations. Their women friends can help by emphatically saying no to degrading, thoughtless sexual behavior and learning to say yes to mutually conscious sexual interaction.

Male students in fraternities and athletics are especially vulnerable to macho stereotypes because of the status the old ways confer. Change takes courage and passion for equity, for which the gender with a history of dominance is not known to pursue. However, it is possible to do, as I discovered in working with members of one of Penn's fraternities.

Some five years after the original edition of *Fraternity Gang Rape* was published, a male student in one of my classes informed me that he was a member of a fraternity that was recolonizing at Penn as a rape-free fraternity. Working with another brother in the fraternity, he wrote a description of all the ways his fraternity was trying to formulate a rape-free environment.

Noel and Josh admitted that fraternities at Penn "propagate sexist attitudes and provide a breeding ground for insecure acts of sexism, racism, and homophobia." According to Noel, Penn's fraternities "tend to be self-segregating entities which seek to maintain the inferior social position of women and minority students through exclusion" and social intolerance. Their fraternity consciously fights against these norms.

QRS (pseudonym) is among the oldest fraternities at Penn, going back to the nineteenth century. It was like all other fraternities at Penn until it was almost forced to disband due to insufficient numbers. At that time, a group of nine first-year males pledged as a group knowing that their numbers would give them control of house decisions.

Noel and Josh were part of a group of brothers who were proud to say that they are "not a real fraternity." Interestingly, although both Josh and Noel treasure their lives in QRS (because of the fun, companionship of respected friends, and community the house offers), both feel that fraternities should be abolished because of the "loud, obnoxious, sexist, racist, homophobic" behavior that characterizes so many.

Most of the brothers in QRS do not participate in the campus inter-fraternity council and prefer to see themselves as "a group of friends," rather than as a fraternity, and their house as "a place to have concerts." Parties are always open to anyone and are either free to everyone or everyone pays, contrary to parties at other houses in which men pay and women are admitted for free. At QRS, heavy drinking is not a requisite for membership and is not a part of initiation. There are no drinking games, and binge drinking does not occur. While some brothers drink to get drunk more than once a week, most don't.

Peer oversight is common. At parties there are always brothers who watch out for women or for house members who have had too much to drink. Josh stressed that "it is clearly not acceptable for someone to take advantage of a drunk woman, because that's rape." There is no talk in the house about getting a girl drunk to have sex, he says. Members are very aware that where there is heavy drinking someone can be exploited. If a female passes out or is very drunk she is watched or escorted home. Both Josh and Noel remember an incident during a party in the fraternity next door, in which several members of QRS came to the aid of a young woman whose shirt was above her waist and who had passed out on their porch, left there perhaps by friends from the party who had deserted her. Their intervention may have saved her life. When they were unable to get her to talk, they took her to the emergency room of a nearby hospital only to learn that she was in a coma and her heart had stopped. Fortunately, they found her in time and she responded to treatment.

Women are not seen as sex objects in the house, but as friends. Unlike other fraternities at Penn, there is no distinction drawn between "girlfriends" and friends and there are no "party girls." Noel says that when he was rushing he would often hear women referred to as "sluts" in other fraternities. However, at QRS this kind of talk is unknown. According to Josh, a brother who acted "inappropriately" with a woman would be severely reprimanded, perhaps even expelled from the fraternity. The brothers are not afraid of strong women. There are women's studies students who are regulars at the house, along with outspoken feminists and activists. Noel quotes one of them:

> I guess there's a few brothers who make sexist jokes, but I don't know how seriously people take them. I remember last year in the middle of midterms I was studying late at night and was feeling sick and tired, and in a span of about five minutes, four people offered their beds to me, not as a sexual thing at all, but just because they cared.

One QRS brother started the Men's Association for Change and Openness (MAChO) and is an active participant in Penn's student peer-counseling group for sexual health. Another brother displays a "Refuse and Resist" sticker on his door, proclaiming, "Date rape: cut it out or cut it off." In a 1993 pamphlet advertising QRS as the site of the National Anarchist gathering, the brothers wrote, "Although QRS is a frat, it is generally a friendly place, along with being a safe haven for women."

Eight years later, when Claire went to the QRS frat for a party during her first year at Penn, she was struck by how friendly the brothers were to their women guests. As she remembers it:

> It was spring fling and I was pretty, very, very drunk and was sitting on their porch, staring at a wall. They were all really sweet to me and

let me sit there and talk to them the rest of the night and then one of them walked me home. He was in my econ recitation. He took me to a concert a couple weeks later and was a gentleman again. He was a math major and wanted to go to grad school and for fun he made chain-mail vests. My impression was that they all were artistic, smart, sweet, and rebellious . . . but even though I didn't fit in at the house . . . they were all really nice to me. I definitely believe they were a rape-free fraternity. They were too nice and too removed from the scene to ever really want to mess with victim crimes or violence.

Most interesting about QRS in light of the homophobia described in this book is its acceptance of homosexuality and bisexuality. Homophobia does not become the basis for males to prove their virility to one another in this frat. Indeed, because of its openness about sex and acceptance of homosexuality, QRS has earned the reputation on campus of being "the gay frat" or "faggot house." Josh comments on this reputation and what it means to him:

QRS's attitudes about homosexuality are complex, but fundamentally tolerant and respectful. Some brothers revel in rumors that we are the "gay frat." It is rumored that a few years ago a few of the brothers were involved sexually, and one of our most involved alumni is homosexual.

Although most of Penn's fraternities are now willing to admit that they have had or have a few homosexual brothers, such honest acceptance of homosexuality is unusual. QRS brothers are proud of being called the "gay frat." Evidence of this is the humorous statement in the letters given prospective pledges offering bids, which ends with the phrase "we are all gay." This is a positive take on the concept of *casualization* through joking. The joking in this case, however, removes the prejudice and phobia with which the word "gay" is usually associated.

Eleven years after working with Josh and Noel, I interviewed two current students involved with QRS in 2006. Len and Lena (pseudonyms) confirmed that the house culture Josh and Noel described was still accurate. Their description of this culture suggested to me that there was now an even stronger ethic of sexual equality, including the desire to admit women as pledges.

In separate interviews, Len and Lena both said that the fraternity was "inclusive" in accepting anyone who wants to join. With respect to initiation, there is what is called a *f—k you* policy in which the initiate can reject any behavior that is uncomfortable. They also think of the house as a collective rather than a fraternity. Most parties are attended by people who like the band scene at the house, usually people known to the brothers. The women who hang out at the house all refer to themselves as brothers and are called brothers. Lena says that the party atmosphere she has observed at the house is neither predatory nor is "scoring" the goal.

She sees the house as a refuge from the frat scene. About fraternity parties, she said:

> I don't like the look in their eyes, leering at me and other women when we walk in, sizing us up. The only way I would go to a Penn fraternity party is if a brother hosted me for an evening. That way I would feel shielded from the predatory behavior. QRS is a safe atmosphere, which is why I go there. I am accepted as one of the brothers. We are like a family. Sure, there is sibling-like rivalry, but that is natural in a family atmosphere. I don't recall ever seeing a brother take a drunk woman to his room for sex—it would be to take care of her, just like brothers take male guests to their rooms who are drunk to let them sleep it off. Parties are not about hooking up. We play some music and dance. We are anti-frat—a collective. I like to use the word co-op to describe the atmosphere. It is also diverse; there are black brothers, Asian brothers, Latinos, even women—but that's informal. Everyone is equal, even the pledges. It is a haven for all of us. I know students who would have left Penn if it were not for our fraternity.

THE NEW SEXUAL REVOLUTION

The anti-rape discourse associated with the new sexual revolution carries with it a philosophy that sees sexual expression as taking place in an existential and social arena based on sexual equality. The new sexual revolution is as much about women's as men's desire. Women express their feelings because they understand and are aware of their sexual selves. Knowing themselves, saying Yes is easy; so is saying No emphatically. Women do not service men, they interact with them. Same-sex sexuality is not rejected; it is understood as part of what being human is all about.

The new sexual revolution embraces activism on many fronts. At Penn, activism in 2006 focused on women's empowerment on campus. Supported by the Penn Women's Center, in the past few years the empowerment movement was developed by a group of undergraduate women who organized the Penn Consortium of Undergraduate Women, an umbrella organization representing more than twenty campus women's organizations. The highlight of their effort is the annual Women's Week. The week is part of the V-Day Campaign, an international campaign in eighty-one countries housed on college campuses and in communities worldwide. The highlight of the V-Day celebration all over the world is a production of Eve Ensler's *The Vagina Monologues*, which becomes the focus for large-scale benefits, innovative gatherings, films, and other campaigns to educate and change social attitudes with respect to violence against women.

In February 2006, Women's Week at Penn was called "The Feminist Future" and featured a keynote address by Gloria Steinem. As elsewhere, the celebration of V-Day included a production of Eve Ensler's play, enacted by undergraduate women. In the spirit of the V-Day Campaign's mission to stop violence against women, in the weeks after the performance the local dialogue continued in two of Penn's fraternities, one of which had hosted Tucker Max. This development demonstrates another mechanism for disseminating a rape-free discourse.

Generally speaking, five central values contribute to the various activities I associate with the new sexual revolution for social and sexual change: *knowledge, control, choice, consent, communication,* and *oversight. Knowledge* means understanding the cultural, social, and individual roots of the human sexual appetite. Knowledge also means exploring one's sexual self rather than modeling the male and female roles mirrored on Internet pornography.

The current access to Web porn raises serious questions about unfettered sexual freedom as an end in itself. Like freedom of speech, which allows all kinds of racist and sexist dialogue, and the right to carry guns, which results in innumerable deaths, sexual freedom has all sorts of potential consequences beyond those we usually consider. In addition to ignorance about the relationship between rape and alcohol, there is general ignorance about the many ways the sexual culture of pornography is a formula for sexual self-abuse.

John M., a writer on the Web page "Quitting Pornography," provides a vivid description of feeding what he thought were normal sexual needs through pornography. He writes:

> Pornography became a way of life. I spent all my money on it. I had to have it to keep going, to face life. From about fourteen years on I would think about sex all day long. I carried it on me. I had it hidden in my bedroom.

When he married, John M. thought his wife could take the place of pornography because he needed pornography to have sex. He tried to fit her into the pornography scenes that excited him by asking her to do degrading things to herself such as have sex with other girls and animals. Yet, even this didn't satisfy him. He realized that he wanted pornography more than he wanted her. In his story on the Quitting Pornography Web page, he says:

> I would rather be alone with my sex books than be with her. My addiction was growing so fast I could hardly keep up with it. It always wanted more. It kept getting sicker all the time. I need more books, more degrading sex, more abusive sex. Pornography showed me new ways of abuse and self-abuse.

Finally, after having three children, his wife left him. His addiction became worse and he started abusing himself even more than before. As things went from bad to worse he withdrew altogether from family and friends. When he went for counseling he was told that his use of pornography was normal and that he needed to get rid of the shame that he was feeling and give in to the feelings that led him to masturbate ten times a day and still not feel relief. Relief came when he started to go to Sex Addicts Anonymous. The twelve steps followed by SAA, modeled after the twelve steps of AA, saved him. Through this program he was able to take control of his life.[20]

When John M. was counseled that his feelings were "normal," he encountered the ideology of the second sexual revolution—that the sexual appetite can be neither self-abusive nor abusive of others, that the more sex the better, that it is impossible ever to have too much sex, even if getting sex cuts into every moment of one's waking life. When John M. started going to Sex Addicts Anonymous, he was exposed to a new way of thinking that teaches that control is necessary to guard against crossing the fine line between excess and abuse. Thus, *control* must be considered in tandem with *consent* and *choice*. Control is also relevant to oversight, such as when individuals at a party intervene to prevent hooking up when one or both partners are smashed.

When I use the word "choice" as a basic value of the new sexual revolution, I do not use it in the way it was used during the second sexual revolution, as in a woman's right to choose an abortion. To my mind, "choice" renders the issue of abortion mute.

I like to think of choice as follows: All individuals should have the right to choose whom they have sex with, how they have it, under what circumstances, and with what protective measures. Choice always operates in a climate of communication, which means verbal consent. Discussing safe sex is part of consent. Choice and consent are also related to knowledge and self-control. John M.'s wife consented at first to his abusive needs and then left the marriage. Had his wife understood better the source of John M.'s runaway sexual appetite and where it would probably lead him, she may not have consented in the first place. Knowledge about sex as an appetite that, like any other appetite, can be abusive to the self as well to others is the first step toward understanding the role of control in sexual behavior.

Choice includes sexually charged verbal communication. The idea that men and women communicate passion through language—which means listening for the Yes and responding to the No—is at the core of the new sexual revolution. Verbal consent is neither prudish nor puritanical. It can be highly erotic.

In his powerful love story, *Snow Falling on Cedars,* David Guterson paints a compelling scene in his account of the history of the relationship between a young Anglo man and a Japanese American woman. The story takes place on an island off the coast of the state of Washington. It is a sad but beautiful story of the unrequited love the young man feels for the young woman he adores. She also loves him, but cultural differences, circumstances, and family expectations make it necessary for her to reject him. As their love is about to be expressed physically after many years of knowing one another, he whispers into her ear.

"Just say yes. . . . Just tell me yes, tell me yes. Say yes to me. Say yes, oh god say yes" (1995:214).

She, however, pulls away from him and at that point he realizes after years of loving her that they will never be together.

Hermann Hesse's *Narcissus and Goldmund*, published in English during the 1960s, betrays the philosophy of the second sexual revolution. This novel tells the story of two medieval men whose characters are diametrically opposed. Narcissus, an ascetic monk, is firm in his religious commitment, and Goldmund, a romantic youth, is hungry for knowledge, worldly experience, and women. The two men are like twins in their opposition. Like twins they are bonded by a special feeling for one another that marks their lives more than love of God or love of woman. Referring to Goldmund's penchant for women with whom he rarely talks, the narrator muses about the uselessness of words in lovemaking:

> Words [are] unnecessary in love. . . . But in spite of all she had said, he still saw love in her eyes. . . . He believed her eyes more than he believed her words (1968:110).

Although the events of the novel are set in a different culture and time period, the sexual culture described is reminiscent of the male bonding and disregard for women that marked the American sexual culture as I was growing up and the one Natalie and Claire describe as still firmly in place in some parts of campus.

The mission statement for many of the campus conferences on sexual assault and harassment articulate the philosophy of the new sexual revolution. "We are not just anti-rape activists," students say, "we are advocates for a 'gentler, kinder' sexuality," one in which partners are in an equal relationship. At one of these conferences held in 1999 at the University of Wisconsin, Madison, the mission statement could be taken as a manifesto for the New Sexual Revolution:

> Sexual violence is more than just a crime it is part of the society we live in. Everything from attitudes to advertisements contributes to an environment in which rape is both allowed and accepted. Our goals are to be proactive and dissolve the foundations of sexual violence. We are challenging sexual and cultural norms that contribute to sexual violence. By emphasizing and striving for equality, we can challenge this crime of power and fear. By fostering relationships of communication,

love, and respect we can take a giant step in the struggle to end sexual violence.

Fostering relationships of communication, mutual choice, and respect makes *casualization* inoperative, be it with respect to sex, race, or the other life-threatening social issues of our times. Altruism and empathy extend outward toward everyone in the community, including sexual partners. Those who do so are capable of deep feeling. They take action because they are compassionate and caring, knowing that their efforts will probably not stem the tide of irresponsibility and self-indulgence that propels the current rush to destroy the planet. Although many of us think it may be too late, compassion and love are the only honorable ways for living life. More and more people are beginning to think about the history of how we got to this dreadful point in order to see a way into the future. This book is part of that thinking. How we care for one another, especially whether we protect the vulnerable, including mothers and children, is a measure of our stewardship of life on this planet.

NOTES

1. Despite the statistic that campus sexual assault remains a continuing problem, the public remains divided in its opinion on who is at fault. A survey of the Internet discussion about the Duke case in the weeks after it was first reported demonstrates the numbers involved in discussing the issue. This survey suggests that there is a sharp gender divide in the opinions expressed. According to this survey:
  • 80 percent of more than 90,000 female bloggers and chat roomers think some players are guilty, though no charges are filed.
  • 80 percent of more than 150,000 male bloggers and chat roomers believe the team may be victim to an extortion scheme (*USA Today*, April 12, 2006 by Eric Brady).
2. http://dolphin.upenn.edu/~staar/manual/introduction.html.
3. http://freud.psy.fsu.edu/~womenstudies/conferences.htm.
4. http://www.rainn.org/programs/social-norms/data-sources.html.
5. Zailckas (2005:217).
6. Interview, spring 1994; see Sanday 1996:272–73.
7. http://www.antioch-college.edu/Campus/sopp.
8. http://www.antioch-college.edu/Campus/sopp/adda.html.

9. Sanday 1996:278–79.

10. Ibid.

11. Ibid.

12. Supreme Court of New Jersey [State in Interest of M.T.S., 1992, 129 N.J. 425–46]. (See also Sanday 1996:279–82.)

13. Lefkowitz 1997:21.

14. Quoted in *Newsday*, March 4, 1993.

15. *Newsday*, March 17, 1993; see also Lefkowitz 1997:406–7.

16. Wisconsin Statutes @ 940.225 (1994). See also Schafran 1994:8–9.

17. Illinois Compiled Statues Annotated. 720 ILCS 5/12–17 (1995).

18. Annotated Revised Code of Washington (ARCW) @ 9A44.010 (1994). See also Sanday 1996:282–83.

19. See discussion in Sanday 1996:283–85.

20. http://saa-recovery.org/.

Bibliography

Ageton, Suzanne S. 1983. *Sexual assault among adolescents.* Lexington, Mass.: D. C. Heath.

Barry, Kathleen. 1984. *Female sexual slavery.* New York: New York Univ. Press.

Beauvoir, Simone de. 1952. *The second sex.* New York: Vintage Books.

Belsey, Catherine. 1980. *Critical practice.* London: Methuen.

Biemiller, Lawrence. 1984. For Colby College's doomed fraternities. *Chronicle of Higher Education* 28 (2):7.

Bowden, Mark. 1983. The incident at Alpha Tau Omega. *Philadelphia Inquirer Magazine* (11 Sept. 1983). From the *Philadelphia Inquirer.* Used by permission.

Brenner, N. D., P. M. McMahon, C. W. Warren, & K. A. Douglas, 1999. Forced sexual intercourse and associated health-risk behaviors among female college students in the United States. *Journal of Consulting and Clinical Psychology* 67:252–59.

Brownmiller, Susan. 1975. *Against our will: Men, women and rape.* New York: Simon and Schuster.

Caplan, Pat, ed. 1987. *The cultural construction of sexuality.* London: Tavistock.

Dworkin, Andrea. 1987. *Intercourse.* New York: Free Press.

Ehrhart, Julie K. and Bernice R. Sandler. 1985. Campus gang rape: Party games? In *Project on the Status and Education of Women.* Washington, D.C.: Association of American Colleges.

Estrich, Susan. 1987. *Real rape.* Cambridge, Mass.: Harvard Univ. Press.

Fisher, Bonnie, Francis T. Cullen, and Michael G. Turner. 2000. *The sexual victimization of college women.* National Institute of Justice and Bureau of Justice Statistics, Department of Justice.

Ford, Richard. 1986. Rules of the house. *Esquire* 105 (6).

Foucault, Michel. 1980. *History of sexuality.* New York: Vintage Books.

Freud, Sigmund. 1959. *Group psychology and the analysis of the ego.* New York: W. W. Norton.

Gaylin, Willard. 1982. *The killing of Bonnie Garland.* New York: Simon and Schuster.

Geertz, Clifford. 1973. *The interpretation of cultures.* New York: Basic Books.

Girard, Rene. 1987. Generative scapegoating. In *Violent origins,* ed. Walter Burkert, Rene Girard, and Jonathan Z. Smith. Stanford: Stanford Univ. Press.

Gold, Jodi and Susan Villari, eds. 2000. *Just sex: Students rewrite the rules on sex, violence, activism, and equality.* Lanham, Md.: Rowman and Littlefield.

Goodchilds, Jacqueline D., Gail Zellman, Paula B. Johnson, and Roseann Giarrusso. 1988. Adolescence and the perceptions of sexual interactions outcomes. In *Sexual assault,* vol. 2, ed. A. W. Burgess. New York: Garland Publishing Co.

Goodenough, Ward Hunt. 1963. *Cooperation in change.* New York: Russell Sage Foundation.

Gottlieb, Alma. 1990. Reflections on "Female Pollution" among the Beng of Ivory Coast. In *Beyond the second sex,* ed. Peggy Reeves Sanday and Ruth Gallagher Goodenough. Philadelphia: Univ. of Pennsylvania Press.

Griffin, Susan. 1981. *Pornography and silence.* New York: Harper Colophon Books.

Guterson, David. 1995. *Snow falling on cedars.* New York: Vintage Books.

Henriques, Julian, Wendy Hollway, Cathy Urwin, Couze Venn, and Valerie Walkerdine. 1984. *Changing the subject.* London: Methuen.

Hesse, Hermann. 1968. *Narcissus and Goldmund.* New York: Farrar, Straus and Giroux.

Hollway, Wendy. 1984. Gender difference and the production of subjectivity. In *Changing the subject,* ed. Julian Henriques, Wendy Hollway, Cathy Urwin, Couze Venn, and Valerie Walkerdine. London: Methuen.

Horney, Karen. 1967. *Feminine psychology.* New York: W. W. Norton.

Hughes, Jean O'Gorman and Bernice Sandler. 1989. Harassing women, a college sport. In *New directions for women,* 18(1) (Jan.–Feb.):22.

Kopytoff, Igor. 1990. Women's roles and existential identities. In *Beyond the second sex,* ed. Peggy Reeves Sanday and Ruth Gallagher Goodenough. Philadelphia: Univ. of Pennsylvania Press.

Koss, Mary P. and Sarah L. Cook. 1993. Facing the facts: Date and acquaintance rape are significant problems for women. In *Current controversies on family violence,* ed. Richard J. Gelles and Donileen R. Loseke, 104–19. Newbury Park, Calif.: Sage.

Koss, Mary P. and Thomas E. Dinero. 1987. Predictors of sexual aggression among a national sample of male college students. Paper presented at the New York Academy of Sciences Conference on Human Sexual Aggression: Current Perspectives, 7 January, New York City.

Koss, Mary P., Christine A. Gidycz and Nadine Wisniewski. 1987. The scope of rape: Incidence and prevalence of sexual aggression and victimization in a national sample of higher education students. *Journal of Consulting and Clinical Psychology* 55:162–70.

Koss, Mary P. and Kenneth E. Leonard. 1984. Sexually aggressive men: Empirical findings and theoretical implications. In *Pornography and sexual aggres-*

sion, ed. Neil M. Malamuth and Edward Donnerstein, 213–32. New York: Academic Press.

Laqueur, Thomas. 1990. *Making sex: Body and gender from the Greeks to Freud.* Cambridge, Mass.: Harvard Univ. Press.

Lederman, Rena. 1990. Contested order: Gender construction and social structure in Mendi. In *Beyond the second sex*, ed. Peggy Reeves Sanday and Ruth Gallagher Goodenough. Philadelphia: Univ. of Pennsylvania Press.

Lefkowitz, Bernard. 1997. *Our guys: The Glen Ridge rape and the secret life of the perfect suburb.* Berkeley: Univ. of California Press.

Lemaire, Anika. 1977. *Jacques Lacan.* London: Routledge and Kegan Paul.

Lepowsky, Maria. 1990. Gender in an egalitarian society. In *Beyond the second sex*, ed. Peggy Reeves Sanday and Ruth Gallagher Goodenough. Philadelphia: Univ. of Pennsylvania Press.

Lerner, Gerda. 1986. *The creation of patriarchy.* New York: Oxford Univ. Press.

Lewis, Magda and Roger I. Simon. 1986. A discourse not intended for her: Learning and teaching within patriarchy. *Harvard Educational Review* 56:457–72.

Malinowski, Bronislaw. 1929. *The sexual life of savages in north-western Melanesia: An ethnographic account of courtship, marriage and family life among the natives of the Trobriand Islands, British New Guinea.* New York: Harcourt Brace Jovanovich.

Max, Tucker. 2006. *I hope they serve beer in hell.* New York: Citadel Press.

Meigs, Anna. 1990. Multiple gender ideologies and statuses. In *Beyond the second sex*, ed. Peggy Reeves Sanday and Ruth Gallagher Goodenough. Philadelphia: Univ. of Pennsylvania Press.

Mitchell, Juliet. 1982. Introduction—I. *Feminine sexuality*, ed. Juliet Mitchell and Jacqueline Rose. New York: W. W. Norton.

Mohler-Kuo, Meichun, George W. Dowdall, and Mary Koss. 2004. Correlates of rape while intoxicated in a national sample of college woman. *Journal of Studies on Alcohol* 65:37–45.

Murphy, Yolanda and Robert F. Murphy. 1974. *Women of the forest.* New York: Columbia Univ. Press.

Nadelson, Leslee. 1981. Pigs, women, and the men's house in Amazonia: An analysis of six Mundurucu myths. In *Sexual meanings*, ed. Sherry B. Ortner and Harriet Whitehead. Cambridge: Cambridge Univ. Press.

Ortner, Sherry. 1978. *Sherpas through their rituals.* Cambridge: Cambridge Univ. Press.

Pateman, Carole. 1988. *The sexual contract.* Stanford: Stanford Univ. Press.

Poole, Fitz John Porter. 1981. Transforming "natural" woman: Female ritual leaders and gender ideology among Bimin-Kuskusmin. In *Sexual meanings*, ed. Sherry B. Ortner and Harriet Whitehead. New York: Cambridge Univ. Press.

Reich, Wilhelm. 1963. *The sexual revolution*. New York: Farrar, Straus and Giroux.

Remick, Lani Anne. 1993. Consent standard in rape. *University of Pennsylvania Law Review* 141:1103–51.

Sanday, Peggy Reeves. 1981a. *Female power and male dominance*. New York: Cambridge Univ. Press.

———. 1981b. The socio-cultural context of rape: A cross-cultural study. *Journal of Social Issues* 37(4):5–27.

———. 1986. Rape and the silencing of the feminine. In *Rape: A collection of essays*, ed. Roy Porter and Sylvana Tomaselli. London: Basil Blackwell.

———. 1988. The reproduction of patriarchy in feminist anthropology. In *Feminist thought and the structure of knowledge*, ed. Mary M. Gergen. New York: New York Univ. Press.

———. 1990a. Androcentric and matrifocal gender representations in Minangkabau ideology. In *Beyond the second sex*, ed. Peggy Reeves Sanday and Ruth Gallagher Goodenough. Philadelphia: Univ. of Pennsylvania Press.

———. 1990b. Introduction. In *Beyond the second sex*, ed. Peggy Reeves Sanday and Ruth Gallagher Goodenough. Philadelphia: Univ. of Pennsylvania Press.

———. 1996. *A Woman scorned: Acquaintance rape on trial*. Berkeley: Univ. of California Press.

———. 2003. Rape-free versus rape-prone: How culture makes a difference. In *Evolution, gender, and rape*, ed. Cheryl Brown Travis, 337–62. Cambridge, Mass.: MIT Press.

Schafran, Lynn Hecht, esq. 1994. Understanding sexual violence. National Judicial Education Program to Promote Equality for Women and Men in the Courts, State Justice Institute.

Schlegel, Alice. 1990. Gender meanings: General and specific. In *Beyond the second sex*, ed. Peggy Reeves Sanday and Ruth Gallagher Goodenough. Philadelphia: Univ. of Pennsylvania Press.

Smith, Michael Clay. 1988. *Coping with crime on campus*. New York: Collier Macmillan Publishers with the American Council on Education.

Spindler, George and Louise Spindler. 1987. *Interpretive ethnography of education: At home and abroad*. Hillsdale, N.J.: Lawrence Erlbaum Associates. (See article by R. G. Goodenough, Small group culture and the emergence of sexist behavior: A comparative study of four children's groups, 409–44.)

Tanner, Nancy. 1981. *On becoming human*. Cambridge: Cambridge Univ. Press.

Tjaden, Patricia and Nancy Thoennes. 2006. Extent, nature, and consequences of rape victimization: Findings from the National Violence Against Women Survey, http://www.ncjrs.gov/pdffiles1/nij/210346.pdf.

———. 2000. Extent, nature, and consequences of intimate partner violence: Findings from the National Violence Against Women Survey. NCJ 81867,

July 2000, Research Report, http://www.ncjrs.gov/pdffiles1/nij/183781 .pdf.

Vance, Carol S. 1984. Pleasure and danger. In *Pleasure and danger*, ed. Carol Vance, 1–28. London: Routledge and Kegan Paul.

Warshaw, Robin. 1988. *I never called it rape: The Ms. report on recognizing, fighting and surviving date and acquaintance rape.* New York: Harper and Row.

Weeks, Jeffrey. 1985. *Sexuality and its discontents.* London: Routledge and Kegan Paul.

Zailckas, Koren. 2005. *Smashed: Story of a drunken girlhood.* New York: Viking.

Index

Acquaintance rape: date rape drugs, 7; fraternity gang rape, 2; hook-up sexual culture (University of Pennsylvania), 219; prevalence on campuses, 53–54, 202–203; second sexual revolution, 19; ubiquity of, 20

Acquaintance Rape Task Force (University of Pennsylvania), 200

Affirmative consent, 225

Affirmative verbal consent: advantages of, 225–226; anti-rape movement, 20; Antioch College, 219; definition, 221; feminism, 20; Glen Ridge (New Jersey) case, 224–225; New Jersey Supreme Court decision (1992), 220, 222–226; new sexual paradigm, 201; one-sex model of sexuality, 201, 220; safe sex, 201

Against Our Will (Brownmiller), 6

Alice (U. student): acceptance of fraternity life on its own terms, 192; on "asking for it," 73, 81; attraction to power, 82; drinking, 67, 73, 76; identification with fraternity brothers, 193; on Laurel, 70–71, 73; on life at XYZ fraternity, 67–68; on motivation of women who attend fraternity parties, 66; on riffing, 89; seeking acceptance, 67, 69, 77; suspicious about gang rape of Laurel, 69; time spent with XYZ brothers, 71; as a "wench," 69; on XYZ brothers, 74; on XYZ Express, 68–69, 70, 71, 74

Amy (rape victim): acceptance of fraternity life on its own terms, 192; anal sex, 115; boarding at a fraternity, 113; courting danger, 116–117; drinking, 117; identification with fraternity brothers, 193; ménage à trois situations, 112; pregnancy, 112–113; proving attractiveness to men, 112; rape of, 113–116, 117; seeking acceptance and power, 109; shocking friends, 112

Anna (U. student), 74–82; acceptance by XYZ brothers, 75–76, 77–78; acceptance of fraternity life on its own terms, 192; attraction to power, 75, 82; being "butt-fucked," 76–78; circle dancing, 75, 77, 78–79; Ed and, 74–75, 76–77; equating XYZ Express and rape, 37, 81, 85–87, 92, 108; friendship with XYZ brothers, 37; identification with fraternity brothers, 193; on Laurel, 1; legal definition of rape, 84; "male-identified attitudes" of, 76, 78; motivation of women who attend fraternity parties, 66; as a "regular," 74; as subject of gossip among XYZ brothers, 81

Anti-rape movement: affirmative verbal consent, 20; courses in ethics, 31–32; at Duke University, 201; "pro-pleasure principle," 201; response to, 198; at University of Pennsylvania, 5–6, 199–201

Antioch College, 219–222, 225

Aristotle, 11, 12

"Asking for it": Alice on, 73, 81; drinking, 35, 72–73; drug use, 35; partying and getting drunk, 81; provoking male sexual aggression, 106–107; putting oneself in a certain situation, 73, 81

Association of American Colleges, 33

"Beaching a girl," 60

Beauvoir, Simone de, 193

Belsey, Catherine, 180

"Bimbos," 69

"Bitches," 61

"Blacked-out hook-up," 203, 212, 219

Blaming the victim in: fraternity gang rape, 35, 42, 120–121, 160–161; gang rape, 25; rape, 2; XYZ Express, 2–3, 134

"Blue-balled" excuse, 135

Bob's story, 166–171

Bok, Derek, 29–30, 31–32

About the Author

Peggy Reeves Sanday is Professor of Anthropology at the University of Pennsylvania. Her many books include *Women at the Center: Life in a Modern Matriarchy, A Woman Scorned: Acquaintance Rape on Trial, Divine Hunger: Cannibalism as a Cultural System,* and *Female Power and Male Dominance: On the Origins of Sexual Inequality.*